Wittgenstein and Other Minds

This book offers an innovative and compelling exploration of the other minds problem, drawing mainly on the later Wittgenstein, but also on figures from the "Continental" tradition, such as Levinas, Husserl, and Heidegger.

For all these thinkers, the problem of other minds is not primarily an epistemological problem about our knowledge of the mental lives of other creatures, but rather a problem that basically concerns the way in which we think about the mind as such. Søren Overgaard argues that if we conceive of the mind in the way Wittgenstein is urging us to conceive of it – that is, if we understand mental life as world-involving, embodied, and expressed – then we can provide an account that steers clear of a number of traditional pitfalls. In particular, we can accommodate two seemingly conflicting intuitions about the accessibility of the mental lives of others. One intuition is that it is wrong to claim that the minds of others are essentially inaccessible to direct experience. The other is that it is equally wrong to claim that the mental lives of subjects are completely accessible to an outside spectator. Philosophers have often emphasized one intuition at the expense of the other. Overgaard, however, argues that both are equally essential to an understanding of intersubjectivity, and that the idea of mental life as something that is expressed in bodily behavior is what allows us to accommodate them both. This idea also leads us to the (arguably Wittgensteinian) insight that the other minds problem has an irreducible ethical aspect.

Søren Overgaard is Research Councils UK Fellow and Lecturer in Philosophy at the University of Hull. He is the author of *Husserl and Heidegger on Being in the World* (2004).

Routledge Studies in Twentieth-Century Philosophy

1 **The Story of Analytic Philosophy**
   Plot and Heroes
   Edited by Anat Biletzki and Anat Matar

2 **Donald Davidson**
   Truth, Meaning and Knowledge
   Edited by Urszula M. Zeglén

3 **Philosophy and Ordinary Language**
   The Bent and Genius of Our Tongue
   Oswald Hanfling

4 **The Subject in Question**
   Sartre's Critique of Husserl in *The Transcendence of the Ego*
   Stephen Priest

5 **Aesthetic Order**
   A Philosophy of Order, Beauty and Art
   Ruth Lorland

6 **Naturalism**
   A Critical Analysis
   Edited by William Lane Craig and J. P. Moreland

7 **Grammar in Early Twentieth-Century Philosophy**
   Richard Gaskin

8 **Rules, Magic and Instrumental Reason**
   A Critical Interpretation of Peter Winch's Philosophy of the Social Sciences
   Berel Dov Lerner

9 **Gaston Bachelard**
   Critic of Science and the Imagination
   Cristina Chimisso

10 **Hilary Putnam**
    Pragmatism and Realism
    Edited by James Conant and Urszula Zeglén

11 **Karl Jaspers**
    Politics and Metaphysics
    Chris Thornhill

12 **From Kant to Davidson**
    The Idea of the Transcendental in Twentieth-Century Philosophy
    Edited by Jeff Malpas

13 **Collingwood and the Metaphysics of Experience**
    A Reinterpretation
    Giuseppina D'Oro

14 **The Logic of Liberal Rights**
A Study in the Formal Analysis of Legal Discourse
Eric Heinze

15 **Real Metaphysics**
Edited by Hallvard Lillehammer and Gonzalo Rodriguez-Pereyra

16 **Philosophy after Postmodernism**
Civilized Values and the Scope of Knowledge
Paul Crowther

17 **Phenomenology and Imagination in Husserl and Heidegger**
Brian Elliott

18 **Laws in Nature**
Stephen Mumford

19 **Trust and Toleration**
Richard H. Dees

20 **The Metaphysics of Perception**
Wilfrid Sellars, Critical Realism and the Nature of Experience
Paul Coates

21 **Wittgenstein, Austrian Economics, and the Logic of Action**
Praxeological Investigations
Roderick T. Long

22 **Ineffability and Philosophy**
André Kukla

23 **Cognitive Metaphor and Continental Philosophy**
Clive Cazeaux

24 **Wittgenstein and Levinas**
Ethical and Religious Thought
Bob Plant

25 **Philosophy of Time: Time before Times**
Roger McClure

26 **The Russellian Origins of Analytic Philosophy**
Bertrand Russell and the Unity of the Proposition
Graham Stevens

27 **Analytic Philosophy without Naturalism**
Edited by A. Corradini, S. Galvan and E. J. Lowe

28 **Modernism and the Language of Philosophy**
Anat Matar

29 **Wittgenstein and Other Minds**
Rethinking Subjectivity and Intersubjectivity within Wittgenstein, Levinas, and Husserl
Søren Overgaard

Wittgenstein and Other Minds

Rethinking subjectivity and intersubjectivity within Wittgenstein, Levinas, and Husserl

Søren Overgaard

NEW YORK AND LONDON

First published 2007 by
Routledge
270 Madison Avenue, New York, NY 10016

Simultaneously published in the UK by
Routledge
2 Park Square, Milton Park, Abingdon, Oxon OX14 4RN

© 2007 Søren Overgaard

Typeset in Times New Roman by Taylor & Francis Books

Routledge is an imprint of the Taylor & Francis Group, an informa business

Transferred to Digital Printing 2009

All rights reserved. No part of this book may be reprinted or reproduced or utilized in any form or by any electronic, mechanical, or other means, now known or hereafter invented, including photocopying and recording, or in any information storage or retrieval system without permission in writing from the publisher.

Library of Congress Cataloging in Publication Data
A catalogue record for the book has been request

British Library Cataloguing in Publication Data
A catalogue record for this book is available from the British Library

ISBN10: 0-415-95593-9 (hbk)
ISBN10: 0-415-80306-3 (pbk)

ISBN13: 978-0-415-95593-5 (hbk)
ISBN13: 978-0-415-80306-9 (pbk)

In loving memory of Meta Overgaard

Contents

Acknowledgments		x
List of abbreviations		xii
	Introduction	1
1	Exposing the conjuring trick	10
2	Catching reality in one's net	28
3	Being some body	45
4	Externalism, realism, and Wittgenstein	63
5	The opposite of solipsism	83
6	The transcendence of the other in Husserl, Sartre, and Levinas	103
7	The play of expression	120
8	Responding to faces	141
9	Concluding remarks	158
	Notes	162
	Bibliography	187
	Index	197

Acknowledgments

This book is a result of three years of postdoctoral research at the Danish National Research Foundation: Center for Subjectivity Research, University of Copenhagen, Denmark. The Carlsberg Foundation funded the first two years. At a later stage the project was funded by the Nordic Research Council for the Humanities (NOS-H) through the NOS-H research project "Rearticulations of Reason" led by Leila Haaparanta. Many crucial revisions were made during the nine months in which my work was funded by NOS-H. The final round of revising and polishing took place in the spring of 2006 and was funded by the Center for Subjectivity Research.

The book would hardly have seen the light of day were it not for the unique research environment provided by the Center for Subjectivity Research. The creation and preservation of this environment is first and foremost due to Dan Zahavi. I am greatly indebted to Dan for his interest in and support of this book project, and for his extensive comments on all parts of the manuscript, in all stages of its becoming. I am grateful as well to other past and present researchers at the center for their (in some cases crucial) comments on parts of the manuscript. Thor Grünbaum, Eva Schwarz, and especially Lisa Käll (who commented extensively on the whole manuscript) deserve thanks on this account.

I have also benefited from discussions with people outside the Center for Subjectivity Research. David Cockburn, Bob Plant, and Sami Pihlström read, and offered valuable remarks on, portions of the manuscript. Special thanks are due to Anne-Marie Christensen, who had a formative impact on the argument of Chapter 8 (which is not to say that she agrees with everything I say in it). I would also like to thank an anonymous reviewer for Routledge, whose perceptive remarks led to a couple of improvements at a late stage.

On a more personal level, I am grateful to Kirsten Overgaard, Jens Overgaard, and Deborah Vlaeymans, for their unwavering interest and support. I dedicate this book to the memory of my grandmother Meta Overgaard (1914–2006), who knew my vocation before anyone else did (including me).

Parts of the book have appeared previously in other publications of mine. An earlier version of Chapter 1 was published as "Exposing the Conjuring

Trick: Wittgenstein on Subjectivity," in *Phenomenology and the Cognitive Sciences*, vol. 3, 2004, 263–86, © 2004 Kluwer Academic Publishers. It is reprinted here with kind permission of Springer Science and Business Media. A longer version of Chapter 4 appeared in a paper entitled "The Private Language Argument and Externalism," published in the *Danish Yearbook of Philosophy*, vol. 39, 2004, 17–48. It is used here by permission of the journal and its publisher, Museum Tusculanum Press. Part of Chapter 3 appeared in the article "Heidegger on Embodiment," published in the *Journal of the British Society for Phenomenology*, vol. 35, 2004, 116–31. It is used with kind permission of the editor, Dr. Ullrich Haase. Chapter 7 is a revised version of an article titled "Rethinking Other Minds: Wittgenstein and Levinas on Expression," published in *Inquiry*, www.tandf.no/inquiry, vol. 48, 2005, 249–74. The material is reprinted here by permission of Taylor and Francis. I am grateful to all the mentioned journals, editors, and publishers for permission to reuse previously published material.

List of abbreviations

This list only includes works to which frequent references are made. References to all other works, including other works by Wittgenstein, Levinas, Husserl, and Heidegger, are made using the author–date system. Bibliographical information about the latter works is found in the Bibliography.

Works by Ludwig Wittgenstein

BB — *The Blue and Brown Books.* Ed. R. Rhees. Oxford: Blackwell, 1958.
CV — *Culture and Value: A Selection from the Posthumous Remains.* Revised 2nd edition. Ed. G. H. von Wright and H. Nyman, trans. P. Winch. Oxford: Blackwell, 1998.
LW I — *Last Writings on the Philosophy of Psychology*, vol. I. Ed. G. H. von Wright and H. Nyman, trans. C. G. Luckhardt and M. A. E. Aue. Oxford: Blackwell, 1982.
LW II — *Last Writings on the Philosophy of Psychology*, vol. II. Ed. G. H. von Wright and H. Nyman, trans. C. G. Luckhardt and M. A. E. Aue. Oxford: Blackwell, 1992.
PI — *Philosophical Investigations.* Trans. G. E. M. Anscombe. Oxford: Blackwell, 1963.
PO — *Philosophical Occasions 1912–1951.* Ed. J. Klagge and A. Nordmann. Indianapolis: Hackett, 1993.
PR — *Philosophical Remarks.* Ed. R. Rhees, trans. R. Hargreaves and R. White. Oxford: Blackwell, 1975.
RPP I — *Remarks on the Philosophy of Psychology*, vol. I. Ed. G. E. M. Anscombe and G. H. von Wright, trans. G. E. M. Anscombe. Oxford: Blackwell, 1980.
RPP II — *Remarks on the Philosophy of Psychology*, vol. II. Ed. G. H. von Wright and H. Nyman, trans. C. G. Luckhardt and M. A. E. Aue. Oxford: Blackwell, 1980.
T — *Tractatus Logico-Philosophicus.* Trans. D. F. Pears and B. F. McGuinness. London: Routledge and Kegan Paul, 1961.
Z — *Zettel.* Ed. G. E. M. Anscombe and G. H. von Wright, trans. G. E. M. Anscombe. Berkeley: University of California Press, 1967.

Works by Emmanuel Levinas

CPP *Collected Philosophical Papers.* Trans. A. Lingis. Pittsburgh: Duquesne University Press, 1998.
OB *Otherwise than Being or Beyond Essence.* Trans. A. Lingis. Pittsburgh: Duquesne University Press, 1998.
TI *Totality and Infinity: An Essay on Exteriority.* Trans. A. Lingis. Pittsburgh: Duquesne University Press, 1969.

Works by Edmund Husserl

CM *Cartesian Meditations: An Introduction to Phenomenology.* Trans. D. Cairns. Dordrecht: Kluwer Academic Publishers, 1995.
TS *Thing and Space: Lectures of 1907.* Trans. R. Rojcewicz. Dordrecht: Kluwer Academic Publishers, 1997.
ZPI *Zur Phänomenologie der Intersubjektivität. Zweiter Teil: 1921–1928.* Ed. I. Kern. The Hague: Nijhoff, 1973.

Works by Martin Heidegger

BT *Being and Time.* Trans. J. Macquarrie and E. Robinson. Oxford: Blackwell, 1962.
GAP *Grundbegriffe der aristotelischen Philosophie.* Ed. M. Michalski. Frankfurt a. M.: Klostermann, 2002.

Works by Jean-Paul Sartre

BN *Being and Nothingness: An Essay on Phenomenological Ontology.* Trans. H. E. Barnes. London: Routledge, 1989.

Introduction

[Y]ou must see something that sheds a new light on the facts.

(CV, 45)

Without other people, human life would be emptied of most of its content; indeed it would hardly be recognizably human. Most of what we consider central to our lives – and central to our lives being *human* lives – is bound up, in one way or another, with the existence of others in the shape of parents, siblings, children, friends, lovers, foes, casual acquaintances, and so forth. In fact, other people or "minds" are not only at the center of our lives. They also constitute a central theme for philosophical reflection, at least since the seventeenth century. In 1641, Descartes stated that

> if I look out the window and see men crossing the square, as I just happen to have done, I normally say that I see the men themselves [...]. Yet do I see more than hats and coats which would conceal automatons? I *judge* that they are men.
>
> (Descartes 1984, 21)

Descartes could not have known what impact these remarks would have on posterior philosophy. In particular, there is no evidence that it ever occurred to Descartes that there was any special difficulty concerning our "judgments" about other minds (cf. Avramides 2001, 50 and *passim*). In a way, this is evident in the quotation just given. The problem Descartes is sketching there seems to differ from what we know as the problem of other minds in that the former, unlike the latter, is extremely easy to solve. We don't have to make do with the mere judgment that the hats and coats that we look at from our window conceal real people; we can, if we want, walk down in the street and lift some hats and coats to see what they conceal. But the problem of other minds, especially as it has been handed down to us filtered through Cartesian metaphysics, has no such easy solution. So while Descartes was unaware that there should be any special problem about others, this thought has occurred to numerous later philosophers – especially those who, like Descartes, have been persuaded that some version of dualism is true. For if the visible, tangible body is one type of thing or substance, and the soul or mind is another type of thing or substance – an invisible and intangible substance – then tearing off the coats and hats of people in the street is ultimately a useless effort. On the Cartesian view, all I will be able to discern under those hats and coats are *bodies*; and what I am really inquiring about when I ask whether these creatures are "men" is whether they have souls or minds, not whether they have bodies. A host of problems is cropping up here – among them the problem we know as the problem of other minds.[1] Most philosophers have phrased this problem in Cartesian (i.e. skeptical) terms: I *think* I know that I am surrounded by other people; but to what do I have cognitive access? Is it not merely an outer shell, comparable to Descartes' hats and coats, which might as well hide an automaton as a real, minded person? And if so, do I or can I then know that there are other people here? How could I possibly justify such a knowledge claim?

In other words, we are used to think of the problem of other minds as an epistemological problem (cf., e.g., Hyslop 1995, 5–14). It is a problem about our *knowledge* of the contents, and even existence, of minds other than our own. How do I know what another person really feels when her hand gets jammed in the door? How do I know that she feels anything? Indeed, once I start to think about it, how *can* I possibly know that she is not simply a mindless robot or a *zombie*?[2] However, as Anita Avramides has recently argued, these epistemological qualms are rooted in a particular way of replying to a more fundamental question – "a question about what the mind is" (Avramides 2001, 4). Not that there cannot be any legitimate worries about our knowledge of other minds; of course there can. But the notion that there is a *fundamental* epistemological difficulty hereabouts, a difficulty concerning the very possibility of achieving knowledge about the existence of any minds other than one's own – this notion is the result of a particular way of conceiving of the mind (or subjectivity) in the first place. For example, if we think about the mind as constituting an inner realm of its own, separated in various ways from the "external" world, then something like the epistemological problem of other minds is likely to pop up sooner or later, precisely in virtue of the way in which we have conceived of the mind. At bottom the other minds issue, according to Avramides, is hence a conceptual or ontological problem rather than an epistemological one.

But could it be that we should cast an even wider net? Could it be, for example, that the question about other minds is not merely an ontological or conceptual question, but also intrinsically bound up with questions of a moral or ethical nature? Perhaps our very notion of a "mind" or a "subject" involves ideas of how it is appropriate to treat a subject – of the attitudes and reactions that "befit" a minded creature. Stanley Cavell seems to suggest such an ethical dimension to the other minds problem when he insists, for example, that Wittgensteinian criteria for the pain of another demand a response from me, impose a call upon me "for comforting, succoring, healing" (Cavell 1979, 81). As Cavell puts it, "in the case of, for example, 'acknowledging another's pain,' I know in a general way what I am called upon to do that goes beyond my feat of cognition, viz., to express sympathy, or impatience, something that incorporates his suffering" (ibid., 429). The example of pain is just a special case of Cavell's general idea that to experience another human being's inner life is to respond to a call, a call for acknowledgment (ibid., 84). If such thoughts are not completely farfetched, then properly addressing the problem of other minds ultimately means discussing issues ranging from ontology through epistemology to ethics.

I think this is the right approach to the issue of other minds or intersubjectivity. Consequently, it is the one I adopt in this book. I also think, along with Cavell, that it is an approach that is characteristic of the later Wittgenstein. According to the latter, the problem of other minds is not an isolated epistemological problem. Rather, it is a problem that has to do with deeply entrenched philosophical ways of thinking about the mind. It is also a problem that has an irreducible ethical or "proto-ethical" aspect, which we may perhaps overlook due to deeply entrenched ways of dividing and relating philosophical problems.

There are two additional reasons why Wittgenstein is an important philosopher in the context of the other minds problem. First, as David Pears has argued, the problem of other minds occupies a central position in the philosophy of the middle Wittgenstein, and it continues to set the course for his later philosophy – even to the point of excluding Wittgenstein from paying due attention to other important issues (Pears 1988, 294, 296, 398–405). Contra the claims of certain other commentators, I believe there is something fundamentally right in Pears' assessment, although it is somewhat problematically phrased.[3] Intersubjectivity is a theme of central interest to Wittgenstein right until the end of his life, as documented by the manuscripts collected in the two volumes entitled *Last Writings on the Philosophy of Psychology*. In other words, Wittgenstein is interesting to look at in this context simply because he lavished enormous efforts on coming to grips with the issue of other minds.

Second, the nature of Wittgenstein's writing makes it well suited for an investigation such as the one attempted in this book. Wittgenstein rarely states and argues for philosophical theses. Rather, he engages in dialogues with various imaginary or real interlocutors, and the point of these dialogues is not primarily to promote a set of fixed philosophical claims. Anthony Kenny has calculated that the *Philosophical Investigations* "contain 784 questions. Only 110 of these are answered; and seventy of the answers are *meant* to be wrong" (Kenny 1959, 235). This lends Wittgenstein's remarks a fruitful open-ended character. He is not trying to foist a particular view on us as much as he is trying to get us to think carefully about certain philosophical issues. To be sure, the point is usually that we need to think *differently* about the issue at hand, but this does not necessarily mean that Wittgenstein has a particular conclusion in mind as the one we have to reach. As he writes in the preface to the *Investigations*, "I should not like my writing to spare other people the trouble of thinking. But, if possible, to stimulate someone to thoughts of his own" (PI, viii).

Wittgenstein's writings can have, and sometimes do have, the latter effect. But, as Wittgenstein himself suspected, they can also have the opposite effect of generating empty philosophical jargon[4] that makes it difficult to think thoughts of one's own, or indeed any clear thoughts whatsoever. One way to avoid getting caught up in Wittgensteinian jargon, and thus to let Wittgenstein's writings have the effect intended by their author, is to compare and supplement Wittgenstein's perspective with the perspectives of philosophers who employ a very different vocabulary and style. In this book, I draw especially on Levinas and Husserl, but to a lesser extent also on Heidegger and Sartre, in an attempt to assemble and develop Wittgenstein's ideas into a compelling account of intersubjectivity. Including such "Continental" thinkers helps to immunize us against at least one variety of a common philosophical disease diagnosed by Wittgenstein: the disease caused by "a one-sided diet" (PI, § 593). This may enable us to shed new light on the problem of other minds.

There is an additional bonus. Some of the new light that we shed on the problem of intersubjectivity may reflect back on Wittgenstein. One of the ideas behind this book is that the comparison with the mentioned Continental thinkers can be used to challenge certain widespread views on the basic drift of Wittgenstein's thoughts on subjectivity and intersubjectivity.

According to some commentators, Wittgenstein offers a "community account" of the mental, or a "social conception of the mind" (cf. the subtitle of M. Williams 1999). Such commentators think Wittgenstein's main achievement is to offer a corrective to a traditional account of the mental that "privileges the subjective over the public and/or social" – a traditional emphasis that continues in the twentieth century "not only in the sense-data theories of Russell and others within the positivist movement, but also in the work of adherents of the phenomenological tradition, such as Husserl" (ibid., 2). There is an obvious danger in the talk of a "social conception of the mind," however: the danger of merely reversing the priorities, privileging the public and/or social over the subjective. And this danger is not to be taken lightly, for, as Husserl and Levinas (among others) have pointed out, the price of downplaying or ignoring the subjective and individual is ultimately to make sociality incomprehensible. A community of no one is not a *community*; without *subjectivity* there is no *intersubjectivity*. Reading Wittgenstein against the background of these basic insights reveals a different picture of this supposed protagonist of a community view. The later Wittgenstein's repeated insistence on the asymmetry of first-person and second- or third-person perspectives, for example, can now be seen as an attempt to show that there is really no alternative here between, say, "individualism" and "anti-individualism."[5] A particular sort of "individualism" is, rather, a precondition for the establishment of a coherent "community view" – a coherent account of sociality. Or so I will argue.

A closely related view that a comparison with Husserl and Levinas may assist us in challenging is the view that a central aim of Wittgenstein's reflections on the philosophy of mind is to contest the very notion of a "self-present subject" (Glendinning 1998, 150).[6] According to Husserl, for example, denying that there exists a subject with a "potential for a distinctively first-personal 'inside take' on its own states" (ibid., 139) is denying the existence of subjects of experience altogether; and our healthy fear of Cartesianism should never prompt us to make such radical (eliminative) moves. Nor, as I will argue, was it Wittgenstein's intention to deny that there exist subjects with first-person "inside takes" on their mental lives. The comparison with phenomenology can help us see how he could avoid eliminating subjectivity while maintaining his critique of Cartesian dualism – or, more precisely, how he could steer a steady course between dualism and its various (behaviorist, reductionist, or eliminativist) opponents.

The theme of intersubjectivity, or other minds, construed broadly in the way indicated, is the main topic of this book. Perhaps the central idea of the book is that we have two sets of seemingly conflicting intuitions about the accessibility of the mental lives of others. (Indeed, I suspect that it is due to these intuitions that philosophers continue to feel a need to address the problem of other minds.) On the one hand, we are inclined to think that it is wrong to claim, as Cartesian dualists would have to do, that the minds of others are essentially inaccessible to direct experience. But on the other hand we feel that it is equally wrong to claim, as behaviorists have done, that the mental lives of subjects are completely accessible to an outside spectator. My view is that both these sets of intuitions reflect important truths, so that if we want to shed new light on the issue(s) of other minds, then we have to find some way to accommodate them both.

The argument of the book, in very brief outline, is as follows. If we understand mental life as having a number of essential features distinguishing it fundamentally from all objects and things – that is, if we understand mental life as *world-involving*, as *embodied*, and as *expressed* – then we can provide an account that steers clear of a number of pitfalls (such as behaviorism and Cartesian dualism), and one that is able to accommodate both of the intuitions just mentioned. In addition, we can make sense of intersubjectivity as having from the outset an irreducible "ethical" aspect. Preempting a possible objection, I should emphasize that none of what I am going to say is intended to constitute a refutation of other minds skepticism.[7] It will be as possible to raise skeptical doubts after my argument has been developed as it has always been. A change that I do hope to contribute to bringing about, however, is the following. By doing justice to the intuitions that motivate skepticism concerning other minds, while at the same time accounting for the cognitive access we have to the mental lives of others, the skeptical problems may be rendered a little more speculative and exaggerated, and thereby a little less interesting and urgent, than they would have seemed beforehand.[8] This in itself is a significant result, even if it is nothing like a refutation of skepticism. With this proviso in mind, I will offer a longer outline of the argument.

There is, as Wittgenstein has seen, a characteristic "conjuring trick" that tends to block or misdirect our vision when we philosophize about the mind or subjectivity. Exposing that conjuring trick is the task of Chapter 1. To put it as briefly as possible, the illusion or trick involves the idea that the mind and everything mental should be understood in terms of objects and their properties, states, and processes. When we think in this way about the mind we are left with alternatives neither of which is very attractive. In Wittgenstein's day, the main alternatives were behaviorism and some version of dualism. That is why much of the discussion that follows in this book centers on these "outdated" positions. (Today the choice seems to be between various types of materialism, but the same conjuring trick is active in these discussions as well.) Once we have adopted the idea of the mind or subjectivity as an object or realm of objects, the question is whether this realm is part of the physical world or whether it constitutes an immaterial world of its own. Many commentators have struggled to place Wittgenstein *vis-à-vis* dualism, behaviorism, and materialism, not realizing that their trouble with making him fit into any of these boxes stems from the fact that Wittgenstein considered these to be false alternatives – alternatives that only present themselves the moment we have taken the apparently innocent, but in reality highly problematical, step of conceiving of subjectivity as something "object-like."

Chapter 2 explores one feature of mental life that becomes enigmatic when the object approach is adopted: *intentionality*. The right way to understand the intentionality of subjective life, so I argue in this chapter, is to see it as intrinsically "world-involving." If we fail to grasp this, then intentionality becomes an unsolvable riddle. More precisely, if we assume that intentional mental phenomena are self-standing mental items that we may characterize independently of any reference to their intentional objects, then we cannot make sense of the "normativity" peculiar to intentional phenomena. That gives intentionality an air of magic. If we abandon the view that mental phenomena are such self-contained items, however, we make room for the insight that it is their "nature" to be directly and immediately world-directed.

It is wrong to think of human embodiment in terms of an "ego" or "mind," in itself nonbodily, that "inhabits" a physical body. Not only because the "ego" in question is likely to seem too "ghostly," but also because the body that this ego is supposed to inhabit will be too thing-like or object-like for us to be able to identify it with *our* body. According to the argument developed in Chapter 3, the problem with this whole approach to human embodiment is that what is essentially a unitary phenomenon deserving a separate, holistic explication – a "living human being," in

Wittgenstein's words – is split into various discrete elements with distinct properties. What we should do, rather, is to conceive of embodiment as part of the configuration of subjectivity: something essential to our being experiencing subjects *at all*. This, however, necessitates not only that the human mind is pulled out into the tangible human body; it also demands that we rethink the living human body, that we understand it as imbued with subjectivity.

Chapter 4 may be viewed as an excursus and could in principle be skipped without loss of understanding of the main argument of the book. However, the chapter picks up some of the loose threads that Chapter 2 has left hanging concerning the internalism–externalism debate and Wittgenstein's place in it. More specifically, it argues (countering some claims made by Gregory McCulloch) that one should not assume that Wittgenstein's commitment to some form of externalism entails a commitment to metaphysical realism. In order to show what is wrong with the latter assumption, the chapter provides a brief exposition of some *Leitmotifs* of the so-called private language argument in the *Philosophical Investigations*. The point is that, while Wittgenstein's private language considerations support an externalist interpretation, they at the same time undercut the realistic position of McCulloch. The "real essences" that, on McCulloch's view, are "tracked" by human understanding are ultimately just "wheels turning idly": they make no difference to any of our practices and are therefore not "part of the mechanism" at all. The chapter also suggests that the kind of perspective from which metaphysical realism looks like an attractive position is an (ultimately fictitious) external perspective *vis-à-vis* human life.

The private language argument is often claimed to be Wittgenstein's final victory over the solipsism that influenced his early thought. While not taking issue with this claim, Chapter 5 proposes to investigate the later Wittgenstein's antisolipsism without directly discussing private language. This permits "see[ing] something that sheds a new light on the facts" (CV, 45). In particular, it makes it possible to correct an idea that many philosophers have believed they have found in the later Wittgenstein: for, contra these philosophers, it is not Wittgenstein's opinion that (to put the point very loosely) emphasizing the importance, uniqueness, or irreducibility of the first-person perspective leads to solipsism. To suppose that it does is precisely to repeat the false move of the solipsist, according to Wittgenstein. There is, on the latter's view, an essential and fundamental difference between the first-person perspective and the third-person perspective on subjectivity. But it is only when we assume that there is an important metaphysical truth about the world in this (*à la*: "Only I am *really* a subjectivity") that solipsism follows. The metaphysical assumption is the one that causes all the trouble – not the idea that the first-person perspective is unique or irreducible. Once we achieve a firm grasp of the idea that the first-person/third-person asymmetry is a "grammatical" feature – a "rule of the game" of intersubjectivity, so to speak – the threat of solipsism vanishes.

8 *Introduction*

An important aspect of the asymmetry in question is the notion that there must be a certain inaccessibility or "transcendence" characterizing the mental lives of other minds. The "otherness" of others is reflected, *inter alia*, in the fact that many aspects of their mental lives may elude us, even when we are doing our utmost to grasp them. Some philosophers – notably Jean-Paul Sartre, but on one reading Emmanuel Levinas as well – have claimed that the full transcendence of another subject cannot possibly be presented in a perceptual experience. Anything that can be so presented, the argument goes, will be reduced to a mere thing or object, and thus falls short of the transcendence characteristic of another subject qua *other subject*. In Chapter 6 I attempt to show that this view encounters insurmountable difficulties. Very briefly put, the problem is that it becomes difficult to see how we can work with an otherness manifestly that of other *minds* or *subjects* if we divorce the presence of the latter entirely from anything that can be perceptually given. So what we ought to do is return to the (basically Husserlian) position that there must be a perceptual manifestation of other minds as other minds; but the structure of this sort of manifestation must be fundamentally different from the manifestation of houses, rocks, and bicycles. Having established that, of course, the really big question presents itself: How are we more precisely to describe the structure of the former sort of manifestation?

Chapter 7 takes on this crucial question. In terms of systematic importance, it is arguably the central chapter of the book. It collects several of the main points of the previous chapters in an attempt to show how we can reconcile the notion that there must be a perceptual manifestation of the mental lives of other people with the idea that others have a dimension of inaccessibility or transcendence. The first part of the chapter reiterates the attack on any conception of mental life that would make it completely separate from manifest bodily "behavior." Then, exploiting what Wittgenstein and Levinas write about *expression* (especially the expressions of the human face), I argue that if we conceive of mental life as something that is expressed in the face and in bodily behavior in general, then we can make sense of both its accessibility and its transcendence. For two closely connected features separate expressive manifestation fundamentally from the manifestation of an object. First, while the notion of "lying open to view" is appropriate for rocks, it cannot capture the variability and dynamics that are characteristic of expression. The way expression unfolds it disrupts (or at least can disrupt) every firm grasp we think we have of it. Second, it is characteristic of expression that its dynamic has *another subject* at its source. In a human face, for example, we experience the *personal* presence of someone, attending (and acting as the source of) the expressive manifestation. So although the mental life of another person is manifested to me in his or her expression, it is manifested in such a way as to reveal its otherness and the fragility of my grasp of it. For as *expressed* to me, as unfolding in this personal dynamic of which I am not the source, it is precisely the other person's mental life – not mine. There are many natural objections to these remarks, of course. I will address them in due course.

In Chapter 8 I follow Levinas in attempting to link expression to considerations of an ethical or "proto-ethical" nature. I try to make it plausible that such a link is also found in Wittgenstein. The argument is essentially as follows. First, some of the remarks of the later Wittgenstein's that have lead commentators to accuse him of advocating behaviorism have a feature in common, which is usually overlooked: these remarks do not so much deny the existence or importance of mental life (in particular the mental lives of others) as counter a deeply ingrained philosophical approach to this phenomenon. Wittgenstein's point, so I argue, is that when we philosophize we often tend to view the recognition of others as other minds or subjects as a purely theoretical process. That is, we conceive it as a question of ascertaining, in an observational mode, the presence of certain features characteristic of "mindedness." In Wittgenstein's optic, however, this is a misconstrual of our involvement with others. To recognize someone as another human being is not merely to discover certain features of an object; it is, rather, something that is already interwoven with characteristic attitudes and normative patterns of reaction. In other words, to perceive another human being is essentially to be presented with something like an ethical demand. The second stage of the argument consists in an attempt to show that this demand is tied up with expression and that we can develop a "proto-ethics" by taking expression as our lead. The term proto-ethics is supposed to indicate that what I have in mind here is something considerably less specific than what we usually expect from a philosophical "ethics." (The relative unspecificity, in fact, is anything but coincidental; it has an important proto-ethical point.) To put it very briefly, the demand in question summons an agent to her personal, indeclinable, and in an important sense unlimited and undischargeable duty to treat other people right. Regarding the question of what, then, is the right way to treat others (what is the correct ethical code?), the demand is silent. What is the right thing to do in a particular case is, on Levinas' and Wittgenstein's view, something it is up to the individual agent to figure out; that is, there is and can be no ultimate ethical code or set of rules. All there is is a constantly present appeal or demand that allocates full responsibility to the moral agent while (and this is in fact the reverse side of the same coin) giving her little more than a hint as to the direction she is to follow.

1 Exposing the conjuring trick

> The decisive movement in the conjuring trick has been made, and it was the very one that we thought quite innocent.
>
> (PI, § 308)

Introduction

Wittgenstein's later philosophy of mind has been the subject of many books and articles since the publication of the *Philosophical Investigations* in 1953. Despite the efforts of many knowledgeable commentators, however, there still is nothing resembling a consensus on what Wittgenstein's position is. Most commentators by now agree that Wittgenstein is opposed to both Cartesianism and behaviorism, that indeed it is central to his philosophy of mind to overcome these alternatives. But at the same time there is substantial disagreement regarding what Wittgenstein's own positive contribution amounts to.

One very fundamental point of disagreement revolves around the way in which Wittgenstein's philosophy of mind ought to be placed in relation to the positions of Cartesianism and behaviorism. While (more or less) everyone rejects the labels of Cartesianism and behaviorism as applied to Wittgenstein, there seems to be significant disagreement regarding what these positions, and Wittgenstein's alternative, actually involve. According to Jaakko and Merrill Hintikka, for example, Wittgenstein has no quarrel with the Cartesian ontology of mind. All he is critical of, they claim, is Cartesian semantics, not Cartesian metaphysics, and in fact Wittgenstein subscribes to a full-blown dualistic metaphysics (Hintikka and Hintikka 1986, 250, 267, 292).[1] Similarly, John McDowell has argued that Wittgenstein is not at all critical of the notion of an "inner world, populated by definite states and processes" (McDowell 1989, 644).[2] McDowell, to be sure, does not endorse the terms Cartesianism and dualism as applied to Wittgenstein, but it is nevertheless rather difficult to see exactly where, if at all, the Wittgenstein he describes parts with Cartesianism. The notion that there are two realms or worlds – an "inner" and an "outer" realm, each populated by its own entities, states, and processes – is surely central to what we usually understand by dualism.

On the other hand, it has recently been claimed that if "behavior" is "defined in terms of physical movements or singular and dateable occurrences," then Wittgenstein is certainly not a behaviorist (Glendinning 1998, 10). But still, it is claimed, "in response to a philosopher who attempts to 'thicken' mere behavior by reference to the presence 'in' or 'behind' it of a self-present subject," Wittgenstein will reply that this subject is a mere fiction (ibid., 10, 150). Now, some behaviorists would presumably agree with the rejection of mere "physical movement" as all there is to mental states – this being more of a primitive (perhaps roughly Hobbesian) form of materialism rather than the kind of behaviorism they would subscribe to.[3] And the rejection of the idea of a subjectivity "in" or "behind" behavior (or dispositions to behavior) is surely characteristic of behaviorism. In other words, it is not at all clear that Glendinning's interpretation avoids committing Wittgenstein to some (even quite strong) version of behaviorism. Similarly, if, according to Wittgenstein, "mental states of affairs" are nothing but "patterns" of behavior (cf. Savigny 1996, 179, 253), then this seems only to confirm his commitment to a sophisticated kind of behaviorism. So how, then, are we to understand Wittgenstein's later philosophy of mind?

In this chapter, I will argue that both interpretations just outlined are fundamentally misguided. Wittgenstein's distance from Cartesianism, on the one hand, and behaviorism, on the other hand, is much greater than these interpretations suggest. Wittgenstein in fact thinks that the opposition between Cartesianism and behaviorism conceals a substantial, and deeply problematic, agreement. The aim of Wittgenstein's later writings on the "philosophy of psychology" is to show how this agreement is a conjuring trick that commits our thinking to a choice between two equally misguided notions of subjectivity.

What I aim to do in this chapter, then, is to follow Wittgenstein's attempt to navigate between the alternatives of Cartesianism and behaviorism (and physicalism). This will provide us with a first sketch of the type of perspective that all the philosophical heroes of my story, albeit in different ways, are trying to overcome. So the point of the chapter is mainly negative, and the discussion is at times rather exegetical in its focus. However, besides undermining what is sometimes presented as the only relevant alternative in philosophy of mind, the chapter also indicates the itinerary to be followed in the subsequent chapters.

Against Cartesianism

Cartesianism or Cartesian dualism is the view that, at least apart from God, there are two radically different kinds of things (or substances) in the world: extended things (spatial and physical things) on the one hand and thinking things (minds, souls) on the other. A human being is thus somehow composed of two quite different kinds of stuff on the Cartesian account: a body, which has a certain extension, color, weight – and which, like all other extended things, can be perceived by one or more of the senses (seen, touched) – and a mind, which I can neither touch nor see. This, of course, does not mean that the mind cannot be accessed at all, for, as Descartes puts it, "I can achieve an easier and more evident perception of my own mind than of anything else" (Descartes 1984, 23). The philosophical problems that this account engenders are well known, but since they play almost no part in Wittgenstein's response to Cartesianism they need not directly concern us at this point. Nor do we have to go into the details of Descartes' argument and conception, since what Wittgenstein is interested in is only the general *picture* (*Bild*) of the human being that emerges from the Cartesian account. For this reason, it is also irrelevant whether the Cartesianism combated by Wittgenstein can in fact justly be attributed to the historical philosopher Descartes or any other past or present philosopher.[4] Independently of all this, the Cartesian *Bild* is a familiar and not entirely unattractive one.

Wittgenstein attacks the Cartesian conception from more than one angle. He is critical towards the notion of "privileged access," expressed in Descartes' claim that nothing can be as easily and evidently perceived as what goes on in my own mind. He also criticizes the related idea of "privacy," i.e. the idea that only *I* can perceive, at least in a direct manner, what goes on in my own mind, and that others can at best deduce facts about my mind from my bodily behavior. Attacking Cartesianism from the other end, Wittgenstein also voices doubts about the conception of "body" and "bodily behavior" that the Cartesian account implies. Some have indeed taken Wittgenstein to imply that the very notion of the mind as something distinct from mere physical behavior is misguided. I will return to this last point later. For the moment, I want to take a closer look at Wittgenstein's criticisms of Cartesianism.

First, is it really true in general that each person only has direct, perceptual access to his or her own mind, and that all others are consequently left with little more than speculations? As Wittgenstein admits, this picture is not without a certain appeal:

> It looks like this: there is something inner here which can be inferred only inconclusively from the outer. It is a picture and it is obvious what justifies this picture. The apparent certainty of the first person, the uncertainty of the third.
>
> (LW I, § 951)

This, as a *general truth*, seems to be implied by the Cartesian conception. After all, no matter how closely mind and body are "intermingled," I can only perceive the *bodily* side of the other, the "outer side." Thus her mind or soul, her "inner," being a radically different thing from the one I perceive, seems at best indirectly accessible to me, in particular via some process of reasoning. It is worth emphasizing that it is this general claim that Wittgenstein questions. That is, as we will see, he is not making the implausible counterclaims that I can *always* perceive directly what goes on in another person's mind and that there is *never* room for uncertainty as to what is going on in another's mind. Rather, by providing certain clear-cut examples, Wittgenstein tries to show that the case is much more complicated than the Cartesian picture would have it.

To address the question of "uncertainty" first, Wittgenstein asks his Cartesian interlocutor whether he can really make sense of certain not uncommon situations:

> If I see someone writhing in pain with evident cause I do not think: all the same, his feelings are hidden from me.
> (PI, 223; cf. LW II, 22)

> "I can only guess at someone else's feelings" – does that really make sense when you see him badly wounded, for instance, and in dreadful pain?
> (LW I, § 964)

> You look at a face and say "I wonder what's going on behind that face?" But you don't have to think that way. And if someone talks to me quite obviously holding nothing back then I am not even tempted to think that way.
> (LW I, § 978, variation)

There are some quite straightforward everyday situations in which the "uncertainty" that is construed as an essential uncertainty on the Cartesian account simply has no place (cf. RPP I, § 137), situations "where only a lunatic could take the expression of pain, for instance, as a sham" (LW II, 33). When I see "someone writhing in pain with evident cause," there can simply be no question that this person is in pain. And when I'm engaged in a frank discussion with a friend, the notion that her "inner life" is in principle hidden from me seems absurd. Of course, as Wittgenstein himself stresses, there are degrees of certainty and uncertainty here: there are clear-cut cases and there are more complicated cases, stretching all the way to the case where I feel I simply cannot figure a person out (PI, 223; RPP II, § 568).[5] But this is simply an important aspect of our psychological concepts themselves (cf. LW I, § 967), not an imperfection or a defect.[6]

But at least the Cartesian would seem to be right in emphasizing that I have no *perceptual* access to the pains, thoughts, and emotions of another. Wittgenstein, however, contests the general claim that I have no perceptual access to the mental phenomena of others, and again he does so by appealing to "phenomenological" evidence, that is, to the phenomena of everyday life as they appear to us in everyday life. As he says, choosing the example of fear: "In general I do not surmise fear in him – I *see* it. I do not feel that I am deducing the probable existence of something inside from something outside" (RPP II, § 170). And more generally:

> Consciousness in another's face. Look into someone else's face, and see the consciousness in it, and a particular *shade* of consciousness. You see on it, in it, joy, indifference, interest, excitement, torpor, and so on. The light in other people's faces. Do you look into *yourself* in order to recognize the fury in *his* face? It is there as clearly as in your own breast.
> (Z, § 220; RPP I, § 927; cf. LW I, § 769; RPP II, § 570)

In many cases, it makes perfectly good sense to say that we *perceive* the fears and doubts of another (LW II, 62), that we see that another is in pain, and indeed that we see that the other person sees this or that. Do we not *see* the happiness of a child receiving her birthday presents? Is it not manifested right there before our eyes, in the face of the child? If so, the Cartesian notion of privacy seems to be contradicted by the phenomena of experience.

The quotations just referred to also cast doubt on the way the Cartesian would construe the external appearance and behavior of a subject. The face, and in fact the whole body of a human being, is not some mere material thing, and its movements not mere physical movements, according to Wittgenstein. Rather, the bodily behavior of another subject is itself, as it were, soaked with the meaning of subjectivity. We see another's hesitation in the movement of her hand, and we see her fear in her face (cf. above), just as we see her eyes casting glances (Z, § 222; RPP I, § 1100), and so forth. As Wittgenstein famously summarized the point (thereby inadvertently providing fuel for the recurring charge of behaviorism), "[i]f one sees the behavior of a living thing, one sees its soul" (PI, § 357).

These issues are intimately connected with Wittgenstein's much discussed notion of "criteria." While it is impossible – in particular in view of the massive attention it has received by commentators – to do justice to this notion in the present context, a word or two must be said about it at this point. Wittgenstein's remark that an "'inner process' stands in need of outward criteria" (PI, § 580) should not be interpreted as a statement to the effect that there are inner processes that we cannot see, and which therefore – if they are to figure at all in our lives – must have external, observable criteria. As *Philosophical Investigations*, section 357 makes clear, we are not at all barred from direct perception of the souls of others. What Wittgenstein seems to be saying, then, is simply that "inner" states cannot meaningfully be conceived of as completely devoid of public accessibility. That a person's jerks and screams are, under suitable conditions, "criteria" for her having a toothache means simply that we see, in her behavior under these circumstances, that she has a toothache.[7]

But the last fortress of Cartesianism would appear to be impregnable. Surely I have some sort of privileged access to my own intentions, thoughts, feelings and so forth. Surely I *know* what I am thinking, and *I know* that I am in pain, in a way that is immune to the mistakes that another might make about my thoughts and pains. Yes and no. According to Wittgenstein, we may perhaps say that I have privileged access to my own pain,[8] if we thereby mean that I usually cannot doubt whether I am in pain, whereas others watching me could entertain doubts about whether or not I am in pain (PI, § 246). I am generally the final authority on whether or not (and typically also where) I am in pain. Wittgenstein in no way denies this; in fact, he advocates what has (since Shoemaker 1968) become known as the principle of "immunity from error through misidentification," at least for certain uses of the word "I." Wittgenstein argues that what he calls the "subjective" use of "I" is immune to error through misidentification. When I use the word "I" "objectively" – for example "I have grown six inches," "I have a bump on my forehead" – it involves "the recognition of a particular person, and there is in these cases the possibility of an error" (BB, 67). (What I took to be a mirror reflecting my image is actually a window, on the other side of which stands my identical twin, who happens to have incurred a bump on his forehead.) But when I use "I" subjectively, e.g. saying "I have toothache," "[t]o ask 'are you sure that it's *you* who have pains?' would be nonsensical" (BB, 67). We should be careful, however, not to assume that this carries over into a general immunity to error concerning our own mental lives. And, more importantly, what Wittgenstein is eager to emphasize is not so much the point that others can make mistakes about my sensations that I cannot make myself, but rather the essential difference between first-person and third-person perspectives on subjectivity. As he notes, it is *possible* to achieve certainty regarding the sensations of another, but clearly the other's sensations do not thereby become my sensations (LW I, § 963). This illustrates the crucial point: my access to my own subjectivity is of another *kind* than the access another has, but not necessarily more certain or accurate.

Consistent with this insight, Wittgenstein is reluctant to express the first-person/third-person asymmetry in terms of knowledge. That is, he resists the idea that I *know* something that the other cannot know, or that I know something with a degree of certainty that the other cannot achieve. One problem is of course that few things are more certain than the fact that a severely injured, fully conscious person who is writhing and screaming experiences pain, and thus that the concept of "knowledge" seems more appropriate here than, say, "belief," even though we are dealing with a third-person perspective. In most cases it clearly makes little sense to say, confronting someone screaming and bleeding after being hit by a car, that I "believe" she's in pain. Rather, there is no question she's in pain: those are the phenomenological facts of the matter. Only secluded armchair philosophers would want to contest them; the rest of us would run for help (or simply panic). But that is not all there is to Wittgenstein's resistance to the use of "knowledge" here. He also claims that the first-person perspective on something like pain should not (in the normal case) be labeled "knowledge" at all (LW II, 92). In other words, when I am in pain it is not strictly correct to say that I "know" I'm in pain, and when I am thinking it is not strictly correct to say that I "know" what I'm thinking. As Wittgenstein provocatively puts it:

> It is correct to say "I know what you are thinking," and wrong to say "I know what I am thinking."
> (A whole cloud of philosophy condensed into a drop of grammar.)
> (PI, 222; cf. Wittgenstein 1969, § 41)

One might of course ask whether Wittgenstein's definition of "knowledge" isn't a bit too narrow (cf. Jacobsen, 1996; Savigny 1996, 220–21); indeed one might doubt that his position really squares with how, in our everyday life, we use the verb "to know" (cf. PI, § 246). It might be that sentences such as "I know what you think" are more common than sentences such as "I know what I think," but clearly there are situations in which we would utter something like the latter sentence. Wittgenstein recognizes this, but claims that those are typically situations where we, as it were, remind somebody of the rules of the game (LW I, § 890). If someone says to me, "You weren't thinking that," I might retort "I know what I'm thinking!," thereby reminding the other person that I am the final authority on the question of what I am thinking. Still, arguably this doesn't show that we are wrong in general to speak of "knowledge" in the first-person case.

However that may be, the point Wittgenstein is trying to make is a more fundamental one. The concept of "knowing," according to Wittgenstein, is a concept that essentially belongs in the "language games" in which such concepts as "doubting," "presuming," and "becoming convinced of" belong as well (PI, 221).[9] Of course, Wittgenstein does not mean to say that "knowing" has no application where there is no doubt and thus no need to become convinced. If he did, that would seem to have the absurd consequence that because I never ever doubt the name of my mother I should avoid saying that I "know" her name. What Wittgenstein is saying is rather that "knowing" has no application where "doubting" *makes no sense* (PI, 221; cf. Wittgenstein 1969, § 58). And, at least in usual cases, it makes no sense to say that I doubt whether it is I or someone else that is in pain. So it seems that we should conclude with David Pears that Wittgenstein's point is that this case is simply "too good to be called 'knowledge'" (Pears 1988, 259).

But I think Wittgenstein's real point has to do with something else than the very favorable nature of the case. Consider these famous remarks from the *Philosophical Investigations*: "It can't be said of me at all (except perhaps as a joke) that I *know* I am in pain. What is it supposed to mean – except perhaps that I *am* in pain?" (PI, § 246; cf. BB, 55). The point, as I interpret it, is that to say something like this is to give the impression that I am strangely distanced and detached from my pain – that I am observing it, obtaining knowledge about it, rather than simply *undergoing* it, suffering. In other words, the deeper reason why Wittgenstein resists the terminology of "knowledge" when applied to the first-person perspective on such phenomena as pain, but sanctions it when it's applied to the third-person perspective, is that the former use seems to imply that my first-person relation to my own pain is that of an observer of what goes on "inside" me. It gives the impression (and this is a picture that seems very much in line with Cartesianism) that, just as others learn of my behavior, thoughts, intentions, and perceptions from perceiving me, so I find out about these things from some sort of "internal observation" of what "goes on in my mind."[10] As if my pains, fears, and so forth were internal facts that I "read off" my inner private field of observation (cf. LW I, § 39; RPP I, § 457). Indeed, as if my subjectivity as such were one great internal "phenomenal field," open to some internal gaze. As if it were something I perceive, at a certain "internal distance," rather than what *I am*. No doubt self-observation is possible, but is this really my *default relation to my own subjectivity*, the subjectivity I am? Wittgenstein's answer is unequivocally negative (cf. LW II, 9–12).[11]

At this point one might object that Wittgenstein, too, fails to do justice to the phenomena. After all, granted that my self-relation isn't accurately described in terms of internal observation, shouldn't we then go one step further and add that neither is my relation to others, at least not exclusively or primarily? But the way Wittgenstein has been presented so far he might give the impression of claiming that, whereas I am not an observer of myself, my relation to others is basically one of observing them, obtaining knowledge about them, or recording their subjective lives. Not only would such a view seem to have dubious ethical consequences; it would also seem descriptively mistaken. As Heidegger has pointed out, the observational relation, while clearly possible, is not the most original type of relation to others; rather, it is itself a modification of a more basic "being-with-others" (cf. BT, 162). Take, for instance, the example where I am having a frank conversation with a friend. Wittgenstein is correct to emphasize that here I would feel no inclination towards the claim that "his thoughts are hidden or inaccessible to me." On the other hand, however, it would seem equally absurd to claim that I perceive or observe his mind or thoughts. Clearly, caught up in the conversation, I am doing no such thing. Rather, I am simply experiencing a being-engaged-with my friend in the subject we are discussing.

There is, I think, good evidence to suggest that Wittgenstein recognizes this phenomenological point.[12] For example, when he denies that I "am of the opinion" that other people have souls, he does not state his own alternative in terms of "knowledge." In fact, he dismisses as nonsensical the idea that I am "certain" that others are not robots (PI, 178). That is, Wittgenstein does not claim that I generally *know* or am certain that other people have souls; rather, he says that my *attitude* towards others is an attitude towards souls (PI, 178; LW I, § 324), or, better, simply an "'attitude

18 *Exposing the conjuring trick*

toward a human'" (LW II, 38). This is significant, because the notion of "attitude" clearly avoids the problematic connotations of observation and thematic knowledge. What Wittgenstein ultimately wants to claim is that we do have "direct," "perceptual" access to other subjectivities, but that this does not entail that our original relation to them is one of thematic perception, observation, and knowledge. These latter are specific possibilities within the *attitude* of being-with-others, i.e. they are "later" than, and presuppose, this fundamental attitude (cf. LW II, 38).[13]

Against behaviorism

A significant number of interpreters have accused Wittgenstein of defending logical behaviorism. Wittgenstein explicitly denounces behaviorism in the *Philosophical Investigations* (PI, § 307), but this has not stopped commentators from speculating that perhaps Wittgenstein's position nevertheless amounts to some sophisticated form of the view. Unfortunately, "behaviorism" is not a term that designates one single clearly defined position; on the contrary, it is used to characterize several very different views. For present purposes, we can distinguish between ontological behaviorism (which claims something about the types of things that exist in the world), logical behaviorism (which claims something about the meanings of and logical connections between our words), and methodological behaviorism (which claims something about the proper method for the science of psychology). In fact, things are even more complicated than this. Ontological behaviorism can thus be of both the eliminative and the reductive kind, whereas Wittgenstein, as far as I can tell, has been accused of no less than three different kinds of logical behaviorism (which we might call "strong," "moderate," and "weak" logical behaviorism). In the following discussion, these positions will be discussed in turn, starting with eliminative behaviorism, then moving on to strong logical behaviorism, reductive materialism, and finally moderate and weak logical behaviorism. (Behaviorism as a research method for scientific psychology need not be discussed here.)

First of all, when Wittgenstein says that seeing the behavior of a living thing is seeing its soul, one might be inclined to accuse him of what we could term eliminative *ontological* behaviorism (or eliminative materialism; I shall not distinguish between these), holding that there is no such thing as a "mind," or a subject, or anything subjective – but only physical behavior.[14] However, Wittgenstein himself complains that this is a misunderstanding of his critique of Cartesianism. Discussing the word "excitement," he remarks: "The misconception that this word means something internal *as well as* something external. And if anyone denies that, he is misinterpreted as denying inner excitement" (RPP II, § 335; cf. PO, 283). Taking another example, Wittgenstein explicitly rejects the idea that he would deny the presence of some "mental" occurrence in remembering. Indeed, he claims that denying this would amount to a denial "that anyone ever remembers anything," which is absurd (PI, § 306). And in a section explicitly devoted to the question of behaviorism, Wittgenstein lets his imaginary interlocutor object: "Aren't you at bottom really saying that everything except human behavior is a fiction?" (ibid., § 307) – to which he replies: "If I do speak of a fiction, then it is of a *grammatical* fiction" (ibid.). In other words, Wittgenstein certainly does not want to make the *ontological* claim that everything but behavior is mere fiction; whatever he wants to claim, it is a claim about "grammar."

This defense, however, might seem to suggest that Wittgenstein would be sympathetic towards a strong version of so-called "logical" behaviorism – the view that to attribute mental states to persons is to attribute to them certain sorts of behavior or dispositions to behavior. This interpretation would not hold that Wittgenstein simply denies the existence of mental phenomena, but rather that he claims that ascriptions of such phenomena to people may "be treated as statements referring to their actual or potential behavior" (Mundle 1966, 35). But a rudimentary knowledge of the central motifs of Wittgenstein's later work is sufficient for the realization that one must dismiss this idea.[15] Wittgenstein would clearly have to reject strong logical behaviorism on the ground that it simply doesn't square with our actual practice of using language. As Wittgenstein declares repeatedly, it is not the task of philosophy to improve on everyday language, but only to describe it the way it actually is (PI, § 124; BB, 28). Is it then the same thing to attribute a certain behavior to someone and to attribute some mental state or activity to someone? Can the one kind of sentence be substituted for the other, and vice versa, in all cases, and without loss or change of meaning? A consideration of quite simple cases will convince us that it cannot. Consider what Wittgenstein says about thinking:

> The word "thinking" is used in a certain way very differently from, for example, "to be in pain," "to be sad," etc.: we don't say "I think" as the expression of a mental state. At most we say "I'm thinking." "Leave me alone, I'm thinking about. ... " And of course one doesn't mean by this: "Leave me alone, I am now behaving in such and such a way." Therefore "thinking" is not behavior.
>
> (RPP II, § 12; cf. RPP I, § 652)

Presumably, similar arguments could be provided for most other "psychological" concepts. What we mean when we say we are in pain is not that we behave or are disposed to behave in some particular way; and when we say of another person that she is in pain we do not thereby say that she behaves in any particular way, nor necessarily that she is disposed to a certain behavior. So this is how Wittgenstein responds to his imaginary interlocutor's accusation of logical behaviorism:

> Then psychology treats of behavior, not of the mind? What do psychologists record? – What do they observe? Isn't it the behavior of

human beings, in particular their utterances? But *these* are not about behavior.[16]

(PI, 179)

Some philosophers, however, will find this type of consideration irrelevant. After all, it only concerns our use of words – but perhaps what we are really interested in is the structure of reality (cf. RPP I, §§ 548–49). Could it not be that, for us, in our daily lives, it does not amount to the same thing to attribute motives, intentions, thoughts, and feelings to others and to attribute particular behavioral or physical states or dispositions to them; and nevertheless, as a matter of empirical discovery, it turns out that these things *are* in fact identical? At one point in time it was not the same thing to *talk* of "Hesperus" and "Phosphorus"; but in fact the two were one and the same *entity*, the planet Venus. Wittgenstein's resistance towards strong versions of logical behaviorism does not rule out some commitment to ontological behaviorism or reductive materialism, though not (as we have seen) of the eliminative kind.

So how would Wittgenstein respond to reductive materialism? There is pretty good evidence that he would not subscribe to that type of view either. In one of the *Remarks on the Philosophy of Psychology*, for example, he writes: "Am I saying something like, 'and the soul itself is merely something about the body'? No. (I am not so hard up for categories)" (RPP II, § 690). Accordingly, he emphatically rejects that the lesson to be learned from his critique of Cartesianism is that the inner is itself something outer (LW II, 62), and he claims that the very notion of "physiological processes" is a "dangerously" misleading one in the philosophy of psychology (RPP I, § 1063). We even find in his writings occasional critical remarks on the even weaker notion that there should *correspond* some definite physical state to every mental state (this is weaker since it does not entail the claim that the two states or types of states are identical):

> No supposition seems to me more natural than that there is no process in the brain correlated with associating or with thinking; so that it would be impossible to read off thought-processes from brain-processes.
> (Z, § 608; RPP I, § 903)

> It is thus perfectly possible that certain psychological phenomena *cannot* be investigated physiologically, because physiologically nothing corresponds to them.
> (Z, § 609; RPP I, § 904; cf. RPP I, § 918)

Wittgenstein's objections to reductive materialism receive their clearest articulation in his discussions of memory. Here, too, he voices doubts about the basic assumption that the phenomenon of memory *must* involve some physiological component (RPP I, § 905), and he also provides sketches of arguments in support of his resistance to the materialist view. Wittgenstein argues that whereas we certainly understand what it would mean for some event to leave a mark on the brain – say, if I am hit so hard on my head that a part of my brain is damaged – we encounter problems precisely when we want to make intelligible that such a physical trace could be the memory itself. He writes:

> An event leaves a trace in the memory: one sometimes imagines this as if it consisted in the event's having left a trace, an impression, a consequence, in the nervous system. As if one could say: even the nerves have a memory. But then when someone remembered an event, he would have to *infer* it from this impression, this trace. Whatever the event does leave behind in the organism, *it* isn't the memory.
>
> The organism compared with a dictaphone spool; the impression, the trace, is the alteration in the spool that the voice leaves behind. Can one say that the dictaphone (or the spool) is remembering what was spoken all over again, when it reproduces what it took?
>
> (RPP I, § 220)

Wittgenstein's claim is that a neuronal process, event, or state of affairs as such cannot be identified with the memory of something past. The reasoning behind this claim is connected with a point we will discuss in the next chapter. Because a neuronal state or event of a particular organism is, presumably, something that can be identified and characterized without reference to anything outside the brain and nervous system of the organism, there is something essential to the "intentionality" or "aboutness" characteristic of memory that cannot be captured by reference to such an event. In principle, information about past events could be inferred from such neuronal traces, just as, say, I can infer from the blisters on my heels that I wore the wrong shoes yesterday. Even though the blisters were caused by my having worn the wrong shoes, however, the blisters themselves are not my memory of the event; and the same, so Wittgenstein appears to claim, goes for the neural "traces" some event leaves behind in my brain. Wittgenstein also seems to be suggesting that to attribute memory of an event to neural states is to commit what Anthony Kenny has termed the "homunculus fallacy" (Kenny 1991). The fact that a person remembers an event that she wouldn't remember if, say, a particular area of her brain was damaged, does not license the attribution of memory to her brain. According to Wittgenstein, it is human beings – not nerves, brains, or Dictaphones – that can be said to remember or forget something.

Whether or not any of these objections to reductive materialism is convincing, at least they show that Wittgenstein cannot very well be construed as an advocate of the view.[17] However, Wittgenstein has been suspected of another, weaker form of behaviorism, which might be termed moderate logical behaviorism. This is the view that, although physical behavior is not all there is, what really "matters," at least as far as the meaning of the words we use is concerned, is behavior. On this interpretation, Wittgenstein should not exactly be accused of claiming that it amounts to the same thing to attribute mental states and behavior to people; it is recognized that the language games we play with "behavior words" are different from the one we play with, e.g., "pain words" (RPP I, §§ 288–89). But, in spite of this, the claim is that according to Wittgenstein what *matters* in the game of attributing "pains" to people, is their behavior rather than whatever might go on in their minds. To be sure, Wittgenstein emphasizes the importance of very "fine shades" of behavior (PI, 203), as well as the wider external circumstances under which that behavior took place, some of which circumstances belong to earlier points in time, etc., etc. These qualifications might serve to distinguish the game of attributing pain to people from the game of attributing mere behavior to them (in which case, presumably, the wider circumstances play a less significant part), but they also clearly show that only behavior and the circumstances of behavior play any part in the game (cf. Pitcher 1964, 299).[18] This sort of interpretation apparently finds support in Wittgenstein's well-known claim that an "inner process" needs external criteria (PI, § 580). Even more importantly, it seems to be the explicit conclusion of one of the most famous passages in the *Philosophical Investigations* – the "beetle in a box" fable:

> Suppose everyone had a box with something in it: we call it a "beetle." No one can look into anyone else's box, and everyone says he knows what a beetle is only by looking at *his* beetle. – Here it would be quite possible for everyone to have something different in his box. One might even imagine such a thing constantly changing. – But suppose the word "beetle" had a use in these people's language? – If so it would not be used as the name of a thing. The thing in the box has no place in the language-game at all; not even as a *something*: for the box might even be empty. – No, one can "divide through" by the thing in the box; it cancels out, whatever it is.
>
> (PI, § 293)

On the moderate logical behaviorist interpretation, the central part of the passage is the sentence where Wittgenstein says that "the thing in the box has no place in the language-game at all." This, such interpreters argue, is the conclusion Wittgenstein is trying to establish. The "feeling," or the subjective state, whatever it is, does not belong in the language game: "it cancels out." But is this really what Wittgenstein is trying to say? No, as the important explanation of the argument documents, the argument is really a *reductio* of the Cartesian way of conceiving feelings and sensations. The passage immediately following the quoted portion reads: "That is to say: if we construe the grammar of the expression of sensation on the model of 'object and designation' the object drops out of consideration as irrelevant"

(PI, § 293). In other words, it is when you construe the mind and mental states as objects of some inner, private realm, inaccessible to others, that the absurd conclusion follows that the mind and mental states can be of no relevance to the games played with our words. Being cut off from the public world, these inner, "ghostly" objects (as Ryle would say) can have no part to play in our common, public language. But that subjectivity and the subjective experience should play no part in our language games is precisely not a conclusion Wittgenstein is prepared to draw. On the contrary, he concludes that if such a conclusion follows from the Cartesian way of setting the stage, then that stage setting must be wrong. Since the subjective feeling of pain *must* play an all-important role in our use of the word "pain," the strict Cartesian separation of inner and outer must be rejected. Just to drive the final nail into the coffin of the moderate behaviorist interpretation of Wittgenstein, here is the man himself explicitly rejecting it:

> But am I not really speaking only of the outer? I say, for instance, under what circumstances people say this or that. And I do always mean *outer* circumstances. Therefore it is *as if* I wanted to explain (quasi-define) the inner through the outer. And yet it isn't so.
> (LW II, 63)

In a classic article, Chihara and Fodor have attributed yet another version of behaviorism to Wittgenstein, viz. what they call "weak logical behaviorism" (Chihara and Fodor 1966, 387). Apparently, this is the view that there exist logical or "conceptual relations between statements about behavior and statements about mental events, processes, and states" (ibid., 386). In Wittgenstein, the term "criterion" marks precisely such a conceptual relation, according to Chihara and Fodor (ibid., 390). Committed neither to the denial of the existence of the mental nor to a denial of the importance of the inner to our use of sensation words and the like, this is indeed a weak type of logical behaviorism.

One commentator has attempted to defend Wittgenstein by replying that the view in question is one "which very few people would want to reject and which surely cannot be a reason for calling someone a logical behaviorist" (Schulte 1993, 160). Clearly, however, this is not the right response. Rather, Chihara and Fodor mischaracterize Wittgenstein's views on certain crucial points. First of all, they seem to fall victim to the misunderstanding of Wittgenstein's notion of "criterion" that I explicitly warned against above (see p. 14). They operate with a notion of criterion according to which a criterion for another person's being in pain is something different from the pain itself, but conceptually or logically connected with it; and they take Wittgenstein to hold that only the other person herself can have "first-hand knowledge of the occurrence of such mental events" (Chihara and Fodor 1966, 386), leaving the rest of us with behavioral criteria instead. However, in contrast to these claims, Wittgenstein holds that we often simply see, and thus indeed have "first hand knowledge" of, someone else's pain. More fundamentally, Chihara and Fodor's dualistic picture of "mental events," on the one hand, perceptually accessible to only one person, and "behavior," on the other, is precisely one Wittgenstein is trying to undermine, as we should know by now. Further, it seems that Chihara and Fodor are committed to a view of body and behavior that is very far indeed from the one propounded by Wittgenstein. Chihara and Fodor claim that Wittgenstein's position is "strikingly similar" to the views of the moderate behaviorist C. F. Hull (ibid., 387). In Hull's use of the word "behavior," however, it refers to mere "colorless" physical movements,[19] whereas Wittgenstein is concerned to emphasize that the human body and human behavior are full of "mental" significance (cf., e.g., Z, §§ 220–21). In sum, the position Chihara and Fodor describe has very little to do with Wittgenstein, and their attempt to attribute "weak logical behaviorism" to Wittgenstein consequently fails.[20]

Finally, it is important to note that there is one crucial point where Wittgenstein must part ways with logical behaviorism, or at least with most versions of it. As I have already mentioned, Wittgenstein grants to the Cartesian the essential difference between a first-person perspective and a third-person perspective on subjectivity. And he emphasizes repeatedly that, in a great many cases, I do not base knowledge of my own subjectivity on the sort of evidence on which others base their knowledge of me. But this does not mean that in my own case I have access to some sort of internal criteria, allowing me to determine whether, for instance, I am in pain or not. As we have seen, Wittgenstein rejects this idea of constant self-observation. In fact, quite in line with his resistance to the notion of "knowledge" being applied here, he claims that my original access to my own subjectivity is based on no criteria whatsoever (PI, § 404). At this point it appears that there is an important agreement between Cartesians and behaviorists; for both seem to think that the mind, in the first-person case as well as from a third-person perspective, must be an "object" of knowledge and observation, whether external observation or some kind of internal observation, or introspection. And precisely this is what Wittgenstein objects to:

> One wishes to say: In order to be able to say that I have t[oothache] I don't observe my behavior, say in the mirror. *And this is correct*, but it doesn't follow that you describe an observation of any other kind.
> (PO, 288; cf. RPP II, § 177)

> Here is the picture: He sees it [viz. "that which is in him"] immediately, I only mediately. But that's not the way it is. He doesn't see something and describe it to us.
> (LW II, 92)

In fact, Wittgenstein wants to carry his criticism of both Cartesianism and behaviorism one step further. We should recall from the beetle in a box fable

(PI, § 293) that Wittgenstein's diagnosis was that we get into trouble when we apply the schema "object and name" to subjectivity. As he explains elsewhere, "[t]he main difficulty arises from our imagining the experience (the pain, for instance) as a thing, for which of course we have a name and whose concept is therefore quite easy to grasp" (LW II, 43). The point, then, is this: Subjective life is not an object, not a thing, according to Wittgenstein – but nor is it "nothing" (PI, § 304). The "objectivistic" approach to subjectivity that the "object–name" schema represents is, according to Wittgenstein, the common mistake of Cartesianism and behaviorism. It is the presupposition that we may without further ado use concepts such as "object," "thing," "state," and "processes" to characterize subjectivity and subjective experiences that creates all our difficulties, Wittgenstein thinks.[21] He writes in the *Philosophical Investigations*:

> How does the philosophical problem about mental processes and states and about behaviorism arise? – The first step is the one that altogether escapes notice. We talk of processes and states and leave their nature undecided. Sometime perhaps we shall know more about them – we think. But that is just what commits us to a particular way of looking at the matter. For we have a definite concept of what it means to learn to know a process better. (The decisive movement in the conjuring trick has been made, and it was the very one that we thought quite innocent.)
> (PI, § 308; cf. LW II, 43)

Some commentators pass over this passage rather quickly, referring to it simply as Wittgenstein's somewhat hasty rejection of behaviorism (Schulte 1993, 159; Donagan 1966, 327). But in fact it is a crucial passage, whose critical scope is much wider than such commentators assume. The passage is ultimately a critique of the way most philosophers, including Cartesian dualists, reductive materialists, and various types of behaviorists, approach human subjectivity. Instead of approaching subjectivity without preconceptions about its nature, we uncritically employ such notions as "thing," "object," "process," and "state" to describe it. This is precisely the conjuring trick that commits us to "a particular way of looking" at subjectivity. For now the question becomes whether subjectivity can really be understood in terms of external physical objects and processes, or whether the relevant objects and states must be internal and immaterial, belonging to a private inner realm. But with this way of setting things up we have already gone astray. The culprit is the assumption that subjectivity can be conceived of as some kind of object or thing, that is, as something that "just stands there," to borrow a phrase from John McDowell (McDowell 1998a, 263–78). It is precisely when this assumption is in place that the question becomes one of determining whether subjectivity "stands there" as part of the "external" physical world, or rather constitutes an immaterial "inner world" of its own. In the last analysis, Wittgenstein's complaint against Cartesianism, behaviorism, and reductive materialism is precisely that they are all, in one way or the other, committed to such an "object" conception of subjectivity.

Conclusion

If we are persuaded by the foregoing, then we have at least a rough outline of how *not* to conceive of subjectivity. But that is of course not enough: what we really want is a positive conception. Even though it would be an exaggeration to say that we find a full-blown account of subjectivity in Wittgenstein, at least he gives hints as to how we should positively conceive of it. One of the most important hints is Wittgenstein's notion of the "living human being (and what is similar to it)." The idea, which I touched very lightly on a moment ago in the context of memory, is introduced in an attempt to contrast Wittgenstein's own position with that of behaviorism:

> "But doesn't what you say come to this: that there is no pain, for example, without *pain-behavior*?" – It comes to this: only of a living human being and what resembles (behaves like) a human being can one say: it has sensations; it sees; is blind; hears; is deaf; is conscious or unconscious.
>
> (PI, § 281)

Such passages cast some light on Wittgenstein's rather obscure remarks to the effect that the human body, or the human being, is the "best picture of the human soul" (PI, 178). They also help us see why his contention that to see the behavior of a living thing is to see its soul does not necessarily commit him to behaviorism. Wittgenstein, it seems, wants (so to speak) to cut the ontological cake differently from both Cartesians and behaviorists. Instead of contrasting inner and outer, mind (or soul) and body, Wittgenstein contrasts the whole human being, and what is similar to it, with non-living things such as rocks and bicycles.

This has crucial implications for Wittgenstein's conception of subjectivity. First of all, a human being is not something immaterial, "inner," and hidden; it is not something accessible only to itself. Rather, it is a creature out there in the world, extended and tangible, sensitive and vulnerable to changes in its environment. But this does not entail that it is only an object or a thing among others, or that we can conceive of it exclusively in terms of mere physical behavior. On the contrary, according to Wittgenstein (although he would not put it like this), "human being" is a fundamental ontological category of its own – one that should be contrasted with lifeless material things as well as Cartesian immaterial things, if there are any. To be a human being is to reach out into the world in a way that objects do not: we experience the world, are affected by it, and interact with it. Also, there is something to the Cartesian intuition that my access to myself is in many important ways different from the access that others have to me. There is, on Wittgenstein's view, a fundamental asymmetry between first-person and third-person perspectives on subjectivity. An implicit consequence of Wittgenstein's insistence on the fundamental differences between first-person and third-person uses of psychological concepts is that a first-person "givenness" or mode of presentation, irreducible to any third-person givenness, is an essential aspect of subjectivity. But again, we should not jump to the conclusion that subjectivity must, for that reason, be assigned to some inner, private realm, accessible only to one person. Wittgenstein's point is rather that there are fundamentally different first-person and third-person perspectives on the *one* being, the living human being.

It is the task of the next couple of chapters to show how Wittgenstein's insight into the problematic common assumption underlying much traditional and contemporary philosophy of mind can be used to develop a positive Wittgensteinian account of subjectivity and its place in the world. One of the best ways to develop Wittgenstein's intuitions on this point is, as I hope to demonstrate, through a comparison with philosophers from the so-called "Continental" tradition.

2 Catching reality in one's net

> How was it possible for thought to deal with the very object *itself*? We feel as if by means of it we had caught reality in our net.
>
> (PI, § 428)

Introduction

A central theme – some say *the* central theme (Thornton 1998, vii, 101) – of Wittgenstein's *Philosophical Investigations* is "intentionality" or "aboutness." In fact, the discussion of intentionality not only surfaces in a number of places in this book; it also seems a major theme in various other manuscripts, stretching all the way back to Wittgenstein's early work (Ammereller 2001, 63–73). The basic problem with which Wittgenstein concerns himself is expressed in the following questions: "How [is] it possible for thought to deal with the very object *itself*?" (PI, § 428). "We think about things, – but how do these things enter into our thoughts?" (BB, 38). Reaching all the way to things in the world is what perceptions, thoughts, and wishes seem to do somehow. This is an achievement that seems to call for philosophical elucidation. Wittgenstein, however, does not attempt to answer the mentioned questions directly, by providing a positive account of (the possibility of) intentionality. Rather, his strategy is to try to locate and undermine the assumptions that make intentionality look like a mystery in the first place. He tries to persuade us to view intentional mental states as irreducibly and inherently "world-involving." As long as we retain a firm grasp of this insight, intentionality will not be a mystery to us. But if we fail to do so, then it will become a mystery that we need magic tricks to solve.

In the present chapter, I want to look at some of what Wittgenstein says about intentionality. Lengthy books have been written on the subject of "intentionality" or "aboutness," so the discussion I can offer within the confines of a single chapter is necessarily selective and at times rather swift and superficial. I will attempt to develop one positive extension of Wittgenstein's unmasking of the "conjuring trick" in our way of thinking of the mind, namely the idea that we must understand subjectivity as *essentially involved with the world.* So while what is offered in this chapter may be viewed as an application of Wittgenstein's general – negative – idea that it is a fundamental mistake to conceive of the mental as a domain of objects or items that just "stand there," isolated from the (rest of the) world, it is also intended to provide important clues to his positive views on the nature of the mind.

The concept of intentionality

Let me start out by offering a brief sketch of what philosophers usually mean by "intentionality." The roots of the term "intentionality" are found in the philosophy of Medieval Scholasticism. But the modern use of the term was inaugurated in the late nineteenth century by the Austrian philosopher and psychologist Franz Brentano, who used it to denote a special feature of "mental" (as opposed to "physical") phenomena, viz. that such phenomena, as it were, "contain an object [...] within themselves" (Brentano 1973, 88).

Husserl picked up the term from Brentano, and developed the notion of intentionality further within the framework of his influential phenomenology. As Husserl conceives of intentionality in the *Logical Investigations* and later works, it is a characteristic feature of certain experiences, namely the feature that they relate themselves, in some way or other, to objects. As Husserl says, most of our conscious mental states and processes are, in a variety of ways, "consciousness of something" (Husserl 1982, 201). He gives the following examples:

> [A] perceiving is a perceiving of something, perhaps a physical thing; a judging is a judging of a predicatively formed affair-complex; valuing of a predicatively formed value-complex; a wishing of a predicatively formed wish-complex; and so forth. Acting bears upon action. Doing bears upon the deed, loving bears upon the loved one, being glad bears upon the gladsome; and so forth.
>
> (Husserl 1982, 200)

Despite this apparent omnipresence of the structure of intentionality in mental life it is not Husserl's view that everything that is or belongs to a conscious experience is characterized by intentionality. As he puts it, "we cannot say of *each* mental process that it has intentionality" (ibid., 199). This is one of the points on which Husserl parts with his teacher Brentano. According to the latter, as already mentioned, intentionality is what distinguishes mental phenomena from physical phenomena. Hence "[e]very mental phenomenon is characterized by what the Scholastics of the Middle Ages called the intentional (or mental) inexistence of an object, and what we might call [...] reference to a content, direction toward an object" (Brentano 1973, 88). Presumably, pain would constitute an example of the kind of concrete mental phenomenon that Husserl thinks is not (in itself) characterized by intentionality. A pain, it would seem, has no "pained" object the way a perception has its "perceived" object. A pain obviously has a location, as when my knee hurts, but it seems wrong to think that the knee is in this case an intentional "object" of the "pain" as such (although *my hurting knee*, the pain in its location, may very well become the object of other intentional experiences, as when I can't help thinking about it, focusing on it).[1] Nevertheless, Husserl still thinks intentionality is, so to speak, the milieu in which all of mental life is embedded "in so far as all mental processes in some manner or other share in [intentionality]" (Husserl 1982, 199). Intentionality is thus "part of the configuration of subjectivity" (McCulloch 2002, 134) and in that sense not merely an accidental feature of subjectivity, independently of whether we adopt the Brentanian or Husserlian view.

Note that on Husserl's as well as Brentano's usage of "intentionality" intentional mental states form a class that is wider than the class of "propositional attitudes." "Edmund thinks that roses are red" attributes to Edmund an intentional state that is clearly also a propositional attitude (an attitude toward the proposition "Roses are red"). But it is not clear that "Edmund loves Malvine" and "Edmund sees a rose" attribute propositional attitudes to Edmund (for what would the propositions be?), although both sentences certainly attribute intentional mental phenomena to Edmund in the sense defined above. Edmund's love is object-directed, directed at Malvine; and although such love will typically involve numerous propositional attitudes (such as thinking that Malvine is wonderful and hoping that she loves him in return), it is not clear that Edmund's love for Malvine can be identified with any of these propositional attitudes or any conjunction of them.

Intentional phenomena, it is often said, are *individuated* by their intentional content.[2] What makes my desire for a glass of water different from my desire for a glass of wine is that these two desires concern (are "about") different things. And what makes my belief that Phosphorus is a planet in our solar system different from my belief that Hesperus is a planet in our solar system is the fact that, although the two beliefs in fact concern the same *thing* (the planet Venus), they refer to it under different aspects, or intend it in different ways (cf. Husserl 1970a, 578). It would be possible for a person to hold one of these beliefs while having no opinion about the other. Obviously, for such a person the statement "Hesperus is (the same planet as) Phosphorus" would convey real information. The two beliefs have different content and are thus not identical.

But in fact the reference to intentional content is only part of the story of how we individuate intentional experiences. We also distinguish intentional phenomena in terms of their "quality" or "mode."[3] It is obviously possible to have an imaginative and a perceptual experience, for example, with the same content. I can *imagine* a black cat sitting on the mat and I can *see* a black cat sitting on the mat – two quite different experiences, but with the same content. Similarly, I can hope that I will be offered a glass of wine and I can fear the very same thing. So the "quality" of the intentional experience – perceiving, imagining, dreaming, thinking, hoping, loving, etc. – also plays an essential role in individuating intentional experiences. And together they do the trick. If I want to know what intentional mental state somebody is in and she tells me the quality ("wishing") as well as the content ("that Smith will pay her a visit") of her state, then I have the information I wanted.

The enigma of intentionality

In a sense, nothing could be more trivial than the fact that many mental phenomena display intentionality. Obviously, when I think I think about *something* (although my thoughts may be vague, unspecific, incoherent, etc.). Equally obviously, the something about which I think is very often an object, event, or state of affairs, in the world outside my skin. And, clearly, this is anything but a rare phenomenon. We think innumerable such thoughts every single day, practically never stopping to marvel at what we are doing. So what can possibly make thinking (and other intentional mental phenomena) appear mysterious? According to Wittgenstein, the air of mystery imposes itself when philosophers start reflecting on the nature and achievement of thought:

> "This queer thing, thought" – but it does not strike us a queer when we are thinking. Thought does not strike us as mysterious while we are thinking, but only when we say, as it were retrospectively: "How was that possible?" How was it possible for thought to deal with the very object *itself*? We feel as if by means of it we had caught reality in our net.
>
> (PI, § 428)

However, it is still not entirely clear why there should be something particularly mysterious about this. *Of course* our thoughts and other mental phenomena reach all the way to the things themselves, one might say. We would be in a pretty uncomfortable predicament if they did not. If my visual perception simply stopped short before reaching the pages of Wittgenstein's *Philosophical Investigations*, then there would not be much point in picking up the book, since I would anyway be unable to read it. (And, by the way, could my tactile perceptions reach the book itself? If not, what would it mean for me to "pick it up?") I think Wittgenstein's point is that intentionality starts to look mysterious – and in a way *ought* to look mysterious – once we approach it with a certain type of picture of the mind in hand.

That picture is one in which intentional mental phenomena are depicted as entities, states, or processes characterized by intrinsic properties that have no essential reference to intentional objects. So when Wittgenstein lets his interlocutor remark that thinking "is an enigmatic process and we are a long way off from complete understanding of it" (RPP I, § 1093), the element responsible for the enigma is precisely the idea of thinking being a "process." For considered as a *process* – as something not unlike the solution of an aspirin in a glass of water – thinking does seem to have magical powers, reaching mysteriously beyond itself. Intentional mental phenomena are "normative" in the sense that they prescribe what fulfills them or makes them true. The thought "Roses are red" prescribes what has to be the case in the world for it to be true: it has to be the case that roses are red. How such normative links to the world could be established by chemical processes might legitimately strike one as utterly enigmatic. "For we have a definite concept of what it means to learn to know [such] a process better" (PI, § 308), and that concept does not leave room for a discovery to the effect that a particular process prescribes how the world has to be. It is in this light that one should read remarks such as the following:

> A wish seems already to know what will or would satisfy it; a proposition, a thought, what makes it true – even when that thing is not there at all! Whence this *determining* of what is not yet there? This despotic demand?
>
> (PI, § 437)

The passage follows after two sections in which Wittgenstein has considered the reply that the problem of intentionality "consists in our having to describe phenomena that are hard to get hold of" because they "slip quickly by" (PI, § 436). The aim of section 437, as I interpret it, is to make us see that this reply misconstrues the difficulty altogether. Even if we could get hold of some process that we were inclined to identify with the actual wishing or thinking, it still ought to strike us as utterly mysterious how this process could determine (or "despotically" prescribe) what is not yet there. What Wittgenstein says about "meaning" goes for all intentional phenomena: "[N]o *process* could have the consequences of meaning" (PI, 218).

Note that it is not, according to Wittgenstein, the Cartesian metaphysical conception of the mind as a realm of immaterial inner items, states, and processes that creates the problem of intentionality. In fact, Wittgenstein suggests that immaterialism can be seen, rather, as a response to the problem. If a chemical or other natural process along the lines of the solution of an aspirin cannot do the trick, then it might seem a good move to suppose that we need to envisage a different kind of process altogether – a supernatural kind. Thus "we are tempted to say 'the mechanism of the mind must be of a most peculiar kind to be able to do what the mind does'" (BB, 5). Consequently, we might conceive of thinking as something that takes place in a peculiar "mental world," Wittgenstein says, "imagined as gaseous, or rather, ethereal" (BB, 47). This is natural enough, for, as

McDowell has put it, "magical powers require an occult medium" (McDowell 1998b, 244). But it is clearly not very helpful. Transporting the enigmatic feature into a mysterious ethereal world of its own does not get us any closer to an understanding of the workings of intentionality. Being told that the processes in question are immaterial does not help us understand how they could be such as to be about worldly things and objects.[4] We thus seem unable to make any headway.

The trouble is not that we cannot see how there could be any sort of link between mental phenomena and the world. We can make sense of numerous relations (e.g. various sorts of casual relations) between mental items understood as self-contained items characterizable independently of their relations to other objects, and objects and states of affairs in the world. The problem is rather that we cannot make sense of these relations as relations of the right *kind*. We cannot reconstruct the *normativity* of intentional phenomena.

This is essentially the point Wittgenstein makes already in the *Philosophical Remarks*, when discussing Russell's account of intentionality in *The Analysis of Mind*. In the latter work, Russell rejects Brentano's view "that relation to an object is an ultimate irreducible characteristic of mental phenomena" (Russell 1949, 15). Desire, for example, is not a mental phenomenon bearing an irreducible relation to its desired object, Russell argues. Rather,

> desire [...] is of the nature of a convenient fiction for describing shortly certain laws of behavior. A hungry animal is restless until it finds food; then it becomes quiescent. The thing which will bring a restless condition to an end is said to be what is desired. But only experience can show what will have this sedative effect, and it is easy to make mistakes.
>
> (Russell 1949, 32)

The commitment to behaviorism is neither the only mistake nor in fact the crucial mistake here. On the same page, Russell speaks about desire in terms of a *feeling* of dissatisfaction (that may or may not be satisfied by what we think will satisfy it); so clearly his view is not consistently behavioristic. The crucial mistake, rather, is to identify an intentional mental phenomenon with something – a condition of restlessness or a feeling of dissatisfaction – that can be characterized independently of any intentional object.[5] For such a mental item "stands isolated" insofar as "it does not point outside itself to a reality beyond" (Z, § 236). That leaves Russell with only an "external" empirical link between the desire and what is desired: the object of desire is whatever will terminate the condition of restlessness or feeling of dissatisfaction. As Wittgenstein mockingly comments, this seems to have the following absurd consequence: "If I wanted to eat an apple, and someone punched me in the stomach, taking away my appetite, then it was this punch that I originally wanted" (PR, 64).

Russell could of course appeal to his less behaviorist definition of desire in terms of a feeling of dissatisfaction and object that a punch in the stomach does not give me the feeling of satisfaction that the apple would have given me. But clearly that reply will not do; for any number of things (various drugs, for example) could produce in me a feeling of satisfaction, perhaps greater than that which eating an apple would have given rise to. Yet surely that does not mean that whenever I (think I) desire an apple what I really want is a shot of heroin. As Wittgenstein summarizes these points in the *Philosophical Investigations*,

> Saying "I should like an apple" does not mean: I believe an apple will quell my feeling of nonsatisfaction. [...] And the fact that some event stops my wishing does not mean that it fulfills it. Perhaps I should not have been satisfied if my wish had been satisfied.
>
> (PI, §§ 440–41)

What this whole discussion illustrates is that if one conceives of intentional phenomena as having an "intrinsic nature" that can be characterized without reference to what fulfills them or makes them true or false (cf. Russell 1949, 232), then the external relations one can establish between these mental phenomena and states of affairs in the world cannot reconstruct the normativity essential to intentional mental phenomena. In order to get the normativity right we must understand the relation between the intentional mental state and its intended object as an "internal" relation (PR, 64).

It is an essential fact about my present perception that it is a perception *of a computer screen*. I can hardly describe this perceptual experience otherwise than by referring to its perceived object. Likewise, it is an essential fact about my hope that the weather will be fine tomorrow that it is about *the weather being fine tomorrow*. Again, I cannot describe my hope without referring to its content. Intentional phenomena are, as we put it above (see p. 30), individuated by their content; the content is essential to the mental phenomena being the particular phenomena that they are:

> Expectation is not given an external description by citing what is expected, as is hunger by citing what food satisfies it – in the last resort the appropriate food of course can still only be a matter of conjecture. No, describing an expectation by means of what is expected is giving an internal description.
>
> (PR, 68)

All in all, then, Wittgenstein's point is that we need to abandon the idea that intentional phenomena are inner items that can be characterized independently of any reference to what they are intentionally directed at. We have to understand intentional phenomena as inherently or essentially world-involving. Describing an intentional mental state by means of its object is to give an "internal" description of that state.

Intentionality without objects

Before we move on to outlining the picture of the mind that Wittgenstein is sketching here, we must briefly consider an objection to the argument presented so far. For it might seem that with the notion of intentional phenomena as world-involving we encounter serious trouble. If we want to hold on to the view that intentional mental states are inherently object-directed *and* that they engage with the world *itself*, what do we do then about intentional phenomena that have no (real) objects?[6] In order to describe the intentional phenomena (that seem real enough), we must refer to their objects. Yet objectless intentional phenomena by definition have no objects.

The trouble here does not merely concern marginal cases such as cases in which we think or fantasize about phlogiston, unicorns, or ghosts (to pick the favored philosophical examples). It also concerns perceptual illusions and hallucinations, as well as wishes, expectations, and so forth, in which we apparently intend something that is not yet there, and may perhaps never be (if our wishes or expectations are not fulfilled). In fact, since there is an element of unfulfillment to most if not all intentional phenomena, the problem concerns intentionality as such. Every perception, thought, memory, or wish might be frustrated, exposed as having no real object. So the problem of "empty" or objectless intentional phenomena seems to affect intentionality across the board. Presumably this is part of the reason why Wittgenstein states that the philosophical difficulties concerning wishes, thoughts, and the rest "can all be summed up in the question: 'How can one think what is not the case?'" (BB, 30).

There is a tempting line of thought that we need to avoid when aiming to reply to this question. It is a line of thought discussed extensively in the *Blue Book*. Slightly abbreviated, this is how Wittgenstein presents the problematic conception as arising:

> "How can one think what is not the case? If I think that King's College is on fire when it is not on fire, the fact of its being on fire does not exist. Then how can I think it? How can we hang a thief who doesn't exist?" [...] We may now be inclined to say: "As the fact which would make our thought true if it existed does not always exist, it is not the *fact* which we think." [...] The next step we are inclined to take is to think that as the object of our thought isn't the fact it is a shadow of the fact.
>
> (BB, 31–32)

In other words, if I think (expect, wish, or seem to perceive) something that is not the case or does not exist, then it cannot be the case that this intentional phenomenon reaches out to its object in the world, because there is no object for it to reach out to.[7] When I think falsely that King's College is on fire, there is no state of affairs "King's College is on fire" in the world for my thought to latch on to. Obviously, the very same intentional experience *could* have an object: it could be the case that King's College is on fire. But it seems purely *ad hoc* to allow that in the latter case the thought does latch on to a state of affairs in the real world, when in the former case the very same thought did not reach out to a state of affairs in the world. How can the very same intentional phenomenon reach further in one case than in the other? "The way out of this difficulty seems to be: what we expect [think etc.] is not the fact, but a shadow of the fact; as it were, the next thing to the fact" (BB, 36). In order to accommodate objectless intentional phenomena, we think we have to deny that *any* intentional phenomena reach all the way to the world. In other, more traditional terms, we are led to insert a "veil of ideas" between subjectivity and the world.

Wittgenstein, however, goes on to consider at length the problems that this idea that the object of a thought is a "shadow" of a worldly fact engenders. One fundamental difficulty seems to be that the "shadowy" intermediary objects do not perform the task they were intended to perform. For, as Wittgenstein suggests, "the question now is: 'How can something be the shadow of a fact which doesn't exist?'" (BB, 32). The point is that the "shadows" are still supposed to make sense of intentionality, of mental phenomena being about the world, in the cases where the intended objects exist. So when I think a true thought the "shadowy" object of my thought is precisely the "shadow" of a state of affairs actually obtaining in the world. This, however, seems merely to reproduce the original difficulty. For we can now ask how there can be such a "shadow" of a state of affairs in the world in cases where no such state of affairs obtains. It seems, then, that the original worry that led to introducing the intermediary "shadow" is only assuaged when all links between the "shadow" and the world are severed. And that leaves mind and world out of touch altogether.

A more concrete problem is that the "shadow" conception cannot capture the normativity essential to intentionality:

> For how could we wish *just this* to happen if just this isn't present in our wish? It is quite true to say: The mere shadow won't do; for it stops short before the object; and we want the wish to contain the object itself. – We want that the wish that Mr. Smith should come into this room should wish that just *Mr. Smith*, and no substitute, should do the *coming*, and no substitute for that, *into my room*, and no substitute for that.
>
> (BB, 37)

One may have the feeling that in the sentence "I expect he is coming" one is using the words "he is coming" in a different sense from the one they have in the assertion "He is coming." But if it were so how could I say that my expectation had been fulfilled?

(PI, § 444)

If my original wish that Smith should enter my room did not have the event of *Smith entering my room* as its object, then it is hard to see how the latter event could fulfill the wish. Yet it is precisely only the latter event that does fulfill my wish; no substitutes could do so. And whatever precisely we imagine that the "shadow" is, at least it is clear that it is not identical with, but falls short of, the real event in the world. This was precisely the point of introducing the "shadow" in the first place.

Let us conclude, then, that the "shadow" conception is a dead end. What is Wittgenstein's own alternative? Wittgenstein's "solution" is as simple as it may be "*prima facie* bewildering" (Ammereller 2001, 74). It consists in the claim that objectless intentional phenomena reach out into the world just as much as intentional phenomena whose objects exist. Consider the following passage from the *Investigations*:

> When we say, and *mean*, that such-and-such is the case, we – and our meaning – do not stop anywhere short of the fact; but we mean: *this – is – so*. But this paradox (which has the form of a truism) can also be expressed in this way: *Thought* can be of what is *not* the case.
>
> (PI, § 95; cf. § 429)

To understand Wittgenstein's point, it may be helpful to think of intentionality in analogy to tossing darts. Let us say that, given my basic ability to make the dart fly, there are two different ways in which I may fail to hit the bull's-eye. My dart may *fail to reach* the target (i.e. fall short of it) or it may *miss or fly past* the target (hit the wall, say). Now, the "shadow" conception clearly thinks of objectless intentional phenomena in analogy to the former sort of case. Objectless thoughts fail to make it all the way to their target. Instead, they reach a different target: they hit the shadow, "the next thing" to the target. Wittgenstein, however, suggests a different perspective. He thinks of objectless thoughts in analogy to shooting past the target. Shooting past the target does not contradict, but in fact presupposes, reaching all the way out there. Objectless intentional phenomena reach all the way out in the world, but obviously without hitting their targets out there.

So now we should be able to see what goes wrong in the following exchange: "'The report was not so loud as I had expected.' – 'Then was there a louder bang in your expectation?'" (PI, § 442). When I expect a loud noise there is no loud noise "in my expectation." Noises are usually in the world. Sometimes there are noises "in our heads," say if we suffer from tinnitus or if we are having auditory hallucinations; but there are no noises "in our expectation" when we simply expect to hear the sound of a gun being fired. And if our expectation is disappointed this does not mean that there was a loud noise somewhere else (in our minds), but that there was *no* loud noise anywhere of the sort that we expected.[8] Wittgenstein's basic point is well expressed in an early remark: "what expectation has in common with reality is that it refers to another point in the *same* space" (PR, 70). When I expect a gunshot or that Smith enters my room my expectations reach the "space" of reality; they do not fall short of it. This is precisely the reason why my expectations can be fulfilled as well as disappointed by events in the real world.

Ultimately, what Wittgenstein is suggesting is that we view false thoughts, pure fantasies, illusions, unfulfilled wishes, and so forth as reaching just as far out in the world as true thoughts, imaginations of real things, veridical perceptions, wishes that have come true, etc. None of these intentional mental phenomena "stop[s] anywhere short" of things and events in the world.[9] The possibility of "deficient" or unfulfilled intentional phenomena is simply the flipside of the normativity of such phenomena. If there is always a prescriptive element in an intentional mental state, then it is always possible that reality disobeys the prescription. It is essential to a thought's being *about* the world that it may get the world wrong. It is essential to a wish's directedness at events in the world that actual events in the world can frustrate it. So there really is no difficulty in maintaining that intentionality should be understood as world-involvement in the sense of *inherent directedness* at worldly things and events *themselves*. On the contrary, the fact that we are directly involved with the world also makes it understandable that we can be wrong precisely *about the world*.

The internalism/externalism debate and Wittgenstein's "quietism"

There is one lesson in particular that Wittgenstein is trying to teach us in his discussions of intentionality. As should be clear, the lesson is not that intentionality is some mythical or mysterious type of relation, of which we ought to be highly suspicious as enlightened twenty-first-century philosophers.[10] On the contrary, what Wittgenstein wants us to see is that we *create* the mystery of intentionality precisely when we attempt to explain it in terms of self-contained mental items the nature of which can be explained without reference to any intentional objects. For we can only make sense of such items as having "external" relations to states of affairs in the world, and external relations cannot sustain the "normativity" of intentionality. Taking this route ultimately leaves us with only one option: the option of postulating inexplicable magical powers of the mind. And this seems to indicate that the moment the enigma of intentionality arises it has already become unsolvable. So the thing to do, Wittgenstein suggests, is to abandon the framework responsible for creating the problem.

Yet one might find this response less than satisfactory. There is surely a real question regarding the workings and conditions of possibility of intentionality.

How exactly do mental states manage to connect with the world? Is it an achievement that is in principle independent of the nature and even existence of the world? Or is it rather the case that intentionality or aboutness as such depends upon the existence and perhaps even the nature of the world? These are questions that have attracted significant philosophical attention in the last couple of decades, and surely for a good reason. When we start to wonder about the apparent ability of thought to "catch reality in its net" these are the kinds of things we want to know. And so far Wittgenstein has not been very helpful in providing answers to these questions.

If we call the view that intentionality – the "ability" of mental phenomena to direct themselves at objects – is *independent* of the external world "internalism" and call the opposite view, the view that denies that intentionality has this independence, "externalism," then it might seem obvious that Wittgenstein belongs in the latter camp. After all, I have portrayed Wittgenstein as being committed to the view that intentional phenomena are intrinsically world-involving, stopping nowhere short of the (external) states of affairs that they are about. This might seem to indicate a tangible degree of world-dependence that is incompatible with internalism. Some, indeed, have found here the contours of a strong externalist position – an "in-the-world Wittgensteinianism" – according to which we cannot describe an individual subject's mental state without making "essential mention of aspects of the individual's surroundings" (McCulloch 1995, 99). However, I think there are two reasons why we should hesitate to draw any such conclusion at this point.

First, note that internalism, as I have introduced it here, is essentially a doctrine about the conditions of possibility of intentional phenomena. That is, it says something about what has to be the case for an intentional mental state to obtain. A paradigmatic internalist holds that the external world need not exist for me to entertain the thought (with the quality and content it has) that roses are red. But she is not committed to the claim that this thought falls short of the real world. On the contrary, "[n]ormally, an internalist will hold that many or most of the objects one thinks about actually exist" in the world "outside our ideas" (Crane 2001, 118). What makes this point easy to miss is that the "internalist" doctrine is sometimes identified with the idea that intentional content is "in the head" (Searle 1983, 208; Smith 2004, 167).[11] This creates the impression that when I think that the neighbor's cat is sitting on my lawn, the content of that thought is not a possible state of affairs in the world (that *the neighbor's cat is sitting on my lawn*), but some intermediary "shadowy" state of affairs in my head. Indisputably, this *would* be incompatible with Wittgenstein's views.

However, the impression is misleading. What the internalist insists on is merely that "a thought would remain the same even in possible worlds where its objects did not exist" (Crane 2001, 118). As we have already seen in detail, we have the ability to think about things that do not exist. The internalist's point is simply that, just as we are able to entertain thoughts about unicorns even if no such creatures exist, we would be able to entertain thoughts about roses, cats, houses, and tax returns even though no such things existed. The internalist will agree that if none of these things existed, then obviously a great many thoughts that we are convinced are true would actually be false. But the internalist simply claims that we would still be able to think those same thoughts, with those same contents, even if their objects failed to exist. As Searle summarizes the internalist position, each of our intentional states "must be possible for a being who is a brain in a vat" (Searle 1983, 230).[12] So, in other words, it is far from clear that an internalist would be prevented from adopting the Wittgensteinian view that intentional mental phenomena are "intrinsically world-involving," as long as this is understood as noncommittal with regard to the actual existence of the world. That is, as long as world-involvement is understood in the sense of tossing intentional darts that may never hit any targets, it is hard to see why an internalist should be unable to embrace Wittgenstein's view.[13]

Second, even if Wittgenstein's perspective on intentionality were incompatible with an internalist doctrine this would not entail that Wittgenstein should instead be seen as offering an externalist account. The rejection of internalism need not imply the adoption of a form of externalism. Indeed, in Wittgenstein's case there would seem to be good reason to assume that his sympathies would be neither externalist nor internalist (Glock and Preston 1995). These reasons have to do with what is sometimes referred to as Wittgenstein's "quietism." The gist of the latter is captured in the statements that in philosophy "we may not advance any kind of theory. [...] We must do away with all *explanation*, and description alone must take its place" (PI, § 109). While there is some controversy regarding what precisely Wittgenstein means by "theory" and "explanation," it seems safe to say that the quote gives expression to a general resistance toward what we might term speculative theory building in philosophy. This need not entail resistance to "positive" or substantive philosophy as such; for surely a descriptive account can be every bit as positive as a speculative theory, and Wittgenstein endorses philosophical description.[14] But it will surely involve a rejection of precisely the type of explanatory ambitions that seem characteristic of internalism as well as externalism. It involves a refusal to provide a positive answer to the question "How do mental states manage to connect with the world?" Wittgenstein seems merely to poke fun at this type of query, as in his reply to a related question: "If it is asked: 'How do sentences manage to represent?' – the answer might be: 'Don't you know? You certainly see it, when you use them.' For nothing is concealed" (PI, § 435). So if internalism and externalism are understood as alternative constructive answers to this type of question, then Wittgenstein would belong in neither camp.[15]

Yet this does not rule out that Wittgenstein's sympathies are with one party of this debate rather than the other. Perhaps, as it has been suggested, Wittgenstein would support a "minimalist form of externalism" (Thornton 1998, 123–24). All that I have suggested in this section is that it is not clear that there is any internalist or externalist commitment in the Wittgensteinian account of intentionality as it has been presented so far. In Chapter 4 I will return to the question of internalism and externalism. But for now I want to inquire whether "in-the-world Wittgensteinianism" might, independently of any externalist commitments, be used to capture an insight emerging from Wittgenstein's discussion of intentionality.

Wittgenstein and Heidegger on being-in-the-world

When Wittgenstein suggests that we ought to know how mental states are connected with states of affairs in the world – because "nothing is hidden" (PI, § 435) – the point is to make us reflect on what kind of explanation we want when we ask a question of this sort. Is it that we suspect there is an inner process somewhere, somehow concealed from us, that we need to be made aware of? But in that case, clearly, we are once again asking the wrong kind of question. We are again demanding that intentionality be explained in terms of self-standing inner items, and this route has been shown to lead nowhere. So everything we need is there, our intentional phenomena and their intentional contents: "Since everything lies open to view there is nothing to explain" (PI, § 126). Instead of postulating mental items – whether ordinary physical items or peculiar "ghostly" objects, states, or processes – all we have to do is achieve a firm grasp of the notion that our thoughts, beliefs, wishes, and perceptions are intrinsically world-involving. Intentional mental phenomena latch on to the world directly, immediately. It is of their "essence" to do so.

Though Wittgenstein would not like to put it that way, we can say that what prevents us from feeling content with these statements is an *ontological* presupposition about the mind and mental phenomena. In fact, it is nothing but the "objectivistic" ontological outlook that was exposed in Chapter 1 – an outlook to which dualists may be just as committed as behaviorists and materialists. To be a subject that thinks, believes, perceives, and so forth is not to be (or have) an inner world populated with special inner items to which one has some kind of unique, perhaps even infallible, access. Rather, to borrow a phrase from John McDowell, it is to be or have a peculiar "openness to the layout of reality" (McDowell 1996, 26).

I think one can put Wittgenstein's point into a useful perspective by briefly considering some ideas of Heidegger's. In a brief discussion of what he calls the phenomenon of "knowing the world" (*Welterkenntnis*), Heidegger reaches conclusions that are remarkably similar to Wittgenstein's. Heidegger starts out by remarking that it seems obvious that knowing as such belongs to the knower rather than to that which is known. If I know that the neighbor's cat sits on my lawn it is (obviously) not to the cat or the lawn that this piece of knowledge belongs. But, says Heidegger, even in the knowing subjects, in the "human-Things, knowing is not present-at-hand," at least "it is not externally ascertainable as, let us say, bodily properties are" (BT, 87). The point is that if we look at the extended material "human-thing," then it is hard to see how something like "knowing" – as opposed to height, weight, skin color, etc. – could belong to it. How could a material entity, state, or process be the intentional phenomenon of "knowing that the neighbor's cat is on my lawn?" This is by now a familiar difficulty and it seems to leave only one, by now equally familiar, option. As Heidegger puts it, "inasmuch as knowing belongs to these entities [human things] and is not some external characteristic, it must be 'inside'" (BT, 87). If an external material state, process, or entity won't do, then perhaps an immaterial and internal one will. Just like Wittgenstein, however, Heidegger denies that this move is successful. For now the question arises "of how this knowing subject comes out of its inner 'sphere' into one which is 'other and external'" (BT, 87). Allocating the problematic intentional phenomenon to an inner sphere of its own does not solve any problems.

In fact, Heidegger moves on to suggest that the phenomenon of knowing will continue to present "enigmas" as long as we have not "clarified how it is and what it is" (BT, 87). This may seem somewhat obscure. But the point Heidegger is trying to make is actually very Wittgensteinian: there are presuppositions at work in our way of looking at the phenomenon of knowing and the subject of knowing which vitiate our discussion from the outset. These presuppositions are encapsulated in Heidegger's talk of knowing as something "present-at-hand" in a "human thing." A fundamental message of *Being and Time* is that traditional philosophy has tended to interpret everything – including subjectivity or "Dasein,"[16] as Heidegger prefers to say – as something "present-at-hand." In other words, we assume without question that "present-at-hand" is how everything, including the mind and everything mental, *is*. And this creates many of our problems. Heidegger writes:

> Ontologically, we understand [Dasein] as something which is in each case already constantly present at hand, both in and for a closed realm [...]. Even if one rejects the "soul substance" and the Thinghood of consciousness, or denies that a person is an object, ontologically one is still positing something whose Being retains the meaning of present-at-hand, whether it does so explicitly or not.
>
> (BT, 150)

The phrase "present-at-hand" may, for our present purposes, be understood to refer precisely to the idea under critical scrutiny throughout this chapter, namely the idea of something that has its own intrinsic nature, which can in principle be fully described without reference to anything else. In this sense it occupies or constitutes "a closed realm," as Heidegger says. In Heidegger's terms, to conceive of subjectivity in this way is to conceive of it, initially at least, as *worldless*. This is so independently of whether the "closed realm" is imagined as being material or immaterial. When we take our point

Catching reality in one's net 43

of departure in a worldless, isolated "subject," the mystery or enigma of intentionality forces itself upon us. And Heidegger suggests, like Wittgenstein, that once we have let the mystery arise in this form there is no way of solving it. As the former puts it, if "we 'take our departure' from a worldless 'I' in order to provide this 'I' with an object and a [...] relation to that object, then we have 'presupposed' not too much, but *too little*" (BT, 363). For we have assumed something present-at-hand, something that "stands isolated," and no matter what we subsequently add to this, intentionality is bound to remain a mystery.

Much in line with McDowell's notion of "openness" to the world, Heidegger recommends that we view subjectivity (or Dasein) as essentially a sphere of "disclosedness" (BT, 171). He also, famously, suggests that the phrase "being-in-the-world" (BT, 78) may be used to convey the manner in which subjectivity "exists." The point of the latter phrase is not to convey the notion that as a human being I occupy my little tiny corner of the universe. Rather, the phrase "being-in-the-world" is intended to suggest that, as a subject, I *"inhabit"* the world, *I am involved with it*, or *have* it (BT, 79–80). So to view knowing as a manifestation of "being-in-the-world," alongside other intentional phenomena such as thinking, wishing, perceiving, intending, and so forth, is precisely to view it as inherently world-involving. Or, to put it negatively, it is to refuse to view knowing as an isolated present-at-hand item that could be characterized without essential reference to the content known. It suggests that intentionality, or "openness to the world," is an irreducible essential part of what it means to be a human subject.[17]

Heidegger even comes close to embracing a Wittgensteinian "quietism." This emerges in his response to a hypothetical objection. One might object that given Heidegger's interpretation of knowing as a mode of being-in-the-world "the problem of knowledge is nullified; for what is left to be asked if one *presupposes* that knowing is already 'alongside' its world" (BT, 88)? Heidegger's reply could as well have been made by Wittgenstein:

> In this question the constructivist "standpoint," which has not been phenomenally demonstrated, comes to the fore; but quite apart from this, what higher court is to decide *whether* and *in what sense* there is to be any problem of knowledge other than that of the phenomenon of knowing as such and the kind of Being which belongs to the knower?
> (BT, 88)

Grasping subjectivity as being-in-the-world means grasping that there really can be no problem of connecting mental life with the world. If we cannot rest content with this, Heidegger suggests, it may simply be because we stubbornly demand of philosophy that it provides constructive explanations, rather than phenomenological descriptions. And, as we recall, Heidegger's general point was precisely that if we fail to grasp the phenomenon of being-in-the-world intentionality as such (including the problem of knowledge) becomes an unsolvable enigma. So the constructive explanation we want is one that cannot be given; but nor is there any need for a constructive explanation if we adopt the Heideggerian or Wittgensteinian view (cf. PI, § 126). The "quietist" point is well expressed by McDowell, in terms of the intentional phenomenon of thinking: "The need to construct a theoretical 'hook' to link thinking to the world does not arise, because if it is thinking that we have in view at all [...] then what we have in view is *already* hooked on to the world" (McDowell 1998b, 288). As Heidegger might have put it, the question concerning the link between Dasein and the world does not arise, because if it is Dasein that we have in view at all, then what we have in view "repudiates any such formulation of the question" (BT, 250). Besides, as Heidegger asks, who says the traditional inventory of philosophical problems and questions is the "right" one anyway? Perhaps the right questions to attempt to answer are conceptual or ontological rather than skeptical.

Conclusion

According to Wittgenstein, intentional phenomena connect directly with states of affairs in the world. Intentional phenomena cannot be characterized independently of the objects they are about. And since intentionality is an essential aspect of being a human subjectivity, being a human subjectivity is being involved intentionally with the world. To put it differently, a minded human being is a creature that has "a *point of view on things*," or "*one which has a world*" (Crane 2001, 4). There is really no mystery in any of this; but we make it seem as if there is, or ought to be, if we think that intentional phenomena are self-standing items that can be characterized without reference to their objects. For then the crucial normative involvement with the world is lost, and it cannot be reconstructed.

So when I'm interested in finding out what another person is feeling, thinking, looking at, intending to do, hoping for, afraid of, and so on, I am not interested in disclosing certain peculiar inner facts about her. To think that looking into her "mind" in search of such facts or entities is what will satisfy my desire is to misconstrue the nature of those phenomena that I am interested in. But obviously it is equally wrong to suppose that I am interested merely in her bodily behavior. What I want to know is, rather, what kind of attitude or relation she has toward what intentional content. In other words, what I am interested in is the other's perspective on matters in the world, her comportment and attitude towards things, her ways of relating to things, and so forth. If a subjectivity is "world-involving" in the sense indicated by Wittgenstein, then to know about a subjectivity is to know about *how* it is involved with *what* parts of the world. As simple and quotidian as this observation is, as easy is it to miss it when doing philosophy. For, as Wittgenstein notes, it is easy to overlook something that is constantly before one's eyes (PI, §§ 129, 415).

3 Being some body

> The idea of the ego inhabiting a body [is] to be abolished.
>
> (PO, 225)

Introduction

Hardly any philosopher, no matter how bizarre his or her views on the nature of subjectivity, has been able to overlook the fact that we human beings are bodily creatures. Descartes himself was well aware of this fact. In the *Meditations* he stressed that I am not in the body "as a sailor is present in a ship, but [...] I am very closely joined and, as it were, intermingled with it, so that I and the body form a unit" (Descartes 1984, 56).[1] However, Descartes and numerous other philosophers have at the same time insisted that some fundamental distinction should be drawn between subjectivity (or mind) proper, on the one hand, and the body, on the other hand. And although Cartesian dualism is not the favored ontological position nowadays, the way the body has been handed down to us as a philosophical theme reflects, to a great extent, the original Cartesian setting. In the philosophy of mind, "body" is often simply a heading for the "mind–body problem." More specifically, it typically covers over discussions of the prospects for eliminating the mental, or reducing it to neuronal activities – discussions that frequently center on the problem of mental causation.[2] Thus, it seems that the body is typically understood along Cartesian lines as a physical thing among others, and the question is to what extent the mind can be explained in terms of the properties, states, and processes of such a thing. This discussion actually hides a further Cartesian element. For even if we were to succeed in reducing the mind to the brain we would not thereby have made all traces of dualism vanish. On the contrary, we would be left with the mind/brain on the one hand, and the (rest of the) human body on the other hand, and philosophical questions would arise concerning the relation between the two.

In the present chapter, however, I do not intend to take part in any of these discussions. The body, or embodiment, can be an interesting philosophical theme in quite a different sense than what is reflected in most contemporary mind–body debates. For example, when Wittgenstein introduces the notion of "living human being," he is not only opposing behaviorism and Cartesianism. Nor is he merely urging us to avoid objectifications of subjectivity (although he is certainly also doing that). Rather, he is claiming that subjectivity cannot be reduced to something isolated within the head of an individual – whether construed in material or immaterial terms. The notion of "living human being" is clearly intended to circumvent the idea of subjectivity as something to which a body can merely be an appendix. From the very beginning, phenomenology too has had a keen interest in embodiment. Most famous, perhaps, is Merleau-Ponty's account in *Phenomenology of Perception* and Sartre's chapter on the body in *Being and Nothingness*.[3] However, in lectures dating back to as early as 1907, just six years after the publication of the *Logical Investigations*, Edmund Husserl initiated a study of embodiment that he would continue throughout the rest of his philosophical career. This study, in fact, would become an important source of inspiration to a later phenomenologist such as Merleau-Ponty.

In Chapter 2 I attempted to show that intentionality understood as world-involvement is an essential aspect of subjectivity according to Wittgenstein. I will argue in the present chapter that embodiment is likewise an essential feature of subjectivity. Relying mainly on Husserl, I will start out by delineating some ways in which embodiment is part of our immediate everyday experience of ourselves *as subjects*.[4] But halfway through the chapter I switch to a more methodological discussion, relocating my focus to Heidegger. I think it is crucial in *what way* we conceive of subjectivity as "embodied"; and no one has been more attentive to this issue than Heidegger. In the course of this discussion I will have to revise some rather entrenched views concerning Heidegger. Specifically, it will emerge from this chapter that it is wrong to view Heidegger as uninterested in human embodiment. Quite to the contrary, he is intensely concerned with this phenomenon. Only there are certain pitfalls that the traditional philosophical notions of the body and embodiment contain, which he is intent on avoiding (and we ought to be as well). As I will try to show towards the end of the chapter, these are precisely also pitfalls that Wittgenstein is concerned to avoid.

Perception and embodiment

In various places, Husserl argues that there is no way of making intelligible the constitution of transcendent, perceptual objects without taking into account the perceiver's immediate, yet implicit, awareness of her bodily position, posture, and movement. To articulate this awareness, Husserl employs the concepts of "kinesthetic sensations" or "kinesthesia." His point is that it is only if we consider the momentary visual or tactile sensations as sensations "under particular kinesthetic circumstances" out of a horizon of more or less familiar kinesthetic possibilities that these sensations can yield visual and tactile perceptions of transcendent, spatial objects. Let me briefly review some of Husserl's main ideas.[5]

When I look at a tree in a familiar park, to pick a simple example, the tree presents itself as part of a reality that stretches beyond what is perceptually given to me. At the very least, other parts of the park and of the surrounding city are somehow "there" for me as well, even if I am neither looking at them nor thinking of them. To a great extent these "object-surroundings" are only dimly "present," and they have no well-defined limits. But they are nevertheless an important part of what I experience; a perceptual object does not manifest itself in complete isolation. Using Husserl's idiom, we can say that a tree is perceived as surrounded by a perceptual "horizon" of other objects. But in fact the "horizon" of my tree perception is not exhausted by these open-ended object-surroundings. A perceptual horizon belongs to the perceived tree itself, independently of its surroundings, Husserl claims. The tree is presented as something that I could view from different angles, whereby different sides (for example the presently "invisible" backside of the trunk) would be brought into view, and also as something that could be inspected more closely with respect to the visually presented side or aspect itself (from close range, I might be able to see that someone carved her name in the bark). It is important to emphasize that this "horizon" belongs to the perception as such and is not something imagined or thought about. The concrete perceptual manifestation includes both "proper" and "improper" manifestation (TS, 42–43), as Husserl puts it.

All this of course has to do with the fact that I see the tree from a certain *distance* and *perspective*. But to view something from a particular distance and angle is to be present – as the one who perceives – in the same space as the perceived object. In other words, the world (trees, rivers, mountains, rainbows, etc.) is always perceived from a certain viewpoint *within* it. Being presented in perspectives and ordered in terms of orientations of left and right, near and far, up and down, etc., the perceived world as such refers back to this embedded viewpoint of the perceiver. According to Husserl, the body plays a crucial role in this, in that it has "the unique distinction of bearing in itself the *zero point* of all these orientations" (Husserl 1989, 166). My body is the ultimate *here* to which all the other perceived objects (in varying degrees of "there") refer back; it is "my *point of view on the world*" (Merleau-Ponty 1964a, 5). Husserl notes how my body, again unlike anything in the perceived world, is something I cannot move away from me, and it is thus a "thing" that I only have very limited perceptual access to: "certain of my corporeal parts can be seen by me only in a peculiar perspectival foreshortening, and others (e.g., the head) are altogether invisible to me" (Husserl 1989, 167). The point, of course, is that the body is precisely *me*, the perceiver; it is that without which I would not be viewing things from *somewhere* – that without which the perceived world could not be given in perspectives. As Sartre puts it, "the perceptive field refers to a center objectively defined by that reference and located *in the very field which is oriented around it. Only we do not see this center as the structure of the perceptive field considered; we are the center*" (BN, 317).

Husserl thinks this perspectival structure is essential to the perception of spatiotemporal objects. In the *Ideas*, he claims that even a god, if she is to perceive spatial objects *as spatial objects*, must perceive them the way we do (Husserl 1982, 92). It is thus not merely because we are "finite" creatures that we can perceive spatial objects only in perceptions that exhibit the horizon structure. Rather, it belongs to the "essence" of the objects that they manifest themselves in this way and not another. A completely perceived tree would not be a tree at all. It would, rather, be something inseparable from my instantaneous experience, Husserl argues. Consider the following thought experiment from the *Logical Investigations*: "If percepts [or perceptions: *Wahrnehmung(en)*] were always the actual, genuine self-presentations of objects that they pretend to be, there could be only a single percept for each object, since its peculiar essence would be exhausted in such self-presentation" (Husserl 1970a, 713). We are here to imagine that everything intended in my present tree perception is also *strictly given* in that perception. Suppose I am having such a perception, standing a few feet from an apple tree. Suppose further that at one point I take two steps to the left. It is very unlikely that I could do this without the perceived tree presenting an at least slightly different aspect to me. But, if so, my perception could no longer be a perception of the same unaltered object. This follows immediately from the assumption that *everything* intended was already given in the previous perception; that is, that *all* aspects of the tree were fully manifest. If moving to the side makes me see new aspects (as surely it does), then we would have to say either that *not all aspects* were given to begin with or that I am no longer viewing the same unaltered tree. But *ex hypothesi* all aspects had to be strictly presented from the beginning, so we are left only with the second option.

But why is that option unacceptable? Why is it important that we can have different perceptions of the same object, perceptions that differ in terms of their perceptual content? The reason is as follows. If all aspects of perceived objects are fully manifest, then perceived objects change whenever the perceptual content changes. But in such a scenario no object can be explored further or perceived in different sensory modalities (e.g. touched instead of seen). If this is so, then how can perceptual experiences be experiences *of* something? The perceptual experience would seem to absorb the object, so that there would be no difference between the perceived object and the experience (cf. TS, 97–101). This is reminiscent of Berkeley's doctrine, with its familiar advantages and disadvantages. The good news is that if the *esse* of the things around us is simply their *percipi* (Berkeley 1988, § 3) there is clearly not much room for questioning their real existence while we perceive them (so skeptics would have a hard time). But the bad news is of course that, besides generating the familiar problems about the continuous existence of things, the whole thing blatantly contradicts our unimpeachable intuition that the things we perceive somehow exist "without the mind" (cf. Berkeley 1988, §§ 38, 8–9). So, to use Wittgenstein's term, a perception must to some extent be "unsatisfied" if it is to be a perception of "something outside the process of [perceiving]" (PI, § 438).

Hence a perception of a tree as a three-dimensional thing "out there in the park" – as something transcendent in relation to the perceptual experience – is only possible in such a way that the "properly" manifest is embedded in a horizon of not-properly-manifest (cf. TS, 46). But how is one to account for this embeddedness?[6] In order to answer this question, I will follow Husserl in considering some rather abstract examples. First, let us disregard the surroundings in which, as explained, a perceptual object always appears. Second (this is slightly more difficult), let us assume that we are not yet on the level of perception of spatial objects, but rather are only presented with two-dimensional visual appearances. Our task, then, is to account for how these appearances can achieve transcendent, three-dimensional significance in our perceptions.

Suppose, now, that I am experiencing a rectangular, light blue figure expanding in my visual field. There must, according to our argument above, be a possible situation in which such qualitatively different "proper" perceptual content (or at least *some* qualitatively different content) functions in such a way as to yield a perception of the same, unaltered object. One important thing here is of course the continuity of the visual experience. That is, it is essential that my experience is not like that of watching a slideshow, where I see a number of discrete pictures of blue rectangular figures; rather, it is important that I experience a continuous, unbroken process (TS, 132). But this is not enough, according to Husserl. Whether there is continuity or not, the "proper" visual content, since it is changing dramatically, cannot account for the possibility of perceiving an unaltered object. This is only possible if we take something additional into account, namely the perceiver's immediate awareness of her position, posture, and movement. As already mentioned, Husserl discusses such awareness under the title of "kinesthesia" or "kinesthetic sensations." His idea is that if the momentary visual content does not stand alone, as it were, but presents itself as a visual content under particular kinesthetic circumstances out of a multitude of possible such circumstances, then it becomes intelligible that a change in visual content need not imply a change in perceived object, provided that there is an appropriate change in the kinesthetic circumstances of the visual content. Thus, to return to our example, there is indeed such a thing as a perception of an unaltered, unmoved object, in the case where a light blue, rectangular figure gradually expands in the visual field; this is precisely the experience I am having at this moment, when I bend my neck and upper body in order to move closer to the copy of Russell's *Analysis of Mind* lying on my desk. My unthematic awareness of initiating a particular kinesthetic change constitutes the circumstance under which such an expansion of a figure in the visual field yields a perception of an unaltered, resting book. If the same alteration in the visual field took place under different circumstances, say in a situation of kinesthetic rest, it would have yielded a perception of an object either moving towards me or growing bigger. Likewise, we can now understand how a series of visual patterns that are radically qualitatively different (e.g. in terms of color) can nevertheless yield perceptions of the same unaltered object. The patterns can, for example, be the visual appearances connected with a "cyclic" kinesthetic pattern, such as a continuous movement "around" the object in which I get to see its various, differently colored, sides (cf. TS, 173–75).

In any visual perception of a transcendent, spatial object, then, we find a "constitutive duet" (Husserl 2001, 52). On the one hand there are the visual patterns and on the other hand there is the system of kinesthetic sensations. Interestingly, Wittgenstein airs a similar idea in his middle period work, the *Philosophical Remarks*. Concentrating on the experience of a space stretching out around the perceiving subject, Wittgenstein claims that a "detached, immovable eye wouldn't have the idea of a space all around it" (PR, 102). My experience of such a space depends essentially on my "feeling of the ability 'to turn around'" (ibid.). As Wittgenstein concludes, employing a somewhat dubious terminology, "[t]he resulting space around me is thus a mixture of visual space and *the space of muscular sensation*" (ibid.).[7]

Husserl and Wittgenstein are not simply saying that both kinesthetic sensations and visual appearances must be present to make a perception; they are also claiming that the two experiential components must stand in a particular functional relation to each other. Kinesthetic sensation and visual appearance must be correlated in such a way that "if" this particular kinesthetic sequence is realized, "then" a particular sequence of properly presented aspects follows (Husserl 1989, 62–63). Now we should be able to understand the nature of the horizon that makes possible the visual perception of a transcendent object. The present visual appearance is experienced as an appearance under certain circumstances, namely the present kinesthetic situation.[8] The "distribution" of proper and improper givenness I have at this moment, looking at Russell's book, is thus the result of my having realized this possible kinesthetic situation instead of another belonging to an open-ended horizon of kinesthetic possibilities. I could choose to move closer and inspect the book from a closer range, or from another angle, thereby letting other aspects be properly given (and letting the previously properly manifest aspects recede into the horizon). The "horizonally intended" aspects are precisely intended as *correlates* to the "kinesthetic horizon," the horizon of "freely possible series of movement" (Husserl 2001, 52). In Husserl's rather complicated formulation:

> Just as the actual sequence of the K's [i.e. kinesthesia] is one out of a profusion of unitarily intimate possibilities and just as, accordingly, the K is at any time surrounded by a halo of apprehensional tints, i.e.,

quasi-intentions, which correspond to these possibilities, so the constant intention living in the appearance is encircled by a dependent halo of *quasi*-intentions which first give the appearance its determinate character, as the appearance of a thing.

(TS, 160)

According to Husserl, then, perception implies embodiment in at least two interrelated ways. First of all, the mere fact that we see things in a certain perspective, and perceive them as oriented around us, indicates our bodily presence, as perceiving subjects, in the perceived world. As we have seen, one might envisage a "perception" without this horizon structure, but we have also seen that it cannot be the kind of perception that we have of the world around us. Second, the same perspectival structure essentially refers back to our potential for bodily movement. Perception presupposes that there is more to the perceived object than the strictly presented content; and this "more" is related to the position and movement (and potential for moving) of the perceiver.[9]

Affectivity and need

So far, the body appears as the perceiving subject's "anchorage in a world" (Merleau-Ponty 1962, 144), as well as a field of activities and abilities. With a famous expression of Husserl's, the body is experienced as a sphere of "*I can*" (Husserl 1989, 13, 159; Merleau-Ponty 1962, 137). But Husserl not only discusses embodiment in the context of perception and potential for movement. He also investigates what we might term the "sensibility" or "affectivity" of the body.

As I let my fingers run across the keys on my keyboard, I have certain tactile sensations. Under normal circumstances, I am not attentively aware of these, being occupied with the tactile object (the keyboard), or rather with the text I am trying to write. I can, however, direct my attention in such a way as to become thematically directed at these sensations. In fact, I can do so in two different ways: I can focus on them as revelatory of the touched object (smooth, slightly curved surfaces); or I can attend to them as *my* sensations, as "located" in my hand. The latter case is not one in which the sensations inform me about the *object* "hand" instead of the object "keyboard." Rather, they appear as subjective sensations belonging to the touching hand *as touching* (Husserl 1989, 154). In other words, the same tactile "material" can both present an object to me and present to me my touching hand as precisely that: my touching, that is, *sensing*, hand.

An important variation is the situation in which what is being touched is a part of one's own body. In *Ideas Two*, Husserl writes:

> Touching my left hand [with my right hand], I have touch-appearances, that is to say, I do not just sense, but I perceive and have appearances of

52 *Being some body*

> a soft, smooth hand, with such a form. The indicational sensations of movement and the representational sensations of touch, which are objectified as features of the thing, "left hand," belong in fact to my right hand. But when I touch the left hand I also find in it, too, series of touch-sensations, which are *"localized"* in it, though these are not constitutive of properties (such as roughness or smoothness of the hand, of this physical thing). If I speak of the *physical* thing, "left hand," then I am abstracting from these sensations (a ball of lead has nothing like them and likewise for every "merely" physical thing, every thing that is not my body). If I do include them, then it is not that the physical thing is now richer, but instead *it becomes body, it senses.*
>
> (Husserl 1989, 152)

In this passage, which generated discussion among the major French phenomenologists,[10] Husserl's claim is not simply that I cannot touch my body without one part of the body functioning as *touching* (Husserl 1973, 296). Rather, what makes the situation in which one part of the body touches another part so special is precisely that the "objectified" part of the body is still experienced as sensing as well (ZPI, 57). In other words, the left hand might be a perceived "object" for the right hand, but as I touch it as such it reveals itself as belonging to the perceiving subject: it feels (or I feel) that it is being touched. Moreover, it is possible for me – by a simple switch of focus – to let the touched hand become the touching hand and vice versa (cf. Husserl 1973, 298, 302).

These phenomenological observations suggest something extremely important. Experiences of this kind are obviously not possible for an experiential subject that is separated from the world of tangible things. Rather, in order to be the *subject* of these experiences, I must be someone who can not only touch things, but *be touched* as well. So the perceiving subject is revealed as a perceivable subject, itself part of the perceived world. In making the world manifest the embodied subject itself becomes manifest.

But another aspect of embodiment begins to become discernable here as well. For to say that an embodied subject is a subject that – *as subject* – can be touched is to indicate an affectability or vulnerability on the part of the subject. This is an aspect of embodiment to which Emmanuel Levinas, in particular, has drawn attention. According to Levinas, "[t]he body is neither an obstacle opposed to the soul, nor a tomb imprisoning it, but that by which the self is susceptibility itself" (OB, 195). To be a bodily creature is not only to have power and abilities ("I can"), but also to be susceptible, exposed, and vulnerable. The body is this ambiguity or this vacillation between power and vulnerability, between sovereignty and submission, between "sickness and health" (TI, 164–65, 229).

For Levinas, these considerations indicate the necessity of an addition to Husserl's account of kinesthesia and perception. Although Husserl recognizes that it is part of our embodiment that we can be touched and affected, he does not seem to draw the full consequences of this insight. As Levinas points out, our bodily exposure and affectability are aspects of a basic *dependence* on the world. As examples of this dependence, Levinas mentions our need for nourishment and warmth. These are not only biological necessities, but fundamental aspects of our experience of ourselves as embodied or incarnated. Changes in temperature, for example, not only affect the subject in the sense that they call forth certain qualitative experiences (it is *like* something to feel cold; a distinct sort of unpleasantness is part of this experience), but warmth is also something a subject positively needs. And this is clearly not only a biological fact, but a phenomenological fact as well. When my feet are cold, for example, I *experience* a need to warm them. When I am hiking on a hot summer day, I feel the need for shade, coolness, and water.

The phenomenon of need involves the possibility of satisfaction. When we experience the satisfaction of a need, enjoyment usually results. And there is no further goal within the context of need than satisfaction and enjoyment. According to Levinas, a phenomenologist such as Heidegger has ignored this fact,[11] claiming that the existence of subjectivity (or Dasein) somehow comprises the final *telos* of everything we do. In one sense, of course, this is correct. Biologically speaking, the purpose of eating is to stay alive. But phenomenologically or experientially speaking things look different. "The need for food does not have existence as its goal, but food," Levinas claims (TI, 134). We eat because we are hungry, and we have no further purpose or aim than the enjoyment and satisfaction eating gives us. There is a distinctive moment of sensibility or even sensuality in this that Levinas thinks other phenomenologists (in particular Heidegger, but essentially also Husserl) have overlooked.

Whether this criticism is justified or not is not our central concern here. We need only note the fact that our embodiment is not merely experienced by us as field of activity and power; in addition to this, it also makes us dependent and vulnerable. This must be kept in mind as we continue the attempt to show that a proper grasp of embodiment forces us to rethink subjectivity altogether.

Heidegger on being embodied

As characteristic as Husserl's ongoing concern with embodiment is, so conspicuous and surprising is Heidegger's avoidance of the topic. Many readers have felt an unacceptable gap opening up in the account of *Being and Time* when Heidegger suddenly interrupts a discussion of "the spatiality of being-in-the-world" with the remark that embodiment (*Leblichkeit*) "hides a whole problematic of its own, though we shall not treat it here" (BT, 143).[12] However, some recently published texts from Heidegger's *Nachlass* shed light on his complicated relation to the phenomenon of the body. I will begin my account of Heidegger's contribution to an understanding of human embodiment by briefly reviewing some of the places where Heidegger does have something to say on the topic. In fact, let me narrow down our initial thematic field even more, and only consider places where Heidegger takes a positive stance toward the notions of body and embodiment.

In a 1919 lecture course, Heidegger emphasizes that what he then calls "life" (and will later term Dasein) has an essential relation to embodiment, and he stresses how this is of "fundamental importance" (Heidegger 1987, 210). Scattered remarks to the same effect are found in a number of Heidegger's texts from the 1920s. In *Being and Time* itself, for instance, a human being is described as being "'in' the world in the sense that it deals with entities encountered within the world" (BT, 138). These entities are not simply placed at this or that position in objective space. Rather, they have their proper "place," related to our practical involvement with them, says Heidegger. For instance, my books are either on the bookshelves or, if not, "lying around," which "must be distinguished in principle from just occurring at random in some spatial position" (BT, 136). My books are "lying around" in the sense of "making a mess" on my desk – something that clearly refers to my working involvement with them. Obviously, this tells us something about the human being (or Dasein) as involved with such things. The different utensils precisely have their proper and improper places in relation to the Dasein using them: they are in the way, making it difficult for me to locate something, or placed within easy reach ("an arm's length"), and so on and so forth. All of this refers to the working, grasping, and walking subject. Apart from the more general reference to Dasein's concern and involvement (without which nothing could be "in the way"), the preceding reflections highlight two specific points concerning the involved subject. First, as being "too far away" or "within easy reach," the tools refer to the concerned subject as one to whom there is such a thing as distance. The subject must be characterized by what Heidegger calls "dis-stance" (*Ent-fernung*), i.e. it must be able to encounter distances as such, which means, among other things, to judge them and traverse them. Second, as being "up there" or "to the right," etc., that is, in being located in this or that direction, the tool refers to Dasein's spatial orientation. Tools are not only at a certain *distance* from me, they are obviously also located in a particular *direction*. It is in the context of this last point that Heidegger utters his two sentences on the body: "Dasein's spatialization in its 'bodily nature' is likewise marked out in accordance with these directions. (This 'bodily nature' hides a whole problematic of its own, though we shall not treat it here.)" (BT, 143).

Another place where Heidegger briefly touches upon the notion of embodiment is the following remark: "Dasein is thrown, factical, thoroughly amidst nature through its bodiliness" (Heidegger 1984, 166). This remark, for all its brevity, is not insignificant. As already mentioned, Heidegger describes Dasein as "being-in-the-world." Often, however, he does so in a way that would seem to suggest that what he has in mind is quite different from what we would normally understand by an expression such as "being-in-the-world." Thus, he is very emphatic that the latter should not be understood to signify our being *contained* in something. Heidegger turns to etymological speculation[13] to indicate the more proper understanding of the "in" in "being-in-the-world":

> Being-in [...] is a state of Dasein's being; it is an *existentiale*. So one cannot think of it as the Being-present-at-hand of some corporeal Thing (such as a human body) "in" an entity which is present-at-hand. Nor does the term "Being-in" mean a spatial "in-one-another-ness" of things present-at-hand, any more than the word "in" primordially signifies a spatial relationship of this kind. "In" is derived from "*innan*" – "to reside," "*habitare*," "to dwell." "*An*" signifies "I am accustomed," "I am familiar with," "I look after something."
>
> (BT, 79–80)

One might be inclined to conclude from this that being-in-the-world means simply a practical and theoretical involvement with the world. In other words, one could get the impression that Heidegger is simply repeating the insight gained in Chapter 2, stating that Dasein is intentionally involved with the world. This, however, would be a mistake. Precisely in order to underscore Dasein's quite literal (including spatial) situatedness *in* the world, Heidegger sometimes lets phrases such as "amidst nature" or "in the midst of what there is" (*inmitten des Seienden*) replace or supplement the formulation "in-the-world" (Heidegger 1996, 328). When introducing these phrases, Heidegger complains that the description of Dasein's "being-alongside" worldly entities is insufficient, because "it still looks as if Dasein were some subject hovering over the entities, as it were, even if it is abandoned to them" (ibid.).[14] The point is that even if we are emphatic that the subject cannot be understood without taking its involvement with its surroundings into account it may still seem as if we have the subject on one side and the environing world on the other side. For example, the world-involvement discussed in Chapter 2 is intelligible in the absence of any assumption that the intentional subject is literally placed *in* the world it experiences. But the latter is precisely what Dasein is, according to Heidegger. In contrast to any interpretation that would construe being-in-the-world as meaning simply being-related-to-the-world (in which way ever), it is Heidegger's contention that Dasein is literally situated "in the midst of" the world.

Now, as the quotation above has it, it is precisely in and through its corporeality or embodiment that the human being finds itself in the midst of the world. The same point is expressed in another text, in which Heidegger even states that "Dasein is physical body [*Körper*] and lived body [*Leib*] and life; it does not just have nature as its perceptual object – it is nature"

(Heidegger 1996, 328). Thus, Heidegger can also refer to the body as something that connects the human being – although it has a mode of being of its own – with the being of animals and other creatures and entities not having the mode of being of Dasein (cf. Heidegger 1990, 181).

The facticity or "thrownness" of human beings – the fact that we find ourselves already situated in the midst of things – is something that is above all revealed to us in our affectivity and moods (BT, 175). Bodily situatedness and moods thus appear to be closely connected. This supposition is confirmed by a recently published lecture course, in which Heidegger introduces the topic of embodiment in the context of Aristotle's account of passions or emotions (*páthe*). Heidegger argues that a *páthos* is something that "carries Dasein away" (GAP, 197) and that this phenomenon of being carried away is misunderstood if taken to involve only a part of Dasein, such as its mind or soul (GAP, 122, 177). As he puts it, "[s]trictly speaking, I cannot say: the soul hopes, fears, feels compassion; rather, I can always only say: the human being hopes, is courageous" (GAP, 197). In other words, it is the *whole* human being that is affected by the emotions or passion; and, as Heidegger emphasizes, this also includes the body (GAP, 202, 203, 206, 207).

We should dwell for a moment on Heidegger's motivation for introducing the notion of body in this lecture course. The background for Heidegger's discussion of embodiment is formed by the desire to emphasize that emotions or passions are not merely mental phenomena. This suggests that Heidegger introduces the considerations of the body, not because he has some special urge to enter into this problematic, but rather because he finds it may help to prevent a possible fundamental misunderstanding. The crucial thing is that the kind of "being-carried-away" and being-affected that the *páthe* constitute affects the whole human being, and not just its soul or mind. This is the reason why Heidegger feels he must emphasize that Dasein "as being in the world, insofar as it is affected by the world, *is also affected with regard to its corporeality*, that everything aims at the living *in its full being-there*" (GAP, 202). But Heidegger's defense of this holistic perspective isn't restricted to his treatment of passions and emotions. His agenda as such, as we shall see shortly, necessitates that we take the being of the whole human being into account, without dividing it up into various components or domains. And, as he unambiguously states it, "the whole being of the human being [is] characterized in such a way that it must be grasped as the *bodily being-in-the-world* of the human being" (GAP, 199).

Body and Dasein

In the discussion of *páthe*, Heidegger is dismissive of the traditional conception of passions or emotions as states of the soul, even when such a conception acknowledges the possible existence of "accompanying corporeal manifestations" (GAP, 177). The problem, as Heidegger sees it, is not that this way of understanding *páthe* has forgotten to take the body into account. It is rather the dualistic approach as such: "[O]ne divides the phenomenon in mental and corporeal states that stand in a certain relation to each other" (GAP, 177). Being at pains to grasp the being of the "whole" Dasein, Heidegger cannot accept this dualistic approach. He stresses that the "so-called 'bodily states' in anxiety, joy, and the like, are not accompanying manifestations" (GAP, 198), as if they were merely supplementing otherwise strictly "inner" mental occurrences. Rather, they are integral moments of the phenomena as such. It is thus not only the strictly mentalistic account of passions and emotions, but also accounts in which the notion of "body" figures on one side of a dualistic divide that Heidegger attempts to overcome by stressing that passions affect the "whole" being-in-the-world as such.

In his elaboration of the structure of being-in-the-world, Heidegger is equally keen to issue warnings against a certain characteristic use of the concept of "body." If being-in-the-world means both being-related-to-the-world or being-involved-with-the-world *and* being situated in it, then it is again tempting to divide the issue and say, for example,

> that Being-in in a world is a spiritual property, and that man's "spatiality" is a result of his bodily nature (which, at the same time, always gets "founded" upon corporeality). Here again we are faced with the Being-present-at-hand-together of some spiritual Thing along with a corporeal Thing, while the Being of the entity thus compounded remains more obscure than ever.
>
> (BT, 82–83)

Heidegger is once again out to criticize the philosophical tendency to divide the human being into various components. We are, as Heidegger puts it, accustomed to conceiving ourselves as a unity of body–soul–spirit – a conception which is precisely destructive to the project of understanding our mode of being as such (BT, 82–83). Can our being be "constructed of the being of the material basis, the body, the soul, and the spirit? Is the being of the person the *product* of the modes of being of these layers of being?," as Heidegger rhetorically asks in a lecture course (Heidegger 1985, 125). This worry is what motivates him to utter repeated critical remarks on the philosophical use of the concept of "body." This is the case, for example, when he emphasizes in *Being and Time* that the "substance" of the human being "is not spirit as a synthesis of soul and body; it is rather *existence*" (BT, 153); and when he states that Dasein's spatiality must not be "interpreted as an imperfection which adheres to existence by reason of the fatal 'linkage of the spirit to a body'" (BT, 419).

There are a great number of other passages that one could refer to in this context, but the essential point should already be clear. It is Heidegger's contention that the terminology of "body" furthers conceptions of the human being as *composed* of various different types of entities. It thus supports what we might term an *analytic* conception of the human being – analytic in the sense that it seeks to *dissolve* or *divide* the human being into a number of discrete components. Concepts such as "body," "embodiment," and "corporeality," tend, in the hands of philosophers, to evoke contrasting concepts such as "mind," "soul," and "the mental." To speak of the human body is already to invoke the complementary notion of the human mind or soul; the notions of embodiment and "incarnation" seem to suggest that *something* (e.g. a "pure ego") is embodied or incarnated, and so forth.[15]

Now one could easily take this to mean that Heidegger's agenda is simply to thrash the dead horse of Cartesian dualism. To be sure, Heidegger intends his critique to apply to Cartesianism, but it would be wrong to view the latter as his main target. The main problem is not the Cartesian commitment to an immaterial mind-substance. Rather, Heidegger's point is that we cannot make ourselves intelligible philosophically in terms of various different components or elements that we simply piece together. More precisely, he believes that accounts of this type cannot be phenomenologically confirmed; they do not correspond with the way we actually *experience* ourselves.

Heidegger thinks that in order to improve on this situation we need to do more than just correct a few false moves. For the analytical conception in fact even covers up the real task of philosophy. From Heidegger's perspective, if we subscribe to an analytic view we make it close to impossible to pose the type of question that it is precisely the business of philosophy to pose: the question of the fundamental structures of what there is (cf. Heidegger 1985, 183). Or, rather, this question has tacitly been answered *for us*. If a being such as a human being has both a certain weight, say, and the ability to engage in philosophical discussions, then one version of the analytic view would hold that this is because such a creature has not only a material, physical component, but also a mental component. The properties of the former component (weight, extension, etc.) are different from the properties of the latter component (perception, thought, feelings), and in conjunction these components make it intelligible that the creature in question can exhibit both types of traits. But the crucial point is that both components are implicitly posited as *things* that might have very different properties but nevertheless have in common their occurrence as things. That is, in both cases being is implicitly understood as simply "occurring" – what Heidegger calls "presence-at-hand."[16] Thus, a question has been silently bypassed, viz. the question whether subjectivity as such could have a peculiar *mode* or *manner* of being different from that of merely occurring (cf. Heidegger 1982, 18). Heidegger calls this question – which concerns not only the human being – the "question of being" or the question of the "meaning of being." He believes this "ontological" question is the most fundamental question of philosophy and yet one that has not been posed since Aristotle (BT, 21). And it is not as mysterious a question as it might appear at first sight. In fact, the "conjuring trick" that we have seen Wittgenstein expose has everything to do with the implicit adoption of a certain notion of "being," as I will argue shortly.

The analytic conception, then, is far from harmless. It harbors a certain questionable ontology that is all the more powerful for being implicit and unarticulated (GAP, 272, 275). Heidegger wants to question this prevailing ontology on phenomenological grounds. His critique does not mainly concern Cartesian dualism but, more fundamentally, the type of ontology a dualistic view (or any other analytic view) typically works with. It might be that the emphasis on "body" and "embodiment" provides an antidote to Cartesianism. But this does not necessarily render this emphasis beneficial. To the extent that it furthers an analytic account of the human being, the "body" talk implicitly posits the being of the human being as "presence-at-hand," Heidegger thinks.

It should be clear from the discussion so far that a certain type of criticism of Heidegger's refusal to discuss the body is completely misguided. One cannot accuse Heidegger of lapsing into a mentalistic conception of subjectivity, because such a criticism takes for granted the analytic conception of the human being – precisely the conception that Heidegger is trying to overcome. It is only when one sees the human being as composed of a "bodily" and a "mental" element that the refusal to address the former may legitimately be seen as an inappropriate elevation of the latter. Heidegger rejects altogether this way of conceiving of a human being. Yet, as we have seen above, what Heidegger says about the being-in-the-world of Dasein has everything to do with embodiment. As he puts it in volume eighteen of the collected works, the being of the human being "must be grasped as the *bodily being-in-the-world*" (GAP, 199).

But what, then, is our corporeal or bodily being-in-the-world? A rough outline of an answer to this question can be gleaned from what has been said so far. First of all, what Heidegger has in mind cannot possibly be a physical presence-at-hand in space. As he puts it, "presence-at-hand and occurring within the world must be sharply distinguished from being-in a world, which belongs to the essential manner of being of Dasein" (Heidegger 1976, 240). As human beings we are *in* the world, but we are in it *as* involved, affectively, cognitively, and practically, with the world. We are bodily in the world, in the midst of what there is, but not as a mere thing is there within the world; rather, we are in the world *as* affected by it, *as* practically engaged in it, and so on and so forth. Heidegger writes in his Kant book that with the existence of Dasein the world is "broken into" or "irrupted" in such a way that it is thereby "opened," i.e. disclosed or manifested (Heidegger 1990, 156). This expression conveys both the world-revealing status of subjectivity and its situatedness in the world it discloses.

The bodily being of subjectivity – "thrown" into the midst of things *as* the place where things come into appearance – is what Heidegger tries to capture with the concept of Dasein. According to his own later verdict, the latter term is awkward and unhelpful (Heidegger 2003, 69); but perhaps we should not agree with Heidegger on this point. In fact, maybe Dasein is an adequate term with which to capture the manner of being that belongs to subjectivity. It is composed of the two words *da* ("there" or "here") and *Sein* ("being"). The word "Dasein" is no invention of Heidegger's; in fact, as he himself points out, the word appears quite frequently in German philosophy, e.g. in Kant and Husserl (Heidegger 1982, 28). But while the latter two understand Dasein – "being-there" – to refer to the being-there of *things*, their presence-at-hand, Heidegger interprets the "*da*" of Dasein quite differently (Heidegger 1982, 28). In Heidegger's use of the word, what Dasein conveys to us is that to be a human being is to *be* a "*there*" (BT, 171), that is, to be a "place" or sphere of dis-closedness (*Erschlossenheit*) into which other entities can somehow enter: "In the expression 'there' we have in view this essential disclosedness" (BT, 171). In other words, to be a "there" means first of all to be a place where the world and worldly entities become manifest and articulated – it means being "the peculiar place for the totality of entities" (Heidegger 1996, 360), or the "place of the transcendental," as Heidegger himself says on one occasion.[17] But there is more to it than that. Being a "there" means not only being the place where the world is disclosed; it means being this "place" as something that is *itself* disclosed. As Heidegger puts it in an early lecture course, having the world disclosed means that "*that* entity that is in the world is co-visible. This *co-visibility* is expressed in the *there*" (Heidegger 1994, 288–89). Thus, being a "there" means also being-oneself-disclosed, or being-*exposed*, both to a physical environment and to a social and cultural environment one has not chosen. These points taken together, the notion of Dasein indicates that being a human being is being a "sphere of manifestness" in the double sense of a *manifest* sphere where entities become manifest (Heidegger 1996, 132–37).

All in all, then, it is not the case that Heidegger "holds that the body is not essential" (Dreyfus 1991, 137; cf. 41). Nor should we conclude that the question of body and embodiment is something Heidegger "has not thought through" (Levin 1999, 136). It is quite the other way around: Heidegger clearly does think these things through, and he does think our embodiment is something essential. But the crucial thing is how to articulate this in a way that remains faithful to the phenomenon, and it is by taking this question very seriously that Heidegger is led to abandon the notion of body. I don't think there is any real need for such a radical step.[18] But I do think that Heidegger's analyses indicate that if we want to be able to conceive the being of the human being as bodily being-in-the-world, then there is good reason to pay close attention to how we, as it were, apply the "picture" of embodiment.

Wittgenstein on embodiment

This is the right place to reintroduce Wittgenstein in our story. One might think that at least the Husserlian account of embodiment is one that the later Wittgenstein would reject vehemently. After all, do the *Remarks on the Philosophy of Psychology* not reveal the later Wittgenstein as a relentless critic of the very idea that there are such things as "kinesthetic sensations?"

Let us look more closely at some of the things Wittgenstein writes about kinesthetic sensations and see if things are not after all a bit more complicated.

Wittgenstein clearly criticizes kinesthesia construed as a sensation providing me with information *on the basis of which I can judge the position of my limbs* etc. That is, the target of Wittgenstein's criticism is a view that makes my awareness of my own bodily movement, position, etc. an *indirect affair*, mediated by observation of peculiar, internal entities (cf. RPP I, § 786). If, on the other hand, kinesthetic sensations – or, better: kinesthesia[19] – are identified with my immediate, noncriterial, and nonobservational "knowledge" of my own movement and position, then Wittgenstein has no objections. In fact, his point is precisely that my "knowledge" of these things has such an unmediated structure. The parallels between Wittgenstein's position on this issue and his claims about one's knowledge about one's own thoughts and sensations (broached in Chapter 1) are striking. In both cases, Wittgenstein rejects models that construe the type of awareness in question as a form of criterial knowledge. According to him, I know that *I* am in pain without knowing it "because ... ," that is, without basing this "knowledge" on any criteria; likewise, I simply know that my legs are crossed, without having established this fact on the basis of an observation of the presence of some special sort of sensations (Z, § 481). In both cases what Wittgenstein opposes is an account that makes it seem as if we are dealing here with a special "inner species" of object-knowledge – knowledge that, despite its "inner" subject matter, is nevertheless characterized by the same comfortable distance as other cases of object-knowledge. In other words, just as Wittgenstein's point in rejecting that I *know* what I think is that this puts me at a strange observational distance from the subjectivity that I *am*, so his criticism of "kinesthetic sensations" comes down to this: we must not make our knowledge of our own bodily movement and position look so distanced and mediate as to give the impression that this is not a case of subjective awareness of oneself. But this is simply another way of saying that my awareness of my bodily movement, posture, and position is an awareness of *my own subjectivity*. And having said that, we are forced to conclude that I am aware of myself as an essentially embodied subjectivity.[20]

There are similar points of convergence between Wittgenstein's crucial insight into the problematic assumption common to Cartesianism and behaviorism (and physicalism) and some of Heidegger's central claims in his discussion of embodiment. As shown, Heidegger thinks most if not all of modern philosophy has adhered to a conception of Dasein as something "on hand" or "present-at-hand." This is precisely also the assumption Wittgenstein finds that behaviorism and Cartesianism tacitly share. In both cases, the problematic idea is that, insofar as something is real, or exists, it must be a thing or an object – something that "just stands there."

When Heidegger says that human beings are "in-the-world" what he means is that we are situated "in" the world *as* engaged-in-the-world, inhabiting it, "having" it. Chairs and tables, in contrast, are within the world yet "worldless" (BT, 81); that is, they have their place within the world, but they are not engaged in the world, they don't inhabit it or "have" it. As we have seen, Heidegger firmly resists the attempt to divide the phenomenon of being-in-the-world by attributing world-engagement to a mind or soul, for instance, and situatedness to a physical body. In a similar vein, Wittgenstein speaks of the "illusion that we use [the word 'I'] to refer to something bodiless, which, however, has its seat in our body," and which – in contrast to the body – "seems to be the real ego, the one of which it was said, 'Cogito, ergo sum'" (BB, 69). The idea is not that there is no subject or "ego," but that we should give up the notion that this is something distinct from, yet somehow inhabiting the human body. The Cartesian distinction between "inner" and "outer," or "real ego" and body, is a philosophical construction, rather than anything uncovered by faithful description, according to Wittgenstein and Heidegger (Heidegger 1982, 90; cf. LW II, 84). In contrast to such a "constructive" view, Heidegger repeatedly stresses that he is trying to bring to light the "manner of being" of the *whole* human being as such. In Heidegger, then, the fundamental ontological dividing line is not between an immaterial mind and a material body, but between creatures that are in the world *as having* a world and creatures that are within the world but "worldless." With the notion of being-in-the-world Heidegger conceives subjectivity in such a way that it cannot be equated with mere behavior or physical structures and states, and yet is no "inner sphere," closed off from others and the "external" world. Precisely such a conception is what Wittgenstein, too, is hinting at with his concept of "the living human being" (cf. M. McGinn 1997, 8): It is a fundamental ontological category of its own, and it signifies being "out there" in the world, at once exposed to it and engaged in it.[21] It is a human being of flesh and blood that perceives, thinks, feels fear and pain, goes shopping, plays tennis, and does mental arithmetic – it is neither an "immaterial soul" (PI, § 573) nor a "material body" (PI, § 286).[22]

Conclusion

To be a world-involved subject is to be embodied, to be a *bodily* subject. But, as we have seen in this chapter, it is far from inessential how we articulate this insight. The very notion of *embodiment* seems ideally suited to dualism, suggesting as it does that there is *something* (a soul or a mind) that is embodied. If we want to understand subjectivity itself as bodily – that is, if we want to understand the body as something essential to being a subject or a mind involved with the world – then we need to be cautious about how we use such concepts as body and embodiment. We have to abolish "the idea of an ego *inhabiting* a body" (cf. PO, 225, my emphasis), as Wittgenstein says. But this is no easy task, since the idea in question seems to be a "picture" that all but forces itself upon us the moment we start speaking, philosophically at least, about the body.

4 Externalism, realism, and Wittgenstein

Here I should like to say: a wheel that can be turned though nothing else moves with it, is not part of the mechanism.

(PI, § 271)

Introduction

According to Wittgenstein, there is no ego inhabiting a body. But there is, as we have seen, a bodily subjectivity inhabiting a world. Indeed, I have argued that being embodied and having a world – "catching reality in one's net" – are essential to being a subjectivity. But the full implications of these Wittgensteinian ideas might not be immediately evident from the discussion so far. In Chapter 2 I briefly considered to what extent Wittgenstein might be sympathetic towards so-called content externalism. I mentioned that some have interpreted Wittgenstein as a staunch defender of externalism; but I did not take a stand on the question. In this chapter, however, I want to spell out some of the implications of Wittgenstein's thoughts on mind and world by taking a closer look at his supposedly externalist views. Although initially involving a brief visit to Hilary Putnam's Twin Earth, the investigation will eventually be led into Wittgensteinian waters.

The questions that I want to raise in this chapter concern, first, the extent to which Gregory McCulloch's realistic "in-the-world Wittgensteinianism" can legitimately be spoken of as a form of Wittgensteinianism at all and, second, whether it constitutes an attractive position. My strategy will be to answer both questions in one move, so to speak. As I present some Wittgensteinian ideas that contradict McCulloch's realistic position, I aim to make these ideas compelling enough to undermine that position. After having presented McCulloch's case, I will turn to a simple consideration of Wittgenstein's so-called "private language argument."[1] I will argue that although there is a strong externalistic element in Wittgenstein's discussions of private language, there is an equally strong – and convincing – resistance to metaphysical realism.

"Strong in-the-world Wittgensteinianism"

Suppose that somewhere in a remote galaxy there is a planet very much like Earth. In fact, the planet is a near perfect duplicate of Earth. Just like Earth, this "Twin Earth" has its forests, oceans, mountain ranges, cities, and so forth. Indeed, the people on this planet speak something indistinguishable from English. But there is one difference. Whereas what we call "water" here on Earth has the chemical formula H_2O, what the Twin Earth inhabitants call "water" has the completely different formula XYZ. Twin Earth "water," however, is superficially indistinguishable from (Earth) water, and it plays exactly the same kinds of roles (quenching thirst etc.). Suppose now that the pair of *Doppelgänger* Hilary (on Earth) and Twin Hilary (on Twin Earth), who have had completely parallel lives, including the same contact with (what they have learned to call) "water," both think they want "a glass of water." The author of the story, Hilary Putnam, suggests that even if Hilary and Twin Hilary are type-identical with regard to what is inside their skins, their psychological histories, etc., they nevertheless mean something different when they talk or think about "water," because of the mentioned difference between their environments.

There are two sides to Putnam's classic argument. The first concerns the role of other speakers. Suppose Hilary and Twin Hilary are both rather ignorant when it comes to their local flora. In particular, they do not have very firm grasps of the words "beech" and "elm." They are unable to tell a beech from an elm, and in fact their understanding of *both* words can be adequately summed up in something like this: "a big deciduous tree." Suppose further that the words "beech" and "elm" are "switched" on Twin Earth, so that the Twin word "beech" refers to the kind of tree we would call an elm, and vice versa. Again, the two Hilarys are type-identical (in the inside-the-skin sense) when they utter the word "elm." So do they mean the same thing when they say "elm?" It seems they do not. The meaning that the word "elm" has – *for Hilary too*, when he uses the word – seems not so closely and exclusively tied to his own grasp of the word. Rather, it seems to be more closely connected with the kind of grasp that botanists and other more competent speakers of Hilary's linguistic community have of the word "elm." As Putnam observes, in the switching case "surely we would *not* say that 'elm' has the same meaning on Earth and Twin Earth," even if our twins have the same fuzzy grasp (what Putnam calls "concept") of "elm" and "beech" – namely "big deciduous tree" (Putnam 1975, 245–46).[2]

We thus seem to reach the conclusion that individual "psychological state" and "concept" or "grasp" do not determine the meaning of a word. The linguistic community plays an important part in fixing meaning. This is especially obvious when we look at terms with which an average speaker in a linguistic community cannot do much. Presumably "elm" is an example of such a word. When an average speaker uses it, she does so without a clear grasp of the criteria for something to be an elm. But she may do so because there is a "division of linguistic labor" such that there are others in the linguistic community (experts, or simply more competent speakers) who do know how to tell whether a given tree is an elm, a beech, or an oak (Putnam 1975, 227–29). This, then, is the first part of Putnam's claim: *Meaning is codetermined by the linguistic community.*

To grasp the idea behind the second part of Putnam's claim, let us return to the example of "water." Putnam argues that the meaning of such a natural kind word is codetermined by "local" environmental samples. What *we* mean by "water" is paradigmatically the stuff that is found in *earthly* lakes and oceans: if anything else is to count as water (for us) it must bear "a certain similarity relation to the water *around here*" (Putnam 1975, 234). This should bring out the crucial lesson of the Twin Earth fiction, for there is a clear asymmetry between Earth and Twin Earth concerning the meaning of the (English, earthly) word "water." If we were to discover that the stuff that fills up earthly lakes and oceans had a different chemical structure than hitherto assumed, we would not conclude that, as it turns out, there is no water on Earth. We would rather conclude that water actually has a chemical structure different from H_2O.[3] This case, indeed, is hard to imagine. But it is even harder to imagine something that would count as a case in which all our earthly "water" was not *water*. Things are quite different for Twin Earth, however. If we would discover that the stuff we found up there in lakes and oceans had a different chemical structure than H_2O we *would* conclude that the fluid Twin Earth stuff was not water. It is thus relatively easy to imagine a case where "water" from another galaxy is not *water*. What the word "water" means, then, is not independent of the nature of our (local) environment. If the nature of paradigmatic local samples is discovered to be otherwise than hitherto thought, then the meaning of the word tends to follow that discovery ("water actually has *that* chemical structure"). If more distant and peripheral samples are discovered to be different from what was expected (viz. something with the *same* nature as the local samples), the conclusion might well be that this stuff, although practically indistinguishable from water, isn't water after all. This second part of Putnam's claim can be formulated in the following way: *Meaning is codetermined by the external world.*

So what does all this show? Putnam thinks it provides an important corrective to traditional philosophical semantics. As he ironically puts it, traditional theory of meaning ignores "only two contributions" to the meanings of our words: "the contribution of society and the contribution of the real world!" (Putnam 1975, 245). Contra the traditional approach, the physical and social environments matter to what a speaker means by her words.

Gregory McCulloch has recently argued that there is something of a tension between the two parts of Putnam's externalist position. The second claim – the claim about the dependence of meaning on the (local) environment – is construed by McCulloch as "the doctrine that *the understanding tracks real essence*" (McCulloch 1995, 163). We can easily see why McCulloch puts the point in those terms. Recall, for example, what we just said about "water." What we human inhabitants of planet Earth mean by "water" is, paradigmatically, the stuff in earthly lakes and oceans. We don't give up talking about "water" no matter what discoveries about the microstructure of this stuff we make. Our understanding of "water," that is to say, follows or "tracks" the "essence" of this local stuff *whatever that essence might be*. What we mean by water is *this* stuff; whatever its hidden, possibly forever hidden, *real* essence (as supposed to what we might at this or that point in time *think* the essence of water is) might be – it will be "tracked" by our understanding.

According to McCulloch, this second claim of Putnam's does not sit well with the first claim. Presumably, McCulloch does not want to deny that a linguistic community has some role in fixing meaning; but the problem is that the introduction of the community obscures what McCulloch thinks is the central point in Putnam's argument, namely the point that "understanding tracks real essence." For

> the existence of experts who can distinguish samples of a substance from superficially similar things is elsewhere said by Putnam not to be necessary for the understanding's tracking of real essence. As he puts it, "the extension of the term 'water' was just as much H_2O on Earth in 1750 [when no one knew this] as in 1950" (MM: 224). Indeed, it is not clear that this point requires even the *existence* of other speakers: on the face of it, it is just a claim about an individual's understanding tracking the unknown facts about real essence.
>
> (McCulloch 1995, 178)

In fact, in a section aptly titled "Let's be realistic," Putnam divorces the meaning (the "real essence") of "gold" from our ability to discover it "even in principle" (Putnam 1975, 238). And if Putnam is willing to go that far – if, that is, my understanding of "water," "gold," etc. tracks real essence no matter whether I or anyone else is even in principle able to discover this real essence – then why does he need the reference to expert speakers? Indeed, why the reference to anyone else at all? Is it not just a question of "an individual's understanding tracking the unknown facts about real essence?" Putnam's discussion of these issues in fact illustrates a quite different point than the one intended, according to McCulloch, namely the point "that speakers can get hold of words they do not really understand" (McCulloch 1995, 178). For the discussion shows that Putnam simply does not understand the words "beech" and "elm" – that they are "pretty meaningless *to him*" (ibid., 179).

Now, one might worry that McCulloch turns "understanding a word" into an all-or-nothing affair. Putnam, it seems, certainly has some understanding of "beech" and "elm"; there are, in fact, quite a number of moves in language games that Putnam would be able to make with these words, given his "concept" of them (for instance, he could correct people who think "elm" is the name of a species of coniferous tree). If this sort of vague or (very) imperfect understanding were not allowed to count as some sort of understanding, wouldn't we have to say that most words are "pretty meaningless" to most of us?[4] Yet this is not the crucial point here. The crucial point is that if Putnam's claim is that our "understanding tracks real essence" no matter whether we will ever be able to discover the real essence in question, then the reference to the existence of expert speakers, or even to other speakers as such, is completely unnecessary. When Putnam does refer to such things it gives the impression that he is arguing for a quite different type of externalism, namely one that denies that "the mind is self-contained with respect to the doings of other speakers" (McCulloch 1995, 180). But this is dangerously misleading. For the latter kind of externalism is compatible with the denial of the Putnamian insight that McCulloch thinks is crucial, in that here "there is nothing like a real essence which the understanding is said to track" (ibid.).

By now the motivation for McCulloch's critique of Putnam should begin to become clear to us. McCulloch is concerned to use the Twin Earth fiction to argue for what he calls "a very strong form of in-the-world Wittgensteinianism" (McCulloch 1995, 181). An in-the-world Wittgensteinianism will

> make essential mention of aspects of the individual's surroundings, and the more inclusive and specific these descriptions are allowed to be, and the more they mention comparatively remote aspects of the world [...], the more extreme will be our form of in-the-world Wittgensteinianism.
> (McCulloch 1995, 99)

So the "strength" of McCulloch's version of the view has a lot to do with an emphasis on realism already implicit in his talk of "unknown facts about real essence" and clearly discernible in his dissatisfaction with Putnam's emphasis on the linguistic community. We have not learned the lesson McCulloch wants us to learn from Putnam's fiction if we do not see it in the light of "realism, the view that things can have their own nature which goes beyond how they impinge on us" (McCulloch 1995, 174). We "must be prepared to admit that something could, possibly, impinge on our awareness in normal conditions in exactly the same way as water yet still fail to be water" (ibid.). In fact, McCulloch seems to imply that there is no limit to the "remoteness" of the aspects of the world that will be mentioned in his in-the-world Wittgensteinianism. After all, he unhesitatingly describes his version of "in-the-world Wittgensteinianism" as *very* strong (cf. McCulloch 1995, 181), and what could make it *very* strong if not precisely the metaphysical realist assumption that our understanding "tracks real essence" regardless of whether or not it is even *in principle* accessible to us?[5]

But what has this to do with Wittgenstein? McCulloch thinks his realistic externalism can be reconciled with Wittgenstein if we construe "'use', 'form of life', and so on [so] that they too track real essence" (McCulloch 1995, 181). According to this interpretation, to understand the word "water" is ultimately "to participate in certain forms of life which themselves, besides of course involving bodily and other factors, track the differences between e.g. H_2O and XYZ, even when these are unknown to the speakers" (McCulloch 1995, 188). In the next two sections we will inquire to what extent these ideas can be reconciled with Wittgenstein the way McCulloch claims they can.

The private language argument

There are several different arguments that can be distinguished in Wittgenstein's discussions of private language.[6] These strands of argumentation are closely connected, but for the present discussion of externalism it is useful to distinguish between three somewhat different motifs. Each of these will prove important to the discussion of "Wittgensteinian" externalism.

It takes two

If one had to sum up a central feature of Wittgenstein's private language argument, one might perhaps, inspired by a famous remark by Austin, say that it is this: it takes (at least) two to make (linguistic) meaning (cf. Austin 1979, 124). However, as is painfully evident to anyone who has just a superficial acquaintance with the literature on Wittgenstein, it is much debated in which way, exactly, it "takes two" to make meaning. Does it mean that there is no hope for a wolf-child, a neonate Crusoe? Does it mean, in other words, that, given the actual absence of other persons, a person would be unable to construct a language for herself? Or does it mean, rather, that it is impossible to construct a language that is private in the sense that others, if there were any, could not possibly understand it or learn it? In other words, is the point that our Crusoe would be able to construct a language for himself, only not one that others, if he should happen to meet any, were in principle barred from understanding? Would a wolf-child be able to construct a language given a suitable external, nonhuman, environment? Or, again, is some contribution from others what is needed, either alone or in conjunction with such an object-environment?

If these questions were easily given conclusive answers, the debate about Wittgenstein's thoughts on a "private language" would have faded out a long time ago. But the debate seems alive and well. Crucial in the debate has been the correct interpretation of Wittgenstein's remarks on rule following. The question, to put it in very general terms, has been what sort of "practice" it is that is supposed to ensure that there *is* such a thing as following a rule. In the *Investigations*, Wittgenstein writes:

"obeying a rule" is a practice. And to *think* one is obeying a rule is not to obey a rule. Hence it is not possible to obey a rule "privately": otherwise thinking one was obeying a rule would be the same thing as obeying it.

(PI, § 202)

But is he necessarily referring to a *social* practice or could a "solitary" practice work as well? That is the moot point, and the passage does not seem to settle the issue. Other passages are equally inconclusive:

Is what we call "obeying a rule" something that it would be possible for only *one* man to do, and to do only *once* in his life? [...] It is not possible that there should have been only one occasion on which someone obeyed a rule.

(PI, § 199)

Is it the "once" or the "one person" which is important here? The emphasis might seem to be on the first option,[7] but both in section 199 of the *Investigations* and again in the *Remarks on the Foundations of Mathematics* (Wittgenstein 1978, 334) Wittgenstein states that a rule is an "institution," which seems to imply a community of speakers (cf. Savigny 1996, 119).

I will more or less sidestep these questions, however. What is of interest to me in this part of the private language discussion is something that most if not all sides in the debate agree on. Let me indicate what that is.

One of the first to articulate the view that a community is what is needed to make linguistic meaning was Saul Kripke in his book *Wittgenstein on Rules and Private Language*. Based on a detailed and by now classic (but widely repudiated) account of Wittgenstein's rule-following considerations Kripke argued that Wittgenstein's private language argument was leveled against the idea that "the notion of a person following a given rule is to be analyzed simply in terms of facts about the rule follower and the rule follower alone, without reference to his membership in a wider community" (Kripke 1982, 109). Kripke's basic claim is that an individual can only be said to grasp a concept (Kripke focuses on that of addition) if his or her uses of it "agree with those of the community in enough cases, especially the simple ones" (Kripke 1982, 92). Without the possibility of checking one's individual use against an established community use there can be no rule following and hence no language. Some recent commentators, among others Savigny (1996, 94–125) and Meredith Williams (1999), have seconded the Kripkean emphasis on the social community. In Williams' formulation of the view, Wittgenstein is emphasizing the normativity of rules, and "[i]t is only in relation to the structured practice of the community that the individual can engage in normative activity" (M. Williams 1999, 187). Since language essentially is such an activity, it cannot be an individual affair, Williams argues (ibid., 157).

From early on, however, the "community reading" has been met with resistance. Some of the fiercest opponents of the view are G. P. Baker and P. M. S. Hacker.[8] A standard objection to the community interpretation is that it is not the encouraging and corrective responses from other subjects that function as the necessary stabilizers for language, but rather the individual's environment: "[R]eality must be sufficiently stable so that the yardstick typically gives the same result when the same object is measured on successive occasions. Otherwise measurement in particular and the application of concepts to reality in general become pointless" (Baker and Hacker 1984, 44; cf. 1985, 179). To see this, consider Wittgenstein's much quoted example about the putative private speaker keeping track of his sensations (PI, §§ 258–61). When a particular sensation appears, he gives it the name "S," writes it in his diary, etc. But the next time the private linguist is inclined to write "S," how can he know that it is the same sensation again? An answer is immediately forthcoming: He remembers the sensation he had the first time, of course, and recognizes that it is there again. Wittgenstein's point, however, is that the memory of the private linguist must play a role here that is very different from the role memory usually plays in our lives. The problem is not that the private linguist might have a faulty memory of the sensation he dubbed "S," but in a sense the opposite: *there can in principle be no such thing as misremembering,* since whatever *seems* right to the private linguist *is* right. Normally we would be able to check our memory against the testimony of others and against the objects in our environment. But there is no such thing for the private linguist. There can be no independent criteria of success and failure. He is like a solitary marksman on a shooting range, who can only see the target down the sight of his rifle right before he fires, and never again.[9] Here target practice obviously becomes senseless. In the same way rule following (and hence language) becomes meaningless when "*there is nothing independent* to which to appeal" (Hacker 1997, 269). But the appeal, here, only needs to be an appeal to something independent; it does not need to be an appeal to the practice of a linguistic community.[10]

Finally, there are some commentators who do not fit perfectly into either the community camp or the Baker–Hacker camp. David Pears has argued extensively for something that resembles the Baker–Hacker view, but at the same time he is somewhat less dismissive of the community view. According to Pears, Wittgenstein had both community and environment in mind as stabilizing factors, and he would probably have refused "to choose a precise point on the line of escalating deprivations resulting from the solipsist's retreat into his microcosm, and to claim that it is just here that language becomes impossible" (Pears 1988, 364). Nevertheless, Pears thinks there is a certain hierarchy between the two stabilizers:

> The appeal to the community is not final, because factual language, whether spoken by a solitary person or by millions, has to preserve the

constancy required if yesterday's predictions are to come true today. The individual gets confirmation from the community only on the assumption that the community's usage has itself remained constant.
(Pears 1988, 369)

In other words, individual language usage might be answerable to the community, but the community's language usage (as well as the individual's) "is answerable to the world" (ibid.). Both factors are important, but in the end the right kind of physical environment is a more important stabilizer than the social environment.

To sum up, it seems fair to say that there are (at least) three general takes on this first aspect of Wittgenstein's critique of "private language": Some emphasize the necessity of a stabilizing social community; others emphasize the necessity of a stabilizing object-environment; and others again argue that while Wittgenstein sets no precise limit specifying where linguistic meaning becomes impossible, he would hold that if there were not a stabilizing factor – either in the shape of a community or in the shape of a stable object-environment – then language definitely would be impossible. If one of these interpretations is correct, then the immediate consequence of Wittgenstein's private language argument is that he must be committed to *some* form of externalism. Linguistic meaning cannot, it seems, be generated "internally" in a subject, without essential reference to the subject's environment. This is something all the mentioned commentators seem to agree on. In some sense, meaning is codetermined by external factors: a stable world and/or community. Or, to speak the language of Putnam, knowing the meaning of a term is not "just a matter of being in a certain psychological state," where "being in a psychological state" is understood as something that does not presuppose "the existence of any individual other than the subject to whom that state is ascribed" (Putnam 1975, 219–20). Grasping a meaning is something that cannot take place outside some rule-governed practice; and no practice can be rule governed unless there is *something* outside the individual subject and unless this "something" gives the right sort of feedback. On all accounts of Wittgenstein's private language argument that I have sketched in this subsection, meaning, to use a term from Putnam, is *interactional* (cf. Putnam 1988, 36). That is, meanings, according to Wittgenstein, too, simply "ain't in the *head*" (Putnam 1975, 227).

We should also note in passing that the private language discussion is structurally parallel to the discussion between Putnam and McCulloch. A crucial issue is how to place the external emphasis, so to speak: on the world, the community, or both. But all agree that the upshot of the private language considerations is some such external emphasis.[11]

Stage-setting

At one point in his story of the solitary diarist Wittgenstein interrupts the discussion of lack of criteria for rightness and wrongness with a somewhat different consideration: "What reason have we for calling 'S' the sign for a *sensation*? For 'sensation' is a word of our common language, not of one intelligible to me alone" (PI, § 261). The point is not merely that "sensation" happens to be a word that is not private in the required sense. The point is rather that by speaking of "sensation" the would-be private linguist draws upon the full-fledged public language in a very substantial way. Wittgenstein had introduced this claim four sections earlier:

> When one says "He gave a name to his sensation" one forgets that a great deal of stage-setting in the language is presupposed if the mere act of naming is to make sense. And when we speak of someone's having given a name to pain, what is presupposed is the existence of the grammar of the word "pain"; it shews the post where the new word is stationed.
>
> (PI, § 257)

A number of commentators have emphasized the importance of this aspect of the private language argument.[12] What Wittgenstein is trying to show, they argue, is that if the private linguist stipulates that "S" is the name of a *sensation*, then she has helped herself to a crucial category of our normal, public language. "Sensation" makes sense only in contrast to other categories, such as "thought," "emotion," and even words for physical things, states, and processes. When our private linguist says that "S" is the name of a *sensation*, she is, as Wittgenstein points out, indicating the "post" on which this new name is to be placed. But thereby the private linguist tacitly invokes the "stage-setting" provided by our public language. That is, she does not "enter the world of a private language semantically naked," as Robert Fogelin has put it (Fogelin 1976, 161). And if that is so, then her language is not all that private after all: it draws on a public language, which, *inter alia*, contains words referring to things outside the individual speaker.

A tempting move to make for the would-be private linguist, then, is to give up the category of "sensation." When she writes "S," she at least "has *something*" (PI, § 261), it might be insisted. Surely, there is "something there"; she "has" ("senses," but we are not allowed to say that) something, and why can't she simply name this *something* "S" ("*This* is 'S'")?[13] Here Wittgenstein launches a second wave of attacks. First, he points out that the words "has" and "something" also belong to our public language (PI, § 261). So when using these, the private linguist is still not linguistically naked enough, so to speak. Second, supposing that the private linguist could avoid the first difficulty somehow, what she must do then is to perform some private or inner act of ostension. But how is that supposed to work? To put it differently, what is the "*this*" that is being named? Take the example of a "normal" ostensive definition. I point to a big Labrador and tell my little nephew, "This is p." How can this be of any use to someone who does not even have an idea of the category of "p," that is, someone who does not yet know "the overall role of the word in language" (PI, § 30) (are we talking about a color, an animal, etc.)? After all, "p" could be filled in with many different words ("black"; "big"; "a carnivore," "a dog"; "something with four legs"; "Rover") (cf. PI, § 28), and there is no general difference in the way we point our fingers when we are trying to define a color rather than a species of animal. So, assuming that the framework is still lacking, and that we thus do not know at which "post" to place the word "p," it is entirely unclear what has been defined. That is to say, *nothing* (in particular) has been defined. So, to return to our would-be private linguist, what does she accomplish by concentrating her attention on whatever it is that she has? If she has *no framework* in place, what could it possibly mean for her to be defining one thing rather than another (this *type* of sensation; this level of *intensity*; this *particular* sensation; and so forth)?[14]

We may reach the same point from the opposite angle, as it were. This would be to emphasize that my inner act of concentration does not fix any *technique for using the word* "S." What Wittgenstein writes in another context concerning "normal" ostension also holds for "private" ostension:

> One can say: Whoever has a word explained by reference to a patch of color only knows *what* is meant to the extent that he knows *how* the word is to be used. That is to say: there is no grasping or understanding of the object, except through the grasping of a technique.[15]
>
> (RPP II, § 296; cf. PI, § 199)

To speak a language, as already mentioned above, is to partake in a practice rooted in our lives. Even though ostensive definitions play an important role in our lives, they cannot play the role the private linguist needs them to play. For what is "S" to be used *for*; what is its *function*? When and how is it appropriate to use "S," what is the appropriate "technique?" The private linguist would presumably say that "S" is used to signify something (namely *this*), but this in fact says nothing about the *use* of the word (cf. RPP I, § 614). "Signifying" is everything and nothing (just as "this" is everything and nothing), and thus it remains as unclear as before how "S" is supposed to connect up with the linguist's life (cf. PO, 240).

Note that these considerations, too, have broadly externalist implications. The argument shows that a private language cannot be set up from scratch; that attempts to imagine it being set up from scratch are parasitic on the framework of our public language. A private inner act of ostension would be condemned to take place in a complete conceptual and practical vacuum, so to speak: there would be no conceptual and practical framework into which it might be fitted, and no independent criteria of success and failure. In such a vacuum, it would be impossible to get language off the ground.

Wheels turning idly

In his influential review of the *Philosophical Investigations* Norman Malcolm distinguishes an "internal" and an "external" private language argument in Wittgenstein's magnum opus. The "internal" argument roughly corresponds to what has been canvassed above in the sections "It takes two" and "Stage-setting". Whether the decisive stabilizers are interpreted as having their origin in the community or in the world, the "internal" argument has the same form, namely that of a *reductio ad absurdum*: "postulate a 'private' language; then deduce that it is not *language*" (Malcolm 1966, 75). The external argument proceeds in a slightly different way. Here the emphasis is not on the stabilizers necessary for establishing and maintaining meaning, nor on the stage-setting without which ostensive definitions are futile, but rather on the *public import* of private objects, assuming they could be privately dubbed (which the "internal" arguments have said they could not).[16] The crucial passage in the external argument is the story about beetles in boxes, already quoted in Chapter 1 (see p. 22). As explained there, the point of the passage is not to show that the feeling of pain, its subjective qualitative character, is "irrelevant" to the meaning of the word "pain."[17] Rather, Wittgenstein is again putting forward a *reductio*. The problematic assumption is of course the one that makes pain look like a beetle in a box. *If* the sensation of pain is really something essentially isolated from public life; if it is something each of us knows about, identifies, and names, only from his or her own case, *then* it follows, Wittgenstein claims, that the sensation is irrelevant to our use of "pain"-words. The "thing in the box," one might say, is a wheel turning idly (cf. PI, § 271), since "it does not connect with the use (i.e. the meaning) of the word" (M. McGinn 1997, 173). The use of the word, the public practice, cannot revolve around an object that *per definition cannot make a difference to public life*.[18]

Hence, if there *were* essentially private "things" of the "beetle" sort, and if these *could* be dubbed "beetles" by each individual, privately, then these things would, in the public language that we actually speak, be nothing but wheels turning idly. They would have no function or place whatsoever. Again, then, we seem to be driven towards an externalist position: what *I* mean by the word "beetle," given a language shared with others, is not just a question of what goes on inside me. In fact, if what goes on "inside me" were *completely severed* from the public world, it would be entirely irrelevant to my use of the word, according to Wittgenstein (cf. BB, 72–73). In this connection, we should also note the well-known fact that Wittgenstein repeatedly connects meaning with "use." It is controversial what exactly we may conclude from his famous remark that "[f]or a *large* class of cases – though not for all – in which we employ the word 'meaning' it can be defined thus: the meaning of a word is its use in the language" (PI, § 43).[19] But it does associate the meaning of at least some words with the use made of them in language. Now, important to our present concerns is the fact that Wittgenstein occasionally contrasts the "use" or "application" made of a word with what goes on inside the individual speaker. In the *Philosophical Investigations* he emphasizes that what I *mean* is a question of the "use" I make of words, rather than what goes on "in my mind." As he puts it, "What is essential is to see that the same thing can come before our minds when we hear the word and the application still be different. Has it the *same* meaning both times? I think we shall say not" (PI, § 140). I take it that this remark implies that two speakers could be "psychologically indistinguishable" (in Putnam's sense), while the "application" and hence the *meanings* of their words were nevertheless different. If so, it clearly illustrates Wittgenstein's commitment to *some* form of semantic externalism.

So, to sum up the results of this section, there is an externalism in Wittgenstein's private language argument in the following sense: *understanding the meaning of a word (sentence etc.) is not merely a question of what goes on inside an individual, independently of the nature of this individual's (physical and social) environment*. Clearly, this is not without further ado to be identified with Putnam and McCulloch's versions of externalism. In fact, I think it is in an important tension with the externalism advocated by McCulloch. This will be the subject of the next section.

Wittgensteinian externalism and "tracking real essence"

As mentioned, McCulloch intends to make his "in-the-world Wittgensteinianism" fit the realism that he distills from Putnam's Twin Earth example by construing "'use', 'form of life', and so on [so] that they too track real essence" (McCulloch 1995, 181). But will that work? Can one interpret Wittgenstein in this way without *mis*construing his position? The issue is not whether McCulloch is right to attribute a general externalist outlook to Wittgenstein – we have seen that this is correct – but whether Wittgenstein's externalism is of the same type as McCulloch's externalism.

Anthony Rudd has recently argued that McCulloch's Putnamian externalism cannot be made to harmonize with Wittgenstein's views. According to Rudd, Wittgenstein's externalism can be formulated in the following way:

> Understanding is something that is manifested in practice, in using words appropriately in contexts. So the understanding cannot be said to exist apart from the contexts in which the word is used. This is what the slogan "Meaning is use" (*PI* §43) comes down to. It is not a theory about what meaning essentially is; it is a reminder to us of the ways in which we ascribe mastery of a concept to a person.
>
> (Rudd 1997, 501; cf. 2003, 77)

As Rudd goes on to argue, this is hard to reconcile with McCulloch's "tracking real essence." McCulloch emphasizes the contrast between the possibly unknown and unknowable real essence that our words "track" and

76 *Externalism, realism, and Wittgenstein*

the "way things impinge on us," but "if understanding must be manifestable in practice, how could we manifest our grasp of what is supposed to be the reality of things in themselves, *as opposed to the way they might impinge on us?*" (Rudd 1997, 506). Rudd continues his attack on McCulloch's use of Wittgenstein by emphasizing that even if we could make sense of such a grasp of the "real essence" being manifested it is hard to see why we would be interested in this unknowable "real essence" in the first place. According to Rudd, what we ought to say, on Wittgensteinian grounds, is rather this:

> If the stuff is to play some role in our form of life (if it does not, we would have no motive for wanting to include it in our classifications anyway) then it will do so in virtue of the ways it impinges on us.
> (Rudd 1997, 506).

I agree with most of this.[20] Nevertheless, Rudd's central premise is slightly misleading. The problem is this: Rudd links his description of understanding as something that is manifested in practice with "the ways in which we ascribe mastery of a concept to a person." The emphasis is thus on third-person ascriptions of understanding; in order for an individual to truly *understand* a word, she must be able in practice to demonstrate her understanding to others. This is problematic, and for two closely connected reasons.

First, it might seem to rely on a very robust community interpretation of understanding. That is, one might take Rudd to imply that understanding is essentially something a community ascribes to an individual. On this view, there can be no understanding for someone born a Crusoe. But, as we have seen, the claim that Wittgenstein subscribes to this view is widely contested in the literature. It therefore seems odd to presuppose this claim in an argument designed to show that McCulloch's position cannot be defended on Wittgensteinian grounds. McCulloch could surely argue that Rudd precisely misconstrues these "Wittgensteinian grounds." Understanding, of course, cannot be said to exist apart from the contexts in which words are used. But that is not in itself an argument against the idea that understanding "tracks real essence." Such an argument is only mounted the moment we assume with Rudd that "use" essentially refers to "manifestation in practice," which in turn refers to other speakers who, on the basis of the right kind of manifestation in the right contexts, "ascribe mastery of a concept" to the individual person. But what this comes down to is the community interpretation of private language, and nothing prevents McCulloch from rejecting it. In fact, his critical remarks on Putnam's reference to the linguistic community strongly suggest that McCulloch would precisely reject this interpretation.[21]

Second, Rudd's description of understanding almost gives the impression that it can be adequately accounted for in purely behaviorist terms. When

Rudd connects the "practice" and "use" of understanding with its manifestation to others he seems to suggest that understanding is simply a matter of displaying the right third-person-observable behavior under the right circumstances. If so, then Marie McGinn's worry that Wittgenstein is presented as formulating a defense of logical behaviorism (cf. M. McGinn 1997, 130) would be justified. Rudd correctly contests the behaviorist interpretation of Wittgenstein (e.g. Rudd 2003, 106), but one might wonder whether he should not then have couched his argument against McCulloch less exclusively in third-person observational terms.[22]

This is one reason why our discussion of Wittgenstein's private language argument is important: the private language argument precisely investigates the possibility of an individual subject grasping words *in complete isolation*. That is, it (or at least part of it) investigates this possibility from the *inside*, from a first-person point of view (see, e.g., Wittgenstein 1978, 335). The question is whether *I* could understand words and sentences completely independently of the nature of my external (social and/or physical) environment. But the discussion of the private language argument is important in another way as well, in that it allows us to see quite clearly why Rudd is still thoroughly right to claim that McCulloch's externalism is irreconcilable with Wittgenstein's.

Wittgenstein's externalist point in the private language argument concerns the conceptual framework and the stabilizing environment that he holds necessary for linguistic meaning. This makes his view difficult to reconcile with McCulloch's "strong in-the-world Wittgensteinianism." When Wittgenstein emphasizes the importance of a stabilizing environment he cannot possibly mean "the real essence" of the environment as opposed to how things "impinge on us." On the contrary, on the Wittgensteinian view meaning is *interactional*, which means that part of what is important here is precisely how the social and physical environments impinge on the individual. Wittgenstein gives as examples of such stabilizing factors the approval and disapproval, expectation and encouragement that others express to us (PI, § 208); and what matters here is surely how these expressions strike us and influence us. In contrast, the hidden reality of things, precisely insofar as it is hidden, insofar as it does not (or even *cannot*) impinge on the individual, seems irrelevant (cf. PI, § 126). It surely cannot function as any kind of stabilizing framework if it is in principle beyond the cognitive reach of human beings. What must provide stability for the individual speaker is her *experienced* physical and social environment.

Recall also the point that linguistic understanding is something that presupposes a practice. It seems hard to conceive of a practice (whether individual or social; whether manifested in behavior or not) that is concerned with real essences in themselves *as opposed to any way they might impinge on us*. This is Rudd's main point. We can easily conceive of practices that are concerned with the real nature of things – just think of natural science – but what are we to make of the idea of a *human practice* concerned with the *fundamentally inaccessible* nature of things? And if we cannot make sense of such a practice what sense can we make of the suggestion that our understanding "tracks" these inaccessible real essences? Or if understanding, as Wittgenstein also emphasizes, is essentially mastering a *technique*, how do we learn to master the technique of referring to the *Ding an sich* as opposed to the thing as it could ever appear to us? It seems hard, in particular on Wittgensteinian grounds, to make sense of any of this. For Wittgenstein, the reach of our understanding seems much too closely connected with our performances and the kinds of explanations, demonstrations, and examples that we can give, to fit McCulloch's idea of tracking unknown and unknowable essences. The idea that our understanding tracks real essence far beyond what it is within our cognitive capacities to realize seems hard to square, for example, with Wittgenstein's hesitation regarding the extent to which we even understand the question whether "7777" occurs somewhere in the development of π (PI, § 516).[23]

The beetle in the box parable makes explicit the incompatibility of Wittgenstein's private language argument and McCulloch's type of externalism. The gist of this strand of the argument is this: that which cannot connect in any way with human social life – that is, that which cannot possibly make any difference to human social life – cannot be relevant to the "use" we make of words in our common language either. It is a wheel turning idly – no part of the machinery, and thus no part of the "meaning" either. But when McCulloch contrasts the way things impinge on us with the "real essence" of these things, he seems to move dangerously close to ascribing to this "real essence" precisely the role of a wheel turning idly, or a beetle that "cancels out." He seems – if I have interpreted his "very strong form of in-the-world Wittgensteinianism" correctly – to claim that our concepts track the real essences of things, even if the latter are in principle unknowable. But if these "essences" never make any difference to our lives, indeed if they *cannot possibly* make any difference to our lives, then they simply reduce to beetles in boxes. On Wittgenstein's view, as we have seen, a difference that makes no difference cannot matter to the meaning of our words. If anyone has a lingering doubt concerning this characterization of Wittgenstein, they should consider this passage from *The Blue Book*:

> I want to play chess, and a man gives the white king a paper crown, leaving the use of the piece unaltered, but telling me that the crown has a meaning to him in the game, which he can't express by rules. I say: "as long as it doesn't alter the use of the piece, it hasn't what I call a meaning."
>
> (BB, 65)

Wittgenstein' reply, then, to the claim that part of what I mean (what my understanding "tracks") when I say "water" can be something in principle beyond the cognitive reach of a possible community would surely be that "a nothing would serve just as well" (PI, § 304) as this kind of "something."

According to Wittgenstein, "[w]ords have meaning only in the stream of life" (LW I, § 913). What is wrong with McCulloch's interpretation of Wittgenstein is ultimately that it moves the meaning of our words far beyond our lives. The world we live in, surely, is the world we experience and interact with – this is something like an analytical proposition. When McCulloch contrasts the real essence of things with things as they impinge on us in our experiences and activities, he locates the former outside "the stream of life," thereby – at least from a Wittgensteinian point of view – depriving it of any significance to our language use.

Let me end this section with a final reservation concerning McCulloch's use of Wittgenstein. McCulloch's notion of "tracking real essence," that is, tracking the nature of things regardless of how they "impinge on us," seems to imply that our concepts are extremely strong and firm. What I mean is this: the discovery that the feline creatures that many of us keep as pets are in fact robots controlled from Mars (cf. Putnam 1975, 243) is not taken to imply any difficulties for our use of the word "cat." Our understanding, on McCulloch's view, tracks the real (and possibly unknowable) essence of these things, no matter what we might think about them, indeed no matter how bizarrely they might begin to "impinge on us." But is this really convincing? Austin, for one, was critical of the idea that we are conceptually equipped to handle every such situation. As he argues, considering an example resembling one of Putnam's:

> Suppose that I live in harmony and friendship for four years with a cat: and then it delivers a philippic. We ask ourselves, perhaps, 'Is it a real cat? or is it *not* a real cat?' 'Either it *is* or it *is not*, but we can't be sure which'. Now actually, that is not so: *neither* 'It is a real cat' *nor* 'it is not a real cat' fits the facts semantically: each is designed for other situations than this one. [...] Ordinary language breaks down in extraordinary cases. (In such cases, the cause of the breakdown is semantical.) Now no doubt an *ideal* language would *not* break down, whatever happened. In doing physics, for example, where our language is tightened up in order precisely to describe complicated and unusual cases concisely, we *prepare linguistically for the worst*. In ordinary language we do not: *words fail us*.
>
> (Austin 1979, 67–68; cf. 88)

Note that this does not imply a general skepticism regarding philosophical thought experiments.[24] Austin himself relies on one such thought experiment to make his point. Rather, it expresses skepticism with respect to the idea that we are always "linguistically prepared for the worst." If we bear in mind what was said above (see pp. 70–1, 77) about the stabilizing factors of language, it should come as no surprise to us that Wittgenstein is in perfect agreement with Austin on this point. As he says in the *Philosophical Investigations*,

> It is only in normal cases that the use of a word is clearly prescribed; we know, are in no doubt, what to say in this or that case. The more abnormal the case, the more doubtful it becomes what we are to say – if there were for instance no characteristic expression of pain, of fear, of joy; if rule became exception and exception rule; or if both became phenomena of roughly equal frequency – this would make our normal language-games lose their point. – The procedure of putting a lump of cheese on a balance and fixing the price by the turn of the scale would lose its point if it frequently happened for such lumps to suddenly grow or shrink for no obvious reason.
> (PI, § 142; cf. Wittgenstein 1969, § 513)

According to Austin and Wittgenstein, we cannot simply assume the smooth functioning of our everyday language across possible worlds, Twin Earths, cats turning out to be robots controlled from Mars, and so forth. Yet if McCulloch is to drive home his point that such examples show how our concepts track real essence, then he *must* assume that they remain perfectly functioning, even under the most extreme circumstances. His point, as already noted, is precisely that our understanding tracks real essence no matter how things impinge on us. But perhaps our words "water" and "cat" only function in certain language games (say, the game of pointing to a picture of a cat when hearing the word "cat"; pointing to a picture of a robot when hearing the word "robot"; pointing to a picture of a tree when ...; etc.). And if we change the circumstances in such bizarre ways as to make these language games pointless or impossible, then perhaps we simply no longer know what to do with those words. Words, then, simply fail us, as Austin says; they do not continue to operate smoothly in order to track the real essences of things, behind their confused appearances.

Note that this does not undermine the externalist position advocated in the present chapter (although it might cast doubt on the Twin Earth fantasy as a proper route to that position). There is nothing *internalist* about the claim that if we change the environment's feedback the interaction between subjectivity and environment is affected and the meanings of terms may change or even collapse. On the contrary, this seems itself an important *externalist* lesson. If meaning and intentional content are interactional, then one would precisely expect them to be substantially affected by changes in environmental feedback.

Conclusion

Meaning and intentionality are possible only for an *embedded* subjectivity – a subjectivity "in-the-world." This externalist conclusion may very well be labeled "in-the-world-Wittgensteinianism." However, I have argued that we should avoid giving a metaphysical realist interpretation of it. On Wittgenstein's view, our language is tied to our *lives* rather than to mysterious essences transcending the world as we experience it. As tied to our lives, language is also essentially tied to the world; Wittgenstein is, in this sense, clearly advocating a form of "externalism." But it is an externalism with a distinctively human face, so to speak, for the world in question is precisely the world as it impinges on our lives. Of course it is true that things could be different from how they seem to us to be; a broomstick partly immersed in water looks bent to all of us, but it *is* straight. No sane person would deny that. But to divorce the "real essence" of things completely from they way they impinge on us, or possibly could impinge on us, is quite a different matter; and Wittgenstein would reject *this* (distinctly philosophical) move.[25]

Is this "to embrace a very forthright form of idealism," as McCulloch claims (cf. McCulloch 1995, 174)? Or is it, rather, just to embrace our natural (or commonsense) realism while refusing to follow the philosopher who insists on adding something "queer" by demanding that this natural realism "bear metaphysical weight?"[26] I think the latter is true, and that it perfectly illustrates Wittgenstein's attitude to the opposing positions of idealism and realism. In the *Blue Book*, he writes, approvingly, that "the common-sense man [...] is as far from realism as from idealism" (BB, 48). In the *Philosophical Investigations* he elaborates:

> [*T*]*his* is what disputes between Idealists, Solipsists and Realists look like. The one party attack the normal form of expression as if they were attacking a statement; the others defend it, as if they were stating facts recognized by every reasonable human being.
>
> (PI, § 402)

Perhaps the reason why McCulloch thinks he can make our "normal form of expression" bear metaphysical weight is that he is attached to a more fundamental, problematic and distinctly un-Wittgensteinian idea. This is the idea that it is possible to occupy an "external point of view" on language and reality (cf. Crary 2000, 3–4),[27] that is, the idea that it is possible to provide what McDowell has called "a sideways-on picture of understanding and the world" (McDowell 1996, 82). It is only if it is supposed that we can step out of our lives and achieve an external view on the relation between our language and the world that the idea of our language as "tracking real essences," no matter whether we could possibly have any cognitive access to these essences, makes sense. And it is only from this standpoint that the denial of this idea must look like "a very forthright form of idealism." Because seen from an external standpoint (if it were possible) such a denial would amount to either a rejection of the idea that our language and experience hook on to this real world at all (epistemic antirealism) or a rejection of the idea that there is any such world apart from our linguistic and other practices (metaphysical idealism). But the whole thing is an illusion. We cannot adopt such an external viewpoint from which to compare our linguistic practices with the world they connect with. We only have access to the real world, and to the real essences of things, *in and through our lives.*

5 The opposite of solipsism

> Is it impossible to imagine a philosophy that would be the diametrical opposite of solipsism?
>
> (PO, 225)

Introduction

A significant merit of Wittgenstein's so-called private language argument, unmentioned in Chapter 4, is often thought to be its way of dealing with the issue of solipsism. Peter Hacker expresses the views of many commentators when he writes that the private language argument constitutes "Wittgenstein's most important argument against solipsism" (Hacker 1997, 229). This assessment ought to attract attention. For the attack on private language is among the most celebrated of Wittgenstein's arguments, and it is widely regarded as occupying a central position in the *Philosophical Investigations*. So if the function of this argument is to refute (or cure) the solipsist, then solipsism can hardly be a marginal issue to Wittgenstein. He must deem the issue of solipsism worthy of close philosophical scrutiny.

Against this background it may look as if I have turned everything upside down in Chapter 4 by construing the private language argument as an attack on metaphysical realism. And I will continue to turn matters on their heads in the present chapter. For while I think there is something profoundly right about the assessment that solipsism was anything but a minor issue to the later Wittgenstein, I intend to approach this issue more or less without mentioning the private language argument. There is a reason for this. It is not my intention to claim that Wittgenstein's attack on private language is unimportant to a discussion of solipsism. But I do think that often a more or less exclusive focus on the private language argument has deflected philosophers' attention away from the extent to which Wittgenstein takes seriously certain intuitions underlying solipsism (in particular the idea of a fundamental intersubjective asymmetry that I will elaborate on p. 91–102).[1] Setting the question of private language aside will make it possible for us to notice important but often overlooked aspects of the later Wittgenstein's engagement with the issue of solipsism.

Yet how can solipsism possibly be an issue worthy of serious philosophical discussion? If solipsism is either the metaphysical doctrine that only I (*solus ipse*) exist (or that I am the only subject that exists) or the epistemological doctrine that I am the only subject I may know about, then surely solipsism is plainly false and thus "a position to be avoided" (Avramides 2001, 3). I think this is obviously true and reflects Wittgenstein's view as well. However, Wittgenstein urges us to consider carefully how, exactly, solipsism is to be avoided. Some philosophers seem to think that the only way to avoid landing ourselves in one of the varieties of this hopeless position is to eschew in our philosophy of mind any special emphasis on the first-person perspective. This skeptical attitude *vis-à-vis* the first-person perspective may take a number of different forms,[2] but the general worry that unites all of them is perspicuous and understandable. According to *The Cambridge Dictionary of Philosophy*, solipsism is "the doctrine that there exists a first-person perspective possessing privileged and irreducible characteristics, in virtue of which we stand in various kinds of isolation from any other persons or external things that may exist" (Vinci 1995, 751). The problematic (epistemological or even metaphysical) isolation is, it would thus seem, so inseparable from the notion of a privileged and irreducible first-person perspective that to adopt the latter notion is *eo ipso* to embrace solipsism. Under such circumstances, any philosopher intent on avoiding solipsism must, in order even to qualify as a candidate, begin by repudiating the idea "that there exists a first-person perspective possessing privileged and irreducible characteristics."

It is not unusual for philosophers who share the worry I have just mentioned to claim to find support for their perspective in the writings of the later Wittgenstein.[3] And the thought seems natural: If there is anything the later Wittgenstein teaches us – in his private language argument and elsewhere – it is that the traditional philosophical privileging of the first person leads to various absurdities, solipsism being a prominent example. But let us be careful here. There are two distinct claims that should be held apart. That the solipsist is a paradigmatic example of the kind of philosopher that needs to be shown the way out of the fly-bottle seems true. After all, Wittgenstein writes: "The solipsist flutters and flutters in the flyglass, strikes against the walls, flutters further. How can he be brought to rest?" (PO, 258). However, saying this is not yet saying that it is an emphasis on the first-person perspective that causes all the trouble. Detecting Wittgenstein's opposition to solipsism is one thing; diagnosing what is the root of the problem is quite another thing.

Before I attempt such a diagnosis, I will complicate matters slightly. Interestingly, there are a few dissenting voices who claim that Wittgenstein is not all that opposed to solipsism. Kripke, for example, claims that the later Wittgenstein "still thinks that the solipsist's terminology illuminates an important philosophical truth" (Kripke 1982, 143). David Bell goes even further, contending that "the private language argument, far from comprising a rejection and refutation of solipsism, is in a number of crucial respects an endorsement and development of it" (Bell 1996, 168). In support of his view, Bell directs attention to the fact that a tendency

> characterizing Wittgenstein's later philosophy as a whole is his insistence on the massive, categorical, and often incommensurable differences between (a) cases in which a person gives expression to his or her own subjectivity, as against (b) cases in which someone reports on the psychological states of another.
>
> (Bell 1996, 170)

According to Bell, this "vision of the asymmetry" between the first-person and the third-person perspective on subjectivity is precisely what solipsism expresses (ibid.). Against this background, we can understand why the author of the "Solipsism" entry in the *Cambridge Dictionary of Philosophy* lists Wittgenstein as an exponent of "psychological solipsism" (cf. Vinci 1995, 751).

So there are authors who claim that Wittgenstein provides us with an effective antidote to solipsism; and there are other authors who find him sympathetic to solipsism, at least in some form. Clear-cut oppositions such as this one, however, often rest on some shared assumption(s) (a truth we saw illustrated in Chapter 1 of this book). In the present case, I suspect that both parties of the debate are precisely committed to something like the following conditional: If we adopt the view that the first-person perspective is in some sense irreducible and privileged, then we have to embrace some form of solipsism. One party consequently claims that Wittgenstein resists the "pull of the first-person" (Avramides 2001, 203) and thus steers clear of what Sartre has dubbed "the reef of solipsism" (BN, 223); whereas the other party contends that Wittgenstein fully embraces the first person and the solipsism that goes with it. I want to argue, however, that both parties are wrong, because the conditional they endorse is wrong. And – less importantly, perhaps, but I will argue for this as well – the conditional in question is not one Wittgenstein endorses. In other words, the claim I will attempt to substantiate in this chapter is the claim that whereas the later Wittgenstein correctly emphasizes the irreducibility of the first-person perspective, he also, and again correctly, denies that this entails any commitment to solipsism. In fact, if we want our philosophy to be "the diametrical opposite of solipsism," then we precisely have to resist the temptation to bypass or downplay the first-person perspective.

I will argue for these claims in a rather roundabout way. First, I will raise the stakes by way of sketching a (Husserlian) position that will strike many, and has struck many, as obviously solipsistic.[4] Then I will show how the early Wittgenstein's apparent commitment to solipsism was based on

86 *The opposite of solipsism*

considerations very much like the ones Husserl elaborated. Finally, however, I will show how the later Wittgenstein's critical engagement with the solipsism of his earlier self undermines not the intuitions that this was based on, but rather the notion that these intuitions can be used to found any sort of solipsism in the first place.

The "absolutely single ego"

Aristotle famously claimed in *On the Soul* that "the soul is in a way all existing things" (Aristotle 1984, 686 [*De anima*, 431b]). Something like this could have been Husserl's slogan as well. Of course, Husserl would have insisted on a fundamental revision of Aristotle's account of the *way* in which the "soul" is all existing things (as well as a great many nonexistent "things"). According to Aristotle, the soul is "all existing things" in the sense that it "has the power of receiving into itself the [...] forms of things without the matter, in the way in which a piece of wax takes on the impress of a signet-ring without the iron or gold" (ibid., 674 [424a]). In contrast, Husserl's account of how subjectivity can "be" "all existing things" turns on his appropriation and modification of Brentano's notion of intentionality. If intentionality, as suggested in Chapter 2, involves "an openness to the layout of reality" (McDowell 1996, 26), then Husserl's claim is that each subjectivity is "all existing things" in the sense that it is one such place of openness to reality. Stated differently, to be a subject of intentional experiences is to be, or have, a *perspective on the world*. Or, to introduce yet another turn of phrase, one favored by Husserl, to be a subjectivity is to be a place where the world is "constituted." The term "constitution" undeniably has some rather unattractive connotations of subjective idealism. Many of Husserl's early followers, indeed, objected to what they saw as Husserl's straightforward adoption of traditional idealistic ideas. But we need not be concerned with this discussion here. Most of what Husserl says about "constitution" can be articulated in a manner that remains neutral on the question of idealism. It might be useful to begin by briefly outlining a few notions that should *not* be read into Husserl's concept of "constitution."

First of all, to talk about the "constitution" of the world is not to talk about some shadowy subjective world, as opposed to the real, concrete world (contra the ideas about "phenomenology" that the middle Wittgenstein appears to have entertained).[5] A related and not uncommon mistake is to claim that "Husserl's inquiry was to be about *consciousness* and not about the nature of the objects of consciousness" (Cunningham 1976, 7). Both claims are confused. The only reason why Husserlian phenomenology shows any interest in subjectivity is precisely that subjectivity is the "place" where the other minds, trees, tea cups, and oil crises – in short, the *world* – become manifested (cf. Held 2003, 24). The point of phenomenology is thus not to investigate some inner life of consciousness, in abstraction from everything external. Nor does it invoke dubious "subjective" objects as opposed to the concrete physical things out there in the real world. Rather, as Husserl states, it is ultimately the goal of phenomenology to understand the meaning that the *world* (the one and only world) has for us, in natural life, before we start reflecting philosophically on it (Husserl 1959, 481–82).

Second, with the notion of intentionality – in particular the idea of so-called "horizon intentionality" – Husserl is able to avoid the absurdities of Berkeleyan idealism. To say that the world is constituted in or for subjectivity is not to imply that the world is *immanent* to subjectivity.[6] On the contrary, Husserl is explicit that the world is constituted as transcendent. When I perceive a table, for instance, my perceptual intentionality (so to speak) *concerns* the table as such, even though the table as a whole is not, and essentially cannot be, fully and completely presented to me. As explained in Chapter 3, I always see a table in a certain perspective, and from a certain distance, and this necessarily implies that there are parts and aspects of it that are perceptually anticipated – "co-intended," in Husserl's terminology – but not strictly given. It is precisely this "incompleteness" of perception that accounts for the *transcendence* of the perceptual object. And this transcendence is an essential and ineradicable part of the constitution of the object. (The transcendence of a perceptual object is just one example, of course, and it might be worth adding that Husserl considers other subjects to be transcendent in a different and much more radical way.)[7]

Finally, the Husserlian idea of constitution does not imply that there cannot be more than one world-disclosing subjectivity. In fact, Husserl explicitly argues that insofar as subjectivity is to be world-disclosing, it must be conceived of as part of an *inter*subjectivity – a plurality of transcendental subjects, somehow forming a "transcendental community."[8] So there essentially is not one, but a multitude of places of "openness to the layout of reality." Each of us, besides being a carpenter or a philosopher, a son or a daughter, and whatever else we are, is one such place were the world appears. And it seems the "constitution" of the world is ultimately a joint achievement by all of us.

However, while insisting that this notion of "transcendental intersubjectivity" is fundamental to the phenomenological explication of world-constitution, Husserl makes some noteworthy additional remarks on this issue in section 54 of his last work, the *Crisis*. Referring to his exposition of intersubjectivity, Husserl comments, rather surprisingly, that "it was wrong, methodically, to jump immediately into transcendental intersubjectivity and to leap over the primal "I" [*Ur-Ich*], the ego of my epoché, which can never lose its uniqueness and personal indeclinability" (Husserl 1970b, 185). But what is this *Ur-Ich*? Husserl makes this clear elsewhere in the same section, in a passage that deserves to be quoted in full here:

> *I* am the one who performs the epoché, and, even if there are others, and even if they practice the epoché in direct community with me, [they and] all other human beings with their entire act-life are included, for

me, within my epoché, in the world-phenomenon which, in my epoché, is exclusively mine. The epoché creates a unique sort of philosophical solitude which is the fundamental methodological requirement for a truly radical philosophy.

(Husserl 1970b, 184)

If I reflect phenomenologically on how the world appears, I must ultimately appeal to how the world appears *to me*. I am, for me, *the* point where the world is disclosed, so to speak; the point where everything that can ever be part of the experienced world must make itself known. Husserl is explicit that this means that the other transcendental subjectivities that phenomenological analysis bids me to recognize must also, then, ultimately be accounted for in terms of their appearance for *me*. Although I am, as Husserl emphasizes, a subject among subjects, I *cannot possibly recognize myself as such without those other subjects making themselves known to me*. My subjective life is the ultimate frame of reference, without which those other subjects cannot manifest themselves as other, and equal, subjects at all. Thus, there is a clear sense in which I, for me, cannot be just another subject among subjects. There is a sense in which I am precisely the *Ur-Ich* around which my experienced world, including the social world, is centered. This "I" "is, for me, the subject who says it, and says it in the right sense, the *primitive intentional basis for my world*" (Husserl 1969, 237). The peculiar philosophical solitude that this insight places me in is absolute. Husserl stresses that it concerns not "the privilege of I-the-man among other men" (Husserl 1970b, 184), but rather an ego that is, in a way, "the *absolutely single [einzige] ego*," the *only* ego (ibid., 256). According to Husserl, it is essential that we hold on to this insight even if, for "philosophical children," as he says, it is "the dark corner haunted by specters of solipsism and, perhaps, of psychologism, of relativism. The true philosopher, instead of running away, will prefer to fill the dark corner with light" (Husserl 1969, 237).

Perhaps somewhat surprisingly, Levinas defends a similar view. In the preface to *Totality and Infinity*, Levinas describes the book as a "defense of subjectivity" (TI, 26). As he elaborates the sense in which this is so, it becomes patent that his point is reminiscent of what Husserl says: "The alterity, the radical heterogeneity of the other, is possible only if the other is other with respect to a term whose essence is to remain at the point of departure, to serve as entry into the relation" (TI, 36). The term in question is precisely subjectivity. There is more than just a superficial agreement with Husserl in this. In fact, there is not much for Levinas to disagree with when Husserl writes: "The only conceivable manner in which others can have for me the sense and status of existent others [...] consists in their being constituted *in me* as others" (CM, 128). For, as we have seen, this means simply that, *for me*, I am the unique "entry" into the intersubjective relation. For me, intersubjective space opens only here, in me, and nowhere else. This point is one Levinas himself expresses in *Otherwise than Being* when he writes: "It is in me – in me and not in another, in me and not in an individuation of the concept Ego – that communication opens" (OB, 126). So whatever Levinas might find open to criticism in Husserl, it cannot be the asymmetry that the *Ur-Ich* implies.[9] But ought Levinas to have been more critical of Husserl's perspective? After all, prominent Husserl scholars have felt uncomfortable with the notion of the *Ur-Ich* because it has seemed to them ultimately to compromise the symmetry and equality that these commentators deem necessary for a plausible account of intersubjectivity.[10] Indeed, others have claimed that this compromise ultimately commits Husserl to *solipsism*; and because Levinas follows Husserl in emphasizing the first-person perspective, his account, too, is condemned to solipsism (Jacques 1991, 133–60). To see how solipsism enters the picture, let us turn to the early Wittgenstein.

Biting the bullet: solipsism in the early Wittgenstein

Wittgenstein scholars often record with some discomfort that the early Wittgenstein, influenced by Schopenhauer's *The World as Will and Representation*, explicitly toyed with solipsistic ideas both in his notebooks and in the only philosophical book he ever published, the *Tractatus*.[11] In the present section I will briefly sketch why Wittgenstein was, at least apparently,[12] lead to embrace what Peter Hacker calls "transcendental solipsism" (Hacker 1997, 99).

In the *Tractatus* the elaboration of solipsism appears in proposition 5.6 and its subsections. From the beginning it is clear that Wittgenstein's agenda is not to offer a straightforward defense of metaphysical solipsism. Although he claims that what the solipsist *means* to say is correct, Wittgenstein also cautions that it actually cannot be *said*: what the solipsist wants to say is, rather, part of that which "makes itself manifest" or "shows itself" (T, § 5.62). Nevertheless, there is something right about solipsism, and Wittgenstein gives some important hints as to what that might be. First of all, the world is "my world," he claims. The point, however, is not that I am some particularly privileged human being in the world. In fact, Wittgenstein seems to deny that there exists such a thing as "the subject that thinks or entertains ideas" at all. As he says, if I were to write a book called *The World as I Found It*, then the subject "alone could *not* be mentioned in that book" (T, § 5.631.) The world is "mine," then, in the sense that I am the subject experiencing the world, the one *by* whom the world is seen (as well as, presumably, touched, heard, smelled, and savored). As Wittgenstein explains, the subject in this sense is clearly not a *part* of the experienced world, but rather "a limit of the world." But as such a "limit" there is a legitimate place for the subject or the "I" in philosophy (T, § 5.641). In fact, the ego takes center-stage together with the world it reveals: "There are two godheads: the world and my independent I" (Wittgenstein 1961, 74). There can be no question that Wittgenstein is here expressing a transcendental conception of subjectivity, and one that has central features in common with Husserl's conception of subjectivity. For example, Wittgenstein explicitly distinguishes his "metaphysical" self (the "limit of the world") from the empirical, psychological subject that forms part of the world (T, § 5.641).

But what makes this solipsistic? Some of the clearest expressions of the solipsistic implications of Wittgenstein's early views are found in works from the 1930s, when he was no longer persuaded that there was anything essentially right – not even correct-yet-ineffable – about solipsism. (But, as is often the case with Wittgenstein, the way he argues against solipsism shows that he is not himself completely insensitive to the appeal of the view.)[13] In the "Notes for Lectures on 'Private Experience' and 'Sense Data'" Wittgenstein finds the roots of the solipsistic temptation in a special emphasis on "experience" or "consciousness." What he means is "consciousness not physiologically understood, or understood from the outside, but consciousness as the very essence of experience, the appearance of the world, the world" (PO, 255). If I take this notion of world-revealing consciousness seriously, then solipsism seems to follow; for it appears a necessity that the world only appears, *truly* appears, in *my* experience. As Wittgenstein writes in the *Notebooks*, "[t]here really is only one world soul, which I for preference call *my* soul and as which alone I conceive what I call the souls of others" (Wittgenstein 1961, 49). The idea seems clear: I might conceive of others as having souls and as experiencing the world just as I do, but their souls and experiences are things and events in "the world as I find it"; they are never the experiences that reveal the world as such. Only my experiences are world-disclosing in an original sense. A remark from the *Blue Book* brings this out: "Sometimes the most satisfying expression of our solipsism seems to be this: 'When anything is seen (really *seen*), it is always I who see it'" (BB, 61).

This obviously removes all traces of equality and symmetry, and seems to suggest that conferring a special, irreducible status on the first-person perspective eventually commits one to metaphysical solipsism – i.e. the view that there is a fundamental sense in which I am the only existing subject. For the kind of asymmetry that we are working with here seems to deny to other minds precisely that which, following Husserl, we claimed was essential to subjectivity as such: being or having a *perspective on the world*. As Wittgenstein puts it, speaking in the voice of his former, solipsistic self: "'It's no use saying that the other person knows what he sees and not what I see and that therefore all is symmetrical, because there is just nothing else corresponding to my visual image, my visual image is unique!'" (PO, 273). The problem thus seems to be that the very notion of taking a first-person philosophical account seriously – an account of *my* experiences (in *some* sense, even if for obvious reasons we cannot be talking about Søren Overgaard's experiences) – is condemned to solipsism. More precisely, it seems that even if symmetrical intersubjectivity finds a place somewhere in the account, the mere fact that this account ultimately refers everything to *me* – to my experiences as the *only* truly world-disclosing experiences – entails that ultimately there *is* no one but me. Once the first-person perspective is wholeheartedly adopted, then, there is apparently no way to prevent a slide towards metaphysical solipsism. Husserl's talk of an "absolutely single ego" being the intentional "source" of the experienced world seems in every important respect parallel to Wittgenstein's notion of the "I" as the limit of the world. Hence, if the musings of the early Wittgenstein do lead to solipsism, then Husserl (and Levinas), too, must strike this lethal reef.

As mentioned, some commentators think that the later Wittgenstein rejects the whole package. In order to provide "a philosophy that would be the diametrical opposite of solipsism," he discards (they claim) the very notion that there is any "subjectivity" characterized by an irreducible first-person perspective. However, I think this is a mischaracterization of the middle and later Wittgenstein's critique of his earlier views; a characterization, indeed, that repeats the very argumentative steps that the later Wittgenstein would identify as the problematic ones. In the next section I will try to show that the later Wittgenstein's perspective is not all that different from that of Husserl. The important thing is not the correct Wittgenstein exegesis, however, but rather that we see which way is the right way to illuminate that "dark corner haunted by specters of solipsism" of which Husserl spoke.

Solipsism and grammar

One point must be granted to those philosophers who have presented the later Wittgenstein as sympathetic towards solipsism: it is not Wittgenstein's intention merely to ridicule the position or offer a commonsense reply to it. He sees correctly that this sort of thing is of no help in trying to get out of a philosophical difficulty. Rather, one must take the difficulty seriously on an existential level, as it were; one must understand the intuitions that give rise to it and feel the pull towards it, before working one's way out of it. This is the point of the following passage:

> No philosopher lacks common sense in ordinary life. So philosophers should not attempt to present the idealistic or solipsistic positions, for example, as though they were absurd – by pointing out to a person who puts forward these positions that he does not really wonder [...] whether his wife is real or whether only he is real. Of course he does not, and it is not a proper objection. You must not try to avoid a philosophical problem by appealing to common sense; instead, present it as it arises with most power. You must allow yourself to be dragged into the mire, and get out of it.
>
> (Wittgenstein 1979b, 108–09)

In the previous section we allowed ourselves "to be dragged into the mire"; now we have to make our way to the exit. Let us try to retract some of the steps we have taken. The problematic step, as usual, is "one that altogether escapes notice" (PI, § 308). What was the basis for the claim that only *my* experiences are truly world-revealing? We noted that if I were to write the book *The World as I Found It*, describing the world as seen from my first-person perspective, then other people's experiences would figure in the description as part of the world. My own experiences, on the other hand, would not figure in the description, because they would be the experiences manifesting the world (*as I found it!*) in the first place. But it is not yet clear that this is solipsistic. After all, if I were to describe a lecture room "as I found it" on a particular morning the other people mentioned in that description would have a different status than me, because I would be the one relating the story from my own perspective. There is a distinct self–other asymmetry in this kind of description; but in itself this asymmetry does not bring metaphysical or epistemological solipsism about. Something more is needed for this result to obtain.

Before I discuss what more is needed for solipsism to result, let me just note that nothing said so far about self–other asymmetry conflicts with the views of the later Wittgenstein. According to the later Wittgenstein, my mental life has, for me, a very special status compared with the mental lives of others. A Cartesian will want to say this as well, of course, but for Wittgenstein the point is not that my mental life is some array of objects and events that I am in a particularly good position to observe. As we have seen, Wittgenstein's position is in a sense more radical, in that he thinks my mental life is not at all like objects or events that I observe. I can and do sometimes "observe" mental events in the minds of others, he thinks, and to some extent I can adopt a similar attitude towards my own mental phenomena. But my default relation to my own mental life is completely different from and much more intimate than anything that might be captured by the notion of observation (LW II, 9–12). That is why Wittgenstein says that I cannot "know" what I think, but only what others think. His point is not that I cannot have any direct access to my thoughts, but rather that the access I have is too direct and too intimate to be called "knowledge" (cf. Chapter 1). My mental life, according to Wittgenstein, is precisely the life in and through which I am thematically aware of all kinds of objects and events – including the mental states of others. So, on Wittgenstein's view, we have to recognize a basic self–other asymmetry.[14]

The addition that brings solipsism about is the notion that we make a significant (even if possibly ineffable) empirical or metaphysical *discovery* when we recognize this asymmetry, "a discovery about the nature of the world which in some sense contradicts what we take to be the case" (Hacker 1997, 229). In other words, the connecting link between Husserl's *Ur-Ich* and solipsism is the idea that the fact that *my* experiential life is, for me, the only world-disclosing life is something akin to an objective, empirical fact about the world. The solipsist is inclined to say that, *as it happens*, it is in *my* experiences, and in no one else's, that the world appears. Or as Wittgenstein himself puts it, playing the part of the solipsist:

"I am in the lucky position of being in the source of the visual world / field/. It is I who see it!" I have a comfortable feeling while saying this although the statement isn't one of the class of statements which in general give me this kind of feeling. I said it as though I had said "I have more money than anyone else in this place."

(PO, 258)

The middle and later Wittgenstein tries to dispel the illusion of discovery by pointing out that the experiences in question really have no "neighbors," that is, they are not really the experiences of some one person in contrast to others (PO, 229). It is not possible for me to imagine that Mr. Smith's experiences, for example, would be the authentically world-disclosing experiences instead of mine. I cannot imagine a situation in which Mr. Smith's experiential life would disclose the world while "all would be dark within me," because the way the solipsist wants to talk of experiences nothing would *count* as Mr. Smith's experiences – *as opposed to mine* – revealing the world. World-disclosure in the sense in question can only be world-disclosure to me. But if only my experiences *can* be world-revealing there is good reason to think that we have not really made any substantial discovery about the world and that some fundamental confusion is at work here. It is really not the case that my experiential life "*happens* to be alone, but that its *grammatical* position is that of having no neighbor" (PO, 229; partly my emphasis). The solipsist, in effect, construes what is really an essential or "grammatical" feature as if it were an empirical or metaphysical fact. She makes a "grammatical movement" and interprets it as a discovery (cf. PI, §§ 400–01).

To see better how the Wittgensteinian reply is supposed to work, consider another way in which solipsism might be thought to arise from the self–other asymmetry we have pointed out. If I am in severe pain *it hurts* in a way that it does not (from my perspective) when another person is in severe pain. This is obvious. But now, if "pain" when I am the one who is in pain is associated with *hurting*, and if it is otherwise associated with writhing and screaming (but no "real" hurting), then we seem to be dangerously close to a conceptual solipsism according to which "pain" does not have the same meaning in first-person and third-person use, and where, consequently, it is meaningful and legitimate for me to say that "only I feel real pain" (cf. BB, 60). It is the worry that this sort of situation should arise that led some philosophers – apparently inspired by Wittgenstein – to warn that we are best advised to avoid any reference to the first-person perspective as special or privileged. But from the perspective that I claim is Wittgenstein's, these philosophers are being fooled by a "grammatical monster" (PO, 283). They construe what is in fact a grammatical, essential asymmetry as having strong metaphysical commitments; and in order to do away with the "monster" these commitments represent, the philosophers in question think they have to deny or at least downplay the self–other asymmetry. But thereby, of course, they merely repeat the solipsistic mistake. Both sides construe what is a grammatical feature as containing some substantial claim about the structure of the world. One party embraces this claim; the other rejects it. Both sides, however, are equally mistaken in thinking that the uniqueness and irreducibility of the first-person perspective carries such metaphysical commitments in the first place.

Consider now the following familiar passage from the *Philosophical Investigations*:

> If one has to imagine someone else's pain on the model of one's own, this is none too easy a thing to do: for I have to imagine pain which I *do not feel* on the model of the pain which I *do feel*. That is, what I have to do is not simply to make a transition in imagination from one place of pain to another. As, from pain in the hand to pain in the arm. For I am not to imagine that I feel pain in some region of his body. (Which would also be possible.)
>
> (PI, § 302)

These remarks give a rather puzzling first impression. Some commentators have found it hard to see what the problem is supposed to be in imagining pain I do not feel on the model of pain I do feel (e.g. Kripke, 116). If my knee hurts after a fall on the ski slope and I witness a similar thing happen to another (who then screams and holds her knee) I can very well imagine her experience on the basis of my experience.[15] In a sense, we do something like this all the time. Our involuntary grimaces and outbursts when we see another take a nasty fall have a lot to do with our ability to immediately understand her pain on the basis of pain we ourselves have felt on similar occasions.

But Wittgenstein, of course, does not mean to deny any of this. Indeed, we have misunderstood his point entirely if we think he does. The task that is "none too easy" here (this is a wild understatement!) is not to understand, in the mundane sense we have just discussed, pain one does not feel on the basis of pain one does feel (or has felt), but rather something like this: to imagine *how pain feels* when I am not myself in pain. How do I go about doing this if I am not allowed to imagine that *I* am feeling pain in some part of the other's body? Here it is as if there is some special sort of barrier, or a limit that I cannot cross. And in a sense there is; but it is important that we realize in *what* sense. Both the solipsist and her opponent think that we have reached some metaphysical or epistemological barrier that more or less inevitably results from taking one's own pain as a model of the pains of others. They think, in effect, that we have wound up in solipsism. But this is precisely where they both go awry. For the limit we have reached is *grammatical*, and that means that it does not make any sense to want to cross it. There is no wall here that it would be *meaningful* to scale; and for this reason we must resist the temptation to "represent the matter as if there were something one *couldn't* do" (cf. PI, § 374).

A good way to illustrate the point is to take a closer look at the possibility Wittgenstein mentions of my feeling pain in a region of the other person's body. While this sort of thing may be empirically impossible, I can presumably make some kind of sense of the idea that I would feel a terrible pain in an arm apparently belonging to another person.[16] But the thing Wittgenstein asks us to try to imagine here is much more extreme than that. His question, as already noted, is more like the following: How does pain *feel* when I am not feeling it *anywhere*, not even in the other's body? How does pain *feel* when I don't feel any (but the other does)? Of course, it doesn't feel like *anything* (to me), and if it did we were after all not talking about the pain of another person, but rather about my pain – possibly "in another person's arm," but my pain nonetheless. So there is no sense in which these ruminations lead to any solipsistic isolation. The only thing I "cannot do" is to imagine that I would occupy the first-person perspective of another person without making it *my* first-person perspective – that I could have her phenomenal consciousness of pain without myself being the subject of this pain. And the reason I cannot do this is not that there is some metaphysical obstacle blocking my path, but rather that it simply *makes no sense* (cf. M. McGinn 1997, 172).

A convinced solipsist might reply that what I have said so far only goes to show that the solipsistic picture is correct, indeed necessarily so. For we have at most established that the idea of a direct first-person experience of another's mental life is incoherent. And it is possible to accept these points and argue that what they indicate is that *it makes no sense to conceive of any other subjects* – that nonsolipsism is an incoherent position. But there is a deception at work here, and it is one that is active as well in at least some familiar ways of posing the skeptical problem of other minds. A skeptic might insist that first-person access is the only acceptable kind of proof of the existence of others. To silence this sort of skeptic, then, we should, in principle, be able to show that I can have direct experiential access to the other's experiences *as she has them*. In order to *know* that she is in pain and not merely pretending I would have to be able to somehow feel her pain or think her thoughts. But this is obviously a game we should refuse to play. The way the problem is set up here, we can only provide a satisfactory solution by adopting what is essentially solipsism – that is, by admitting something considerably stronger (and crazier) than the skeptical point that we cannot have any reliable knowledge of the existence of others. What this shows is *not* that solipsism is necessarily true, but rather that the problem has been set up in a question-begging way, allowing only the type of evidence that would prove the skeptic's (or solipsist's) point. As Wittgenstein insists, my perceptual access to others cannot possibly be of this first-person type, because this would straightforwardly contradict the proviso that we should be talking about my access to *others*. The skeptical conjuring trick is exposed, then, the moment we become clear about what the skeptic is really saying: "Only I know what I am thinking actually means nothing else than:

only I *think* my own thoughts" (LW II, 56). The latter sentence makes a grammatical or essential point. And it is as absurd to suggest that this grammatical point creates a special problem about other minds (let alone proves that only solipsism is a coherent position!) as it is meaningless to imagine that I might feel the pain of others *as* the pain of others.

Therefore, it is also misleading to conclude from the asymmetry we have emphasized in the present chapter that "[t]here is here a solipsism rooted in living experience" (Merleau-Ponty 1962, 358), and that, accordingly, "[t]he truth of solipsism is there" (ibid., 360). What Merleau-Ponty wants to say with these statements is essentially correct. For example, he correctly sees that "[s]olitude and communication cannot be two horns of a dilemma, but [must be] two 'moments' of one phenomenon" (ibid., 359). But his ways of articulating this important insight are at times potentially misleading:

> In short, just as the instant of my death is a future to which I have not access, so I am necessarily destined never to live through the presence of another to himself. And yet each other person does exist for me as an unchallengeable style or setting of co-existence, and my life has a social atmosphere just as it has a flavor of mortality.
> (Merleau-Ponty 1962, 364)

There would be no reason to disagree with anything Merleau-Ponty says here, were it not for traces of the idea of metaphysical barriers and for the little word "yet." This "yet" seems to confirm his commitment to "the truth of solipsism," for it suggests that there is some kind of tension between my being "destined" never to "live through the presence of another to himself" and the fact that "each other person exists for me." But precisely this is wrong, as we have seen. My inability to live the other's mental life is in fact a *precondition* of her existence for me as another. And surely it is at best confusing to suggest that what is in point of fact a necessary condition for intersubjectivity illustrates "the truth of solipsism."[17]

Whether one agrees or disagrees with my claims concerning solipsism and the first person, however, one may question my use of Wittgenstein to back up these claims. I said at the beginning of this chapter (see p. 83) that I wanted to discuss the question of solipsism without referring to Wittgenstein's so-called private language argument. Some may suspect that I didn't speak the whole truth when I explained that I chose to ignore the latter argument in an attempt to throw new light on Wittgenstein's relation to solipsism. Is the deeper reason for my silence concerning private language not that what Wittgenstein has to say on this theme is hard to reconcile with my celebration of the uniqueness of the first person? I think not. Let me briefly explain why.

The way I presented the private language considerations in Chapter 4 they were critiquing realism. Briefly put, the argument was that any object or state of affairs that is essentially beyond the grasp of a possible human society reduces to a "wheel turning idly" – that is, it is a "nothing," something that can have no part to play in our language games and the lives in which they are embedded. Admittedly, this is a somewhat unusual employment of the private language argument. For one thing, it leaves out the "privacy" of the objects and states of affairs; the "real essences" of McCulloch are no one's "private" objects, because they are conceived of as possibly transcending the grasp of humanity as such. So let us add the element of privacy to the mixture and what we get is something like this: Whatever essentially private objects I have, they dissolve in my hands. Specifically, I cannot devise a language for referring to these objects. But the reason why there is no real objection to my emphasis on the uniqueness of the first-person perspective in this should already be clear. As stressed repeatedly in this book, Wittgenstein's real target is not the notion that each of us has a mental life, a first-person perspective, and the rest. Rather, he is trying to prevent us from misconstruing this life in certain characteristic ways. The sections on "private language" in the *Investigations* contribute to this by attacking not only the assumption that mental life is hidden and "private," but also (and arguably this is the pivotal point) the assumption that the mental is a realm of *objects*. So Wittgenstein's solitary diarist goes awry, *not* in thinking that she has a unique relation to the sensation "S" that she feels (if she does feel something) – the "relation," namely, of being the one who *feels* this – but rather in thinking that the uniqueness in question consists in her unique access to an "object" only she can observe, name, and describe. The private language argument is supposed to demonstrate the incoherence of the latter idea from two different angles:[18] First, if mental life were a special range of objects that we detect and catalog, then we would need criteria for determining whether in a given case we were cataloging an item in the right way. Such criteria are not possible here, which means that "here we can't talk about 'right'" (PI, § 258). The latter, in turn, yields the conclusion that observing and naming objects cannot be the model of our relation to our own mental lives. Second, supposing we did have inner private objects of the relevant sort, they would be irrelevant to our lives anyway. They would have "no place in the language-game at all" (PI, § 293).[19]

To direct a final criticism against the idea that an emphasis on the first-person perspective has solipsistic implications, I will turn next to some of the ways in which one may attempt to "resist the pull of the first person." If it can be shown that some of the most obvious ways to do this fail to make coherent sense, then the asymmetry that I have been advocating will begin to look like the only attractive option.

An asymmetry of the game

It is difficult to speak in general terms about ways of avoiding the pull of the first person without the discussion becoming rather abstract. Hopefully, however, it will be possible to get some notion of the alternatives I am considering – and of what I think is wrong with them. The first idea can be introduced as a merely tactical consideration. Even if it is correct that the self–other asymmetry does not as such lead to solipsism, would it perhaps still not be best to avoid emphasizing it for the simple reason that it might give the *misleading impression* of having solipsistic implications? In other words, could one not say that it is a good idea "to leap over the primal 'I'" (Husserl 1970b, 185), as a matter of tactics as it were, in order not to give the wrong impression to anyone? The idea behind Husserl's concept of the *Ur-Ich* is not that if I look at the world objectively, or *sub specie aeternitatis*, I will notice that "I *am* in a favored position," "the center of the world" (PO, 257). As Wittgenstein suggests, I only have to look at myself in the mirror and point at myself in order for this sort of thing to become obviously ridiculous (ibid.). Rather, it is if I look at things from the *inside*, from my first-person perspective, that I may experience my experiential life as the "source" of the manifested world. But, so the present view goes, I don't *have* to describe things from this perspective. We can describe our own mental lives in such a way that they are merely the mental lives of particular people among others and have no special status. We can adopt an outside view on social life, from which perspective we are all equal and all is symmetrical.

Of course, we can do this sort of thing. But Husserl would insist that we are mistaken if we think that we can bypass entirely our first-person perspective. Although we can look more or less objectively or "panoramically" upon things, we cannot, as argued towards the end of Chapter 4, adopt a completely panoramic view from nowhere upon the world and intersubjectivity. For this would entail stepping out of our embodiment and embeddedness in the world. We can always only see things from *somewhere*, from our own (embodied and embedded) perspective. Whatever more "objective" view I take upon things, it remains a view that *I* adopt; there is no such thing as a viewpoint truly *sub specie aeternitatis*. If for a moment I think of myself as only one human being among millions sitting at their computers around the world, then this is an episode in *my* mental life, and presented to me as such, in the first person. Now, if Husserl's insistence that we do not "leap over" the "primordial I" simply comes down to a reminder of the fundamentally inescapable character of the first-person perspective there is, strangely enough, a distinct moment of respect for my "finitude" – my being merely one human being among others in a social reality that to a great extent transcends our grasp – in the point he is making. Part of what it means to be a finite human being in this sense is precisely that one ultimately cannot escape one's own particular perspective. And tacitly ignoring or downplaying the first-person perspective – even for tactical purposes – can therefore be viewed as tacitly downplaying or ignoring an important aspect of our human finitude.

Not ignoring our finitude means not ignoring the fact that sociality must ultimately be anchored in the various networks of relations between individual human beings – even if it cannot be reduced to those relations – and that therefore it must in each case be realized from a particular embodied and embedded perspective. In each case it is from "my" perspective that social life is realized. I am in a sense the "only" subjectivity,[20] then, but precisely only in the sense that my first-person perspective is the only first-person perspective that I have for accessing the world. But clearly this does nothing to rule out the existence of other subjects, for what it illustrates is simply that I am a particular place where the world appears, a particular embodied perspective on the world, a particular point where "communication opens." If I am essentially such a particular, finite perspective, remaining at this "point of departure," then *for me* I am *the* place where the world opens up. For me, of course, the experiential lives of others constitute themselves in *my* experiences (of perceiving others, of talking to them, of playing soccer with them, and so on and so forth). How could it be otherwise? I am naturally practically unshakable in my belief that things are quite similar from the point of view of another (say, my mother); in fact, the only way in which I can entertain the idea that my subjective life is *not* presented to my mother in *her* experiences is by assuming that she has none – that she is a zombie. All this too, of course, is anchored in *my* subjective life. But there is nothing remotely solipsistic about that, since it just amounts to emphasizing the fact that *I am a particular, finite subjectivity*. The point is basically that if we want to make the social world intelligible in terms of *intersubjectivity* we may not bypass individual subjectivity. And not bypassing individual, finite subjectivity means accepting the grammatical point that at the most fundamental level social space is asymmetrical.[21] So the tactic under consideration would appear not to be so clever after all.

However, there is a way of avoiding the affirmation of self–other asymmetry without giving the impression of ignoring human finitude. One can simply deny any important role to "perspectives" (whether one's own or those of others) altogether (cf. Cockburn 1990, 56–57, 125, 128). If the question of perspectives or "points of view" is simply put to one side we can preserve a pluralism of finite subjects. A further bonus, some have thought, is that we have then cut the last ties to Cartesianism. As Simon Glendinning points out, criticizing McDowell,

> [there is] a significant yet silent agreement between McDowell's conception of subjectivity and the more traditional, broadly Cartesian, conception. Specifically, both assume as coherent a particular interpretation of what it is for a living human being to be a "subject of experience," namely, an interpretation conceived in terms of its potential for a distinctively first-personal, "inside take" on its own states, its presence to its own experiences.
>
> (Glendinning 1998, 139)

To this sort of critique, of course, one should reply the following. The fact that something looks "residually Cartesian" does not in itself show that it is wrong or that it should be denied on Wittgensteinian grounds.[22] And in the present case I think it is clear that the residual "Cartesianism" is not really something it would be wise to give up. If, as we claimed at the beginning of this chapter (see p. 86), to be a subject is simply to have a perspective on the world, then the response we are considering here simply amounts to downplaying or denying subjectivity itself. That can hardly be an attractive position. And, as we have seen, it is not part of Wittgenstein's agenda to deny that being a subjectivity involves having "a distinctively first-personal, 'inside take'" on one's mental life. If anything, Wittgenstein wants to complain that Cartesians have misconstrued this "inside take" in such a way as to make it look far too much like the kind of take we have on "external" objects.

The final alternative approach I will discuss here is based on the following considerations. It makes no sense to deny the importance of perspectives as such. But it does make sense to refuse to attribute any kind of privilege or special status to *my* perspective. Once we discard the idea that *my* first-person perspective is privileged (the idea almost perversely exaggerated in Husserl's conception of the *Ur-Ich*) we are back on the right track. The idea here is not that we should achieve symmetry by adopting an "outside" view on intersubjectivity; but rather that the right "inside" view is one where there is no asymmetry between self and other. This view might look promising at first glance. But if we take a closer look at it we soon realize that it has some severe problems of its own. For what can it mean here to deny any special status to *my* first-person perspective? It seems to imply that the first-person perspectives of others should, for *me*, be on a par with my first-person perspective. The threat this implies is readily intelligible. For it seems to involve the idea of the subjective lives of others being somehow accessible to me in just the same way that my own subjective life is accessible to me. And this idea is in grave danger of collapsing into solipsism. In one of the manuscripts on the philosophy of psychology, Wittgenstein writes: "'But you can't recognize pain with *certainty* just from externals.' – The *only* way of recognizing it is by externals, and the uncertainty is constitutional. It is not a shortcoming" (RPP II, § 657; cf. RPP I, § 141). The point is the already familiar one that if I could have the *same* type of access to the thoughts, feelings, etc. of others as they do themselves this would not amount to repairing some defect. Nor would it amount to the achievement of some "direct" relation to the thoughts and feelings of the other person, as opposed to the usual "indirect" and pedestrian relation through her utterances, gestures, etc. (cf. BB, 185). On the contrary, what is really imagined here is that I occupy the other's first-person perspective on her mental life. If something like this were a meaningful possibility it would merely erase the distinction between me, with my thoughts and feelings, and the other, with her thoughts and feelings. And the result would be a nasty predicament, since it is difficult to see how there could still be a difference between us; and if that difference disappears, then so does the possibility of making sense of *inter*subjectivity. This is why Wittgenstein speaks of a "constitutional uncertainty." As Husserl emphasizes, "if what belongs to the other's own essence were directly accessible [to me], it would be merely a moment of my own essence, and ultimately he himself and I myself would be the same" (CM, 109).

Let me elaborate on this for a moment. It is crucial to see what the response in question really changes in the asymmetrical picture we have sketched. To refuse to let my perspective be the only place where the world opens up *for me* is ultimately to imagine that other places, too, are places where the world opens up *to me*. This is easy enough to imagine, for it amounts to imagining, for example, that I would feel pain in the bodies of others when they fall and that I can see the world from their perspective, that I would think their thoughts, and so forth. If we remind ourselves that the question now is not whether others may *count* for me, be given in my (*"only"*) world-revealing life, as such places where the world opens up (this is something Husserl and Wittgenstein would not dream of denying), but rather whether this world-revealing life would just be *one* such life where the world opens up *to me*, then the absurdly solipsistic nature of the latter idea should become obvious. The idea we have sketched is nothing but the idea of a subjectivity that *lives* the subjective lives of other subjects, and for such a subjectivity there clearly are no others. To the extent that I can truly access the world through the perspectives of others, they are not the perspectives of others.[23] These are what Wittgenstein would call "grammatical" remarks, and it makes as little sense to deny them as it makes sense to deny that "[o]ne plays patience by oneself" (PI, § 248).

When Wittgenstein speaks of a "grammatical point," however, is he not trying to make a point about language (or language use) only? That is, is his claim not that the solipsist directs our attention to a peculiar asymmetry in our ways of *talking* about our own mental life and the mental lives of others, but that she goes awry precisely in construing this grammatical (read: linguistic) fact as one that concerns phenomena, our experience of things? This sort of idea certainly seems to be implied in some of the things Wittgenstein says in his extended discussion of solipsism in the "Notes for Lectures on 'Private Experience' and 'Sense Data.'" At one point, Wittgenstein states that "we speak for example of an asymmetry in our mode of expression and we look on it as a mirror image of the essence of the things" (PO, 209). Yet in later texts Wittgenstein seems to be somewhat less insistent on the (obviously false, in my view) claim that the interpersonal asymmetry merely concerns our "mode of expression." For example, in the *Investigations* (discussing imagination) he makes the methodological remark that one should not inquire into "what happens when one imagines anything," but rather ask "how the word 'imagination' is used." He continues, however, to state that "this does not mean that I want to talk only about words" (PI, § 370). In the course of the argument offered in this book, we have already encountered many passages that testify to the truth of the latter statement.

When Wittgenstein stresses, for example, that "[m]y thoughts are not hidden from [the other person], but are just open to him in a different *way* than they are to me" (LW II, 34–35), he seems clearly to be speaking of thoughts and our access to them, rather than the kind of thing we say about thoughts. So what we are dealing with here is clearly not *only* an "asymmetry in our mode of expression," but a "constitutional asymmetry," an "asymmetry of the game" (LW II, 36) as a whole – the "game" that is intersubjectivity.

Conclusion

If the foregoing arguments are persuasive, then we should now have a rough idea of how it is possible "to imagine a philosophy that would be the diametrical opposite of solipsism" (PO, 225). We need to *affirm* "the doctrine that there exists a first-person perspective possessing privileged and irreducible characteristics," while of course *denying* that this is something "in virtue of which we stand in various kinds of isolation from any other persons or external things that may exist" (Vinci 1995, 751). My first-person perspective is irreducible and privileged in the sense that it is my point of access to the world – my *only* point of access. This is what Wittgenstein calls a grammatical remark. To deny it does not avert some threatening "isolation" from other persons. Rather, it makes it simply impossible to speak meaningfully of subjectivity and sociality in the first place.

To be a finite, individual subject means to be unable to escape one's own – *my* own – perspective. Accessing the social world through the eyes of others, or *sub specie aeternitatis*, from which viewpoint all individual subjectivities appear as mere moments of a larger whole, is not a genuine option. And this is not to be lamented. It is precisely because I am the *Ur-Ich*, that is, because I stay firmly rooted in my own subjective life, in my own perspective, that there can be others for me. To preserve pluralism and thus intersubjectivity we need a subject that stays "absolutely at the point of departure," to recall Levinas' phrase. If I were not, so to speak, condemned to access the world in and through my own *particular* perspective, then I would be condemned to the *solitude* of being the owner of *all* perspectives.

6 The transcendence of the other in Husserl, Sartre, and Levinas

[T]he eye looks. (It casts glances, it flashes, beams, coruscates.) With the eye one may terrify.

(RPP I, § 1100)

Introduction

Intersubjectivity is one of the most difficult topics for any philosopher to address, for one thing because the stakes are so high: We might be held responsible for the ethical and political consequences of our accounts of intersubjectivity, even if, or perhaps especially if, we intended those accounts to be ethically or politically neutral.[1] What we say about the relations between subjects can, in an important sense, never be neutral. But intersubjectivity is also a difficult topic because, perhaps more than other philosophical topics, it involves steering an uneasy course between Scylla and Charybdis. At least this will be so for any philosopher who holds the pluralistic view that intersubjectivity must be a relation between beings that are, in a fundamental ontological sense, separate or independent. For, on the one hand, the relations we describe must then be such as to preserve that separateness of the subjects. If we fail to do that, either one term of the relation will be absorbed by the other or both terms will be absorbed by some overarching third term – and in either case there is no longer a relation *between* subjects. The *inter-* of intersubjectivity has, in one way or another, been replaced by an *intra-*. On the other hand, one must not emphasize the separateness of subjects to such an extent that it becomes a mystery how there can be any sort of contact between them. Here the *inter-* simply becomes incomprehensible. From the viewpoint of pluralism, the result in both cases is some type of solipsism. We may have succeeded in describing relations internal to a subject, but we have precisely failed to make intelligible how there can be any contact *between* subjects – how there can be any *inter-subjectivity*.

This problem, set against its pluralistic background, is a fundamental one for phenomenologists such as Husserl, Sartre, and Levinas.[2] Indeed,

104 *The transcendence of the other*

according to Husserl, it may be the "only truly unsettling difficulty" within the phenomenological program (Husserl 1991, 34). Common to the way Husserl, Sartre, and Levinas approach the problem of intersubjectivity is their insistence that, as a term for the various relations precisely between subjects, intersubjectivity must ultimately be anchored in individual subjects. As was suggested in Chapter 5, intersubjectivity is, at the lowest level, the relations between others and *me*. We must elucidate the nature of *my* contact with others; and we must explain how that can be a contact that sustains our fundamental separateness, even when it unites us ever so closely.[3]

In apparent contrast to other phenomenologists,[4] Husserl, Sartre, and Levinas also have in common the specific concern for what they all term the *transcendence* of the other. That is, Husserl, Levinas, and Sartre agree that it is an especially important and difficult task to account for the other's separateness from me – how she or he can avoid being completely absorbed by my grasp and how we can nevertheless be in contact with each other. If the other is to be truly *other*, then there must be a dimension of her that I cannot know, possess, or dominate completely, a dimension that *transcends* me. On this there is agreement. The Husserlian, Sartrean, and Levinasian ways part, however, the moment we ask how we should account for this "transcendence" of the other. Levinas and Sartre are both critical of Husserl's account. They hold that what Husserl can make intelligible is only a "transcendence wrapped in immanence," or a "transcended transcendence," and not the other's transcendence proper. Yet they do not agree on what is to be the alternative.

In the present chapter I will argue that there is reason to be less dismissive of Husserl's perspective on the transcendence of the other than Levinas and Sartre seem to be. I will try to show that Sartre's account of the other's transcendence suffers from a fundamental weakness that Husserl's account does not have and that Levinas' account need not have. The point I attempt to establish is so obvious that it might appear strange that anyone has ever questioned it. The point is this: we cannot divorce the transcendence of other subjects completely from my ability to perceive them. Part of the difficulty in achieving a firm grasp of this point is that it forces us to reconsider what is involved in *perceiving* other minds. In this chapter I will only try to establish the obvious point; the task of reconsidering the perceptual appearance of others is postponed to Chapter 7.

Husserl on the transcendence of the other

Much discussion of Husserl's analyses of intersubjectivity has centered on the argument found in the fifth of Husserl's *Cartesian Meditations*. In this text Husserl sketches an account of the structure of the perception of other subjects. Just as trees and bicycles have their particular intuitive or perceptual givenness, there is, according to Husserl, an "originary" perceptual experience that presents another subjectivity "in person," in flesh and blood.

Husserl describes this peculiar experience under the title of the "experience" or "cognition of the foreign" (*Fremderfahrung*).[5]

Husserl thinks a perception of another person crucially involves what he calls the passive synthesis of "pairing." The idea is roughly the following. When a foreign physical body (*Körper*), which in certain important respects resembles my own body, enters my perceptual field, it will, as Husserl puts it, "without further ado" receive the meaning "lived body" (*Leib*) in virtue of its analogy to my body. The two bodies will present themselves as a pair, as two of a kind (CM, 111–13). And once I am presented with another *lived* body, according to Husserl, I am presented with another subjectivity. In other words, I can have knowledge of other embodied minds because I am myself an embodied mind. As Husserl writes:

> It is only because I can and must conceive my kinesthetic movement [...] as a movement of my lived-and-physical body [*Leibkörper*] in the same space, and as movement in the same sense as that of other physical bodies, that it becomes possible that an external physical body similar to my lived-and-physical body, and with a similar behavior, becomes graspable as having an "interior," an inner-movement, etc.
> (ZPI, 515)

To present-day philosophers, this will probably sound like old-fashioned reasoning by analogy, with all its familiar problems.[6] But Husserl is very clear that what he is describing is an "analogizing *experience*" that does not involve any conscious or unconscious inferences (CM, 111). In fact he is only making a very simple point: if there is to be intersubjectivity, relations between different subjects, and in particular relations where they experience each other precisely as other subjects, then these subjects cannot be minds in the sense we normally think of as Cartesian. That is, these subjects cannot be conceived of as pure mental entities that are in some fundamental metaphysical sense different and separate from the concrete, physical world; rather, they must be *embodied*. In Husserl's words, "if an ego-plurality is to be able to stand in empathic relations, then it must be a plurality of egos that are related to the same nature, and they must be animalistic, 'body-endowed' egos" (ZPI, 260).

But does this mean that other subjectivities, as embodied, are, or can be, perceptually given to me just as they are given to themselves? It does not. Husserl insists that if there is no dimension of the other that essentially transcends my comprehension, then ultimately there is no other. The contrast with material objects is instructive here. While it is simply impossible to perceive all aspects of a material object at once, or even in any finite process of perception, there is no aspect of a material object that *essentially* escapes my grasp. There is no part of its inside, for instance, to which I am in principle unable to obtain perceptual access. According to Husserl, this means that the "transcendence of the perceivable thing, the thing given to me in my perception as real and as being present in person, is, so we may

106 *The transcendence of the other*

say, *itself only a form of immanence*" (ZPI, 246). My ability to perceptually unveil all aspects of the thing in a sense takes away its alterity, Husserl thinks. It potentially pulls the thing into the sphere of that which I *know*, that which has no power to surprise me.

But there is another contrast we should consider as well. As Husserl says in the *Cartesian Meditations*, whatever is originally presentable and displayable is me myself, or belongs to me as mine (CM, 114). A material thing is something that, in a sense, can belong to me as mine, as we have just seen. But it isn't "me myself"; it is still "not-I," in Fichte's terminology. Rather, the second contrast that Husserl has in mind is obviously the contrast with my access to my own subjective life. As we saw in Chapter 5, it cannot be the case that my access to other subjectivities is of the same type as my access to my own subjectivity, since this idea entails solipsism.

It is important, then, that, although the other must be an embodied subject, she must also have a dimension that necessarily and continuously escapes my comprehension. But this gives a rather curious twist to Husserl's notion of perceptual experience. For while he insists that I *can* perceive others themselves, as opposed to some mere external *Ersatz* (cf. CM, 124), he also claims that this perception must be one that does not *really* present all aspects of the other subject. In other words, Husserl seems to operate with a notion of perceptual experience that is broad enough to encompass even that which can never achieve full perceptual presentation. Referring to the manifestation of the other person, Husserl therefore speaks, paradoxically, of a "verifiable accessibility of what is not originally accessible" (CM, 114). Strictly speaking, the other, qua other first-person perspective on the world, is not accessible; her accessibility is somehow only the accessibility of this strict inaccessibility or this perceptual "limit" (Zahavi 2001b, 153). Or, to put it differently, perceiving another means perceiving something that resists my perception, something that "gets away from me" (Ricœur 1967, 172). Husserl therefore concludes that, in relation to my cognitive grasp, the other must be the *transcendent par excellence*: "*Here we find the only transcendence really worthy of the name*, and everything else we call transcendence, such as the objective world, is *based* upon the transcendence of foreign subjectivity" (Husserl 1959, 495; cf. ZPI, 8–9, 442). This transcendence of the other is of course not the transcendence of a peculiar object that essentially refuses to lend itself to my cognition. It is, rather, as already indicated, the transcendence of another subject, another perspective on the world. To encounter another is in that sense to discover the world's having another "constitutive origin," an origin outside me.

According to Husserl, all this and more belongs to the encounter with another subjectivity. Yet there is one way of approaching another that has a special status. Husserl emphasizes that only what he calls "communicative" acts are truly "social acts" (Husserl 1989, 204). Communicative acts are acts where I "turn" to the other person, as Husserl puts it (ZPI, 166). Turning to the other is first and foremost what I do when I address her, talk to her.

Husserl speaks of this situation of turning to the other as one in which we "look each other in the eyes" (ZPI, 167), something he distinguishes sharply from my looking *at* the eyes of the other, as well as from any attempt to probe comprehendingly into her subjective life (ZPI, 211). "Turning towards the other" or "looking her in the eyes" is precisely what I do when I communicate with her. And such direct communication is not only about transmitting information to another person; equally important is the fact that in direct communication the other is given to understand that her interlocutor *is telling her something*, that he or she wants to communicate something to her (Husserl 1973, 473–75). The point, in other words, is that truly social acts are the kind of acts where I – at the same time as I make the other person do something, announce something to her, or whatever – also let her know that I want her to do this or that I am telling her this. It is thus characteristic of what Husserl calls social acts that I put myself on the line in a certain sense. To perceive another person, to make sure she knows something, to make her do things, even to love her – I can do all of this without her ever becoming aware of my existence. But addressing another person means standing forth, turning towards the other person, and announcing to her (regardless of whatever else one is saying) this act of turning towards her (ZPI, 167).

This, then, is the relation that is the social relation *par excellence*, on Husserl's view: "At the basis of all sociality [...] lies the actual connection of the communicative community, the mere community of addressing and receiving the address" (Husserl 1973, 475). As the quotation makes clear, this paradigmatic social relation is characterized by reciprocity. I not only address the other; I also receive, or respond to, her acts of addressing me. There is a moment of what Michael Theunissen has dubbed "alter-ation" (*Veranderung*) (Theunissen 1984, 89) in this kind of relation. In general terms, to recognize oneself as the one being addressed by the other means to recognize oneself as another person to the other person, as "the other's other" (ZPI, 421). And what this comes down to is the recognition that I am no more (and no less) than one human subject in a community of human subjects standing in relations of "*mutual being for one another*" (CM, 129).

Still, it remains important to Husserl that this type of sociality is not opposed to perception. Looking another in the eyes is not looking *at* the eyes of another. But nor is it divorced from all looking. The others are bodily others, physically present, visually and tactually perceivable. Yet I experience another subject precisely when my perceptual experiences encounter that which they cannot in principle possess or unveil; when they encounter that which *appears as essentially inaccessible*, in a sense still to be clarified.

Sartre on the transcendence of the other

According to Sartre, however, Husserlian intentionality is a mere "caricature" of transcendence (BN, 109); it cannot make real transcendence

108 *The transcendence of the other*

intelligible. Husserl "shut[s] himself up in the *cogito* and deserves – in spite of his denial – to be called a phenomenalist rather than a phenomenologist" (BN, 73). With respect to intersubjectivity, this means that Husserl cannot steer clear of the "reef of solipsism" (BN, 223, 235).

To begin to appreciate why Sartre judges Husserl so harshly, consider an example Sartre discusses in *Being and Nothingness*. Sitting in a park, I notice another man pass by a bench located at the edge of a lawn. What does it mean, Sartre asks, to see this man *as a man*? He replies that it means to notice how the surroundings – the lawn, the benches, etc. – organize themselves around the stranger (BN, 254). According to Sartre, this has the further implication that these surroundings are no longer organized or grouped around me but flee away from me towards a new center in the shape of this man. The green lawn "turns toward the Other a face which escapes me"; "I can not apprehend the green *as* it appears to the Other." The other, in effect, has "stolen the world from me," Sartre claims (BN, 255). Except for Sartre's rather conflict-oriented interpretation, the phenomenon he describes can easily be made sense of on Husserl's model, too, as we have just seen. But Sartre wants to make a quite un-Husserlian point, for he immediately adds that, despite all the reorganization of the surroundings, "*the Other* is still an object *for me*" (BN, 255). We remain at "the level on which the Other is an *object*," and at this level the other's existence as other subject is, as Sartre puts it, "purely conjectural" (BN, 256, 253). If this reorganization of the world is to be truly manifest, and not just a conjecture or a hypothesis, then there must be some other and more original way in which the other subject can present himself or herself to me.

If we want to understand the reasoning behind these claims, we must realize that Sartre works with a philosophical framework that allows for only a very peculiar conception of perception. More precisely, he is committed to roughly the following view. There are basically two mutually exclusive ontological categories, for which Sartre uses the Hegelian terms being-for-itself (*l'être-pour-soi*) and being-in-itself (*l'être-en-soi*) (BN, xxxix). Intersubjectivity is clearly a relation between two or more of the former. Being-for-itself basically has two ways of entering into a relation with other beings: it can be the subject that experiences, in which case it experiences an object; or it can itself enter into a relation as an object, but then that is only possible in and through another being-for-itself as the subject for which it is an object.[7] These notions of subject and object are also mutually exclusive. If the *original* encounter with the other is one in which I am the subject that looks at the other, then ultimately I am looking at an object, not a subject – and it thus remains doubtful whether an intersubjective relation has been established. The fact that I am the one who is looking puts me in the position of subject, and what I am looking *at* can then only be an object, according to Sartre. This logic only leaves one authentic type of intersubjective encounter, viz. that I experience myself as the other's object. This is the only way that I am "able to apprehend the presence of his being-as-subject" (BN,

256). The original presence of the other is hence her presence as "the *one who looks at me*" (BN, 257). Through this look a new dimension of being is added to Sartre's account, namely what he calls being-for-others (*être-pour-autrui*) (BN, 218).

The other's look does not have to be in the shape of two eyes directed at me. The look "will be given just as well on occasion when there is a rustling of branches, or the sound of a footstep followed by silence, or the slight opening of the shutter, or a light movement of a curtain" (BN, 257). In fact these must be paradigm cases for Sartre, since they are situations in which I feel myself to be the possible object of another whom I cannot see and therefore cannot attempt to objectify with my own gaze. Of course, this does not mean that I can only be looked at by another subject who is literally absent or hiding; the point is merely that my exposedness to the look does not necessarily involve my perception of a pair of eyes. For the presence of a pair of eyes in my perceptual field is the presence of a pair of *objects*. And when the other looks at me something quite different is at work: "The Other's look hides his eyes; he seems to go *in front of them*" (BN, 258) – indeed, "the Other's look is the disappearance of the Other's *eyes* as objects which manifest the look" (BN, 268). Subjected to this look, I feel vulnerable, disempowered, and even enslaved, Sartre claims (BN, 259, 265, 267). I am placed, by the other's gaze, in the midst of the world, as her object. But this is precisely what allows me to experience the true transcendence of the other. For she is not with me in the world; she is the one who places me there, the one who "comes toward the world and toward me from all [her] transcendence," in her "trans-mundane presence" (BN, 270). The transcendence of the other is thus her transcendence of my transcendence, understood as her objectification of me.

Sartre's objection to Husserl is that the latter cannot conceive of any such original encounter. According to Sartre, Husserl insists, along with most other philosophers, on founding intersubjectivity on the other's presence to my perception and knowledge (cf. BN, 253, 272). What Husserl describes can only be a situation in which I am the subject directing myself at another as my object, and since the two categories are exclusive the-other-as-my-object cannot at the same time be a subject. Her "subjecthood" becomes merely hypothetical, and thus I am essentially alone.

Heidegger suffers a similar fate. In his critique of Heidegger Sartre emphasizes the importance of the concrete encounter with a particular other. He argues that to locate an openness to the other in the very being of the subject (as Heidegger does in his analysis of *Mitsein*) has the effect of making the concrete "ontic" encounter with another impossible, for which reason Heidegger's account is ultimately solipsistic (BN, 247–49). What Heidegger can make intelligible, according to Sartre, is at most a "totally undifferentiated transcendence" (BN, 428), and it is hard to see how one can get from that to "the experience of particular persons" (ibid.).

Sartre elaborates in great detail the consequences of his own alternative view, for example, in his notorious analyses of love and sadism. In the present

110 *The transcendence of the other*

context, however, we need only discuss the most immediate consequences, beginning with my response to the other's objectification of me. Sartre thinks that my response must be an attempt to objectify the other in turn. On Sartre's account, then, intersubjectivity in its original realization must be conflict (BN, 364). It is a situation of two for-itselfs struggling to objectify each other. But how do I go about objectifying the other? I subject her to my gaze, paralyze her, transcend her transcendence, and turn it into an objective fact in my perceived world. Sartre is acutely aware, however, of the dialectics that this sets in motion. Since my objectification of the other places an *object* before my eyes, I have not achieved what I wanted. What I really wanted to conquer was the other qua subject, the other's *subjectivity*. Yet:

> [As soon as I] look at his look in order to defend myself against the Other's freedom and to transcend it as freedom, then both the freedom and the look of the Other collapse. I see eyes; I see a being-in-the-midst-of-the-world. Henceforth the Other escapes me. [...] [E]verything happens as if I wished to get hold of a man who runs away and leaves only his coat in my hands. It is the coat, it is the outer shell which I possess.
>
> (BN, 393)

It could hardly be otherwise. If the other's presence as a subject is her presence as the one who looks at me, objectifying me; and if her exposure to my gaze merely places an object before my eyes, then my attempt to conquer the other qua subjectivity must fail. This is a profound failure, because my turning the other into an object cannot make the other-as-subject disappear. As Sartre says, "what is certain is that *I am* looked at: what is only probable is that the look is bound to this or that intra-mundane presence" (BN, 277). No matter how many such intra-mundane presences I am able to paralyze with my gaze I am still looked at; I can never catch hold of the other as the one who looks at me. Sartre claims that this reveals that the other who looks at me has an "unnumbered" or "prenumerical" presence (BN, 281–82). It is, then, not really this or that *particular* other that I encounter when I am being looked at, but rather something like Heidegger's neutral *Man*,[8] which is everyone yet no one in particular (cf. BN, 282).

Sartre patiently unfolds the twists and turns of the fundamental conflict that he claims is the most basic form of intersubjectivity. Although much of it looks like a rehearsal of Hegel's dialectics of master and slave, the outcome is not mutual recognition. On the contrary, "we are indefinitely referred from the Other-as-object to the Other-as-subject and *vice versa*. The movement is never arrested, and this movement with its abrupt reversals of direction constitutes our relation with the Other" (BN, 408). Thus "we shall never place ourselves concretely on a plane of equality; that is, on the plane where the recognition of the Other's freedom would involve the Other's recognition of our freedom" (ibid.).

As is obvious by now, Sartre paints a rather bleak picture of intersubjectivity. But it is also a picture that is committed to some problematic claims. First of all, several commentators have noted the strange fact that whereas Sartre is very insistent in his critique of Heidegger that the encounter with the other must be an encounter with a concrete, particular other, Sartre himself ultimately associates the look with a prenumerical other, which is precisely not a particular other at all (Theunissen 1984, 241–43; Zahavi 2002, 271–72). It thus seems that Sartre is inconsistent on this point. In fact he seems to renounce all attempts to make a concrete encounter with a particular other intelligible as an original encounter. Such encounters can ultimately only be encounters with the other-as-object, and thus not original modes of intersubjectivity at all. The original intersubjective encounter is an encounter with an omnipresent, invisible, and strangely abstract other.

But if this much is true the question is whether we cannot push the criticism one step further. More precisely, perhaps it can be argued that once Sartre has taken the step from emphasizing the concrete encounter with a particular other to the view that the original encounter can only be with a "prenumerical" and abstract other, then he ought to acknowledge that we cannot really be dealing with another *subject* after all. Deeply problematic in this context are the mutually exclusive notions of subject and object. Sartre says about these notions: "The difference of principle between the Other-as-object and the Other-as-subject stems solely from this fact: that the Other-as-subject can in no way be known nor even conceived as such" (BN, 293). To the extent that Sartre is trying to make the point that the other subject must, in a sense, escape my grasp in order to be another subject, he is of course right. But if we jump to the conclusion that every other whom I *see* can only be an other-as-object, and not the subject I wanted to reach, then confusion ensues. For we have now introduced a scenario in which the other whom I see can never really have anything to do with the invisible prenumerical other who looks at me. Everything that I see is in principle compatible with my being alone in the world; only my *feeling of being exposed, looked at, in danger* establishes the presence of others as other subjects. But then something like the following problem seems to emerge. What reason is there to think that my being-exposed or my being-in-danger signifies precisely my being-exposed-to-others? What makes it certain or even likely that the "rustling of the branches" indicates my being-looked-at by another? Why doesn't it simply reveal my fragility and vulnerability, thrown into a world that overpowers me, as Heidegger says, or my exposure to the "rustling" of the impersonal "there is," as Levinas would say? Sartre himself admits that "[w]hat I apprehend immediately when I hear the branches crackling behind me is not that *there is someone* there; it is that I am vulnerable, that I have a body which can be hurt" (BN, 259). But then what justifies Sartre's immediate transition to the claim that "I *am seen*" (ibid.)? We must remember that no matter what pairs of oval things I might encounter they are mere objects. They can only be the eyes of an other-as-object on the basis of a more original encounter, an encounter where I am *looked at*. Before the latter establishes the presence of the other-as-subject the existence of the other remains "purely conjectural." This, indeed, was Sartre's reason for accusing Husserl of solipsism. But then how can I know that I am *looked at*? The danger, exposedness, vulnerability, and so forth are all readily intelligible, but what is the justification for interpreting any of these things as the exposedness to *a look*?[9] If there is any philosophical account that makes the existence of the other purely conjectural, it is surely the one Sartre offers.

It may be argued at this point that I have only considered what Sartre says about fear, overlooking his other main example, *shame*. Shame "is in its primary structure shame *before somebody*" (BN, 221); it thus cannot possibly be made sense of in terms of an exposedness to an anonymous threatening environment. This must be granted. But one might ask whether shame really makes sense in the absence of a concrete, particular other in relation to whom one is ashamed. I may be ashamed before my mother but not before my friends, for example; or I might be ashamed of certain actions before anyone, not anyone in the sense of a "prenumerical presence," but rather in the sense of "anyone who might happen to notice." Sartre would deny this, of course. In his discussion of the experience of being caught spying through a keyhole, he claims that what my relief upon discovering that no one was there after all reveals concerns only the "facticity" of the other. That is, when I fearfully turn my head thinking I have been caught, but discover that there is no one behind me, what is canceled is only "the contingent connection between the Other and an object-being in *my* world," not the other's presence as subject (BN, 277). Yet this is quite implausible. It seems to imply that I should now be in a worse situation than if I had discovered someone behind me; for in the latter case I would at least have had the chance to objectify the other in turn. As it is, I know myself to be "seen" by an invisible perceiver. But why my sigh of relief then? Surely what my relief reveals is that my shame has everything to do with the presence, here and now, of concrete particular others, whose eyes I may find are directed upon me. If there is no one there I am relieved. I might choose to give up my enterprise, of course, trembling with the awareness that I could have been caught – but the point is, I was not caught.

Moreover, perhaps shame is too complex a social phenomenon to be of use to Sartre here, where we are dealing with the question of the most original encounter with the other. As Merleau-Ponty has argued, shame is precisely the painful experience it is because it replaces a more original communicative encounter between self and other (Merleau-Ponty 1962, 361). According to Merleau-Ponty, this is the reason why the look of a dog, for example, does not embarrass us. In the latter case we do not feel that the look is a withdrawal away from a more original being-engaged-with-one-another. In contrast, when another person makes herself into a pure "inhuman gaze" this is painful to us precisely because it is a refusal to engage with us and respond to us. This suggests that shame cannot be the original encounter with the other that Sartre takes it to be, since it essentially refers back to other types of encounter with others.

It seems, then, that it is hard to make sense of Sartre's "look" as the most original experience of the other.[10] Fear seems to indicate vulnerability and exposure, but not necessarily the exposure to another's look. Shame, on the other hand, is a complex social phenomenon that seems to refer to other, more original ways of encountering others. Sartre's account consequently appears to be drawn into a nonstarter difficulty: Whatever I see can only be an other (as object) if I have an original experience of an other-as-subject. But since this cannot involve my perception of another it must be a situation in which I am perceived *by* another. But how can my exposure be manifestly an exposure to the gaze of *another*, rather than some impersonal danger, given that there is no concrete being that I might discover in my perceptual field that would count as the other who looks at me? Intersubjectivity cannot get off the ground here.

Ultimately, this has to do with Sartre's extreme version of dualism. But one of the more immediate culprits is Sartre's conception of the structure of perception and knowledge. In Husserl's phenomenological terminology every intentional act has its intentional "object." Thus every perceptual act has its perceived "object." But for Husserl an intentional object does not have to be an *object*, or thing, in any interesting sense. As we have seen, he thinks I can have perceptual knowledge of other subjectivities *as such*. This is precisely what Sartre denies. He thinks knowledge and perception essentially *objectify* or *reify* their intentional objects, turn them into *objects* in some stifling, reifying sense. Therefore the transcendence of the other *as other subjectivity* cannot be made intelligible in terms of perception and knowledge, according to Sartre. As we have seen, however, this view forces him into a position that is, in the last analysis, untenable.

Levinas on the transcendence of the other

Like Sartre, Levinas develops his account of the transcendence of the other in a critical dialogue with, among others, Husserl. Levinas' agenda, however, is very different from that of Sartre. Indeed, on the surface of things, it seems the difference could hardly be greater. While Sartre describes the struggle between two subjectivities, striving to confirm their own freedom by transcending that of the other, Levinas describes "subjectivity as welcoming the Other, as hospitality" (TI, 27). While Sartre describes a necessarily asymmetrical relation with incessant "reversals of direction" (BN, 408), Levinas conceives of intersubjectivity as asymmetrical and *ir*reversible.

The difference between their outlooks is strikingly brought out in Levinas' description of the face. To encounter the other as other, according to Levinas, means to encounter the *face* (TI, 50); and to encounter a face is very different

114 *The transcendence of the other*

indeed from encountering an object of any kind. The face does not manifest itself by its qualities – form, color, smoothness, etc. – but breaks through them, as it were, thereby revealing the inadequacy of my hold on the other:

> The way in which the other presents himself, exceeding *the idea of the other in me*, we here name face. This *mode* does not consist in figuring as a theme under my gaze, in spreading itself forth as a set of qualities forming an image.
>
> (TI, 50)

Especially in *Totality and Infinity*, the notion of the face seems to be omnipresent. Perhaps, however, we can, without doing grave injustice to Levinas' intentions, say that much of what he says about the face revolves around the equivocal notions of "nakedness" and "absence." First of all, the face is "naked" in the sense that it resists, or shakes off, all determinations and characterizations. The other is "*kath'auto*, a being that stands beyond every attribute, which would precisely have as its effect to qualify him, that is, to reduce him to what is common to him and other beings – a being, consequently, completely naked" (TI, 74). But this nakedness is also a sort of absence from the world I perceive (TI, 75). Resisting qualification and characterization, the face withdraws from the world of colors and shapes, it "departs" from and "transcends the world" (CPP, 105). This kind of nakedness, then, looks a lot like the "trans-mundane presence" Sartre speaks of. Just as Sartre emphasizes that precisely when I am subjected to the other's look his eyes disappear and, along with them, his "ugliness, his obesity, and his shuffling" (BN, 276), so Levinas associates the encounter with the other's face with not noticing the color of his eyes (Levinas 1985, 85–86; CPP, 20).

However, the other is also described as "exiled," "cold," and "hungry." She is a "stranger, destitute, or proletarian" (TI, 75), says Levinas. The nakedness of the face extends into the bodily nakedness of the other. Levinas emphasizes that "the whole body – a hand or a curve of the shoulder – can express as the face" (TI, 262), so that there is an "expressivity of the person's whole sensible being, even in the hand one shakes" (Levinas 1990, 59).[11] The second, more carnal and bodily sense of nakedness and unworldly "absence," then, also has to do with the face:

> This gaze that supplicates and demands, that can supplicate only because it demands, deprived of everything, because entitled to everything, and which one recognizes in giving [...] – this gaze is precisely the epiphany of the face as a face. The nakedness of the face is destituteness. To recognize a face is to recognize a hunger.
>
> (TI, 75)

Levinas also speaks of the other's being "exposed to the point of the sword" and of the "total nudity of his defenseless eyes" (TI, 199). This gaze, then, is clearly a quite different gaze from the one we find in Sartre. In Sartre, the other's look is not defenseless and exposed; rather, I am exposed and vulnerable when I am subjected to the other's look. Levinas agrees that the face or the gaze of the other transcends me, withdraws and escapes; but it does not accomplish this by turning me into its object.

What, then, does it do to me? The answer to this question is implicit in what we have already said. The flipside of the other's nakedness-as-resistant-to-categories and her not-being-of-this-world is her nakedness-as-destitute and her being-exiled-in-this-world (TI, 74–75).[12] The face is a strange mixture of destitution and "Height," as Levinas expresses it (TI, 200). But then its transcendence and its resistance to me cannot be the transcendence of someone dominating and objectifying me, someone threatening my freedom. Rather, they must be the transcendence and resistance of someone vulnerable and defenseless, and this gives a completely new meaning to the other's gaze. This is forcefully illustrated by Levinas' point that the face expresses the command "You shall not commit murder" (TI, 199; CPP, 43). As a command, this imperative comes from above me, as it were, and Levinas therefore says that the face is "an infinite resistance to murder," "firm and insurmountable," and that it "paralyzes" my power (TI, 199; cf. CPP, 21). But this is not because the other has a force greater than mine. She might, of course, but that has nothing to do with the kind of resistance that interests Levinas – a resistance any person has just qua having (or being) a "face." This latter resistance is the resistance of someone who essentially "has no resistance" (TI, 199), who is "naked and without resources" (CPP, 167). The other does not challenge me to struggle with her; nor does she command me in virtue of being backed up by an irresistible force that I had better yield to. Rather, the other commands me in something like the way that an infant, precisely in virtue of its total defenselessness and dependence, embodies the very impossibility of murder and commands our care. The other's face addresses what is perhaps better termed an *appeal* to me, an appeal to my goodness or responsibility (TI, 200). The important thing about the face, then, is not the bare fact that it looks at me, but that it expresses itself, speaks to me, draws me into conversation. Being-confronted-with-one-another in conversation is, according to Levinas, the ultimate and irreducible social relation: the relation of *face to face* (TI, 81, 182, 291). Thus, to summarize, the other transcends me as the *one to whose appeal I must respond*.[13]

It seems, then, that we can formulate the essential difference between Levinas' and Sartre's accounts in roughly the following way. Sartre thinks the other's gaze is simply a reversal of my gaze. As the latter is inevitably an objectifying look, according to Sartre, the other's transcendence can only take the shape of her domination of me. But Levinas' precisely wants to deny this reversibility (cf. TI, 101). As Levinas says, with clear (if implicit) reference to Sartre, my exposure to the face of the other does not mean that I now know myself "as a theme attended to by the Other" (TI, 86), nor that the other threatens or limits my freedom, because the "Other measures me with a gaze incomparable to the gaze by which I discover him" (TI, 86). The eye of the other neither shines as an object nor objectifies, as in Sartre's scenario. Rather, it *speaks* (TI, 66). But when Levinas says, *pace* Sartre, that the other's gaze is "incomparable" to the gaze I direct at him, doesn't he then also implicitly acknowledge an important point of agreement with Sartre? Isn't it obvious that, as one commentator puts it, Levinas "agrees with Sartre that when I merely look at the other, the result will be that I deny him his alterity and turn him into an object that poses no threat to my subjectivity" (Visker 1999, 329)?[14] As Levinas says in the early work *Time and the Other*, with clear reference to Husserl:

> The intentionality of consciousness allows one to distinguish the ego from things, but it does not make solipsism disappear: its element – light – renders us master of the exterior world but is incapable of discovering a peer for us there.
>
> (Levinas 1987, 65)

Sartre and Levinas would apparently both say that what I perceive can only be a transcendence "wrapped in immanence" (ibid., 65). Levinas' point, then, must be that the face is precisely not something I see, but rather someone who speaks to me and someone I respond to.[15]

But if Levinas agrees with this we may ask if he doesn't encounter problems similar to the problems we discerned in Sartre's account. If the face is completely divorced from all manifestation, if its speaking to me can never be linked to something perceptually given, in what sense can it then be *someone* who appeals to me? There are several different ways of posing this question. One way is to ask how the other can be exposed, hungry, and vulnerable if she is not of flesh and blood (OB, 74), carnally present in this world, even if she somehow transcends it. How can the appeal be the appeal of specific others, unless it can, ultimately, be tied to specific pairs of eyes? How can a demand or appeal that cannot possibly be linked to some concrete being, encountered in *this* world, be the demand or appeal of a concrete, *personal other*? How could such an otherness forbid *murder*? Would its otherness not be too impersonal, fleshless, or even "faceless?"

Levinas is acutely aware of these problems – perhaps more than some of his commentators. He does insist that a relation with a truly transcendent other cannot be made intelligible in terms of Husserlian intentionality, but this has a lot to do with Levinas' firm conviction that Husserlian intentionality is essentially thematization and objectification. He never stops accusing Husserl of modeling the relation with the other on the "relation with the object, the posited, the *thematic*" (TI, 109, cf. 67, 27, 295). When he argues that the other's transcendence must be divorced entirely from perceptual manifestation, cognition, and indeed from intentionality as such, he has such acts of thematization and object-scrutinizing

The transcendence of the other 117

in mind (cf. TI, 75, 109; Levinas 1987, 97–100). When he is not specifically concerned with perception in this allegedly Husserlian sense, he is clear that it makes no sense to divorce the other's face from all manifestation. Rather, he emphasizes that the very possibility of violence and murder has to do with the fact that the face has a "sensible appearance" (TI, 198). But he also insists that "[t]he Other does not *only appear* in his face, as a phenomenon subject to the action and domination of a freedom; infinitely distant from the very relation he enters, he presents himself there from the first as an absolute" (TI, 215; partly my emphasis). The other is a being "both graspable and escaping every hold," and indeed without this "living contradiction," as Levinas calls it, violence would simply be labor (TI, 223).[16] Violence and respect are only possible with regard to a being that appears, that manifests itself in the midst of the world, vulnerable and exposed, but, paradoxically, appears precisely by also withdrawing from, and transcending, this appearance "by an essential dimension" (TI, 39). In other, equally paradoxical, words, it is essential that the other has a "way of manifesting himself without manifesting himself" (CPP, 66).

The "epiphany of the face," then, is not just another perceptual or cognitive event. According to Levinas, the relation of face to face is not "entirely vision, but goes further than vision" (TI, 290). In fact, many of Levinas' formulations seem to suggest that the epiphany of the face is more correctly described as something that happens *to* my cognition: it is the *disturbance*, *rupture*, or *undoing* of my cognition. The other presents herself *by expressing herself*, which means by breaking through or undoing the perceptually given form in which she appears (TI, 198; CPP, 20, 96), overwhelming or confounding the intentionality that aims at her (CPP, 97–98).[17] This is the limit event of perception and cognition, as it were, where perception turns into something "of another order":

> It is nonetheless true that the very relationship of the *saying* cannot be reduced to intentionality, or that it rests, properly speaking, on an intentionality that fails. It is established with the other man whose monadic inwardness eludes my gaze and my control. But this *deficiency of re-presentation turns into a relation of a superior order*; or more exactly, into a relation in which just the faint outline of the meaning of the superior itself and of another order appears. The Husserlian "appresentation" – which does not reach satisfaction, the intuitive fulfillment of representation – is inverted from a failed experience into a *beyond of experience*.
>
> (Levinas 1998, 71)

As Levinas says elsewhere, the epiphany of the face is where "[p]henomenology can follow the reverting of thematization into ethics" (CPP, 124), into conversation (TI, 51). But as such, as the quotation makes clear, it is precisely not completely separated from perceptual appearance.

Conclusion

What I have sketched in this chapter is ultimately a contrast between two broad approaches to the transcendence of the other. One – the Sartrean – tries to divorce the other's transcendence completely from my cognition and perception; the transcendent other can only be the one that I do not see, the one whose gaze exposes me. But this approach cannot really make my exposedness intelligible as exposedness to the other at all – and thus we cannot account for the transcendence of the other in the way Sartre suggests.

The other model is the Husserlian one. On this model I do perceive the other, and her transcendence is given in my perception. As Wittgenstein says, we *see* the eye of another as something that *looks* (cf. RPP I, § 1100). And the fact that the eye is seen by us does not domesticate the eye and turn it into an object, as Sartre thinks. "I contradict anyone who tells me I see the eye's glance 'just as' I see its form and color" (RPP I, § 1101), says Wittgenstein, and we should concur. Far from being pacified and domesticated, the glance we *see* may objectify and terrify us, and it may make ethical appeals to us. Levinas – albeit not without some straining at the leash – commits himself to this model. It makes no sense, according to Levinas, to divorce the epiphany of the face from all perceptual manifestation. Yet the manifestation of the other is certainly not just another perceptual event. Rather, it is "manifestation without manifestation" (CPP, 66). On this Husserl and Levinas are in agreement. They agree on something else as well. In contrast to Sartre, who thinks the transcendence of the other is paradigmatically revealed in her sneaking up behind me, Husserl and Levinas both link the true presence of the other with the face-to-face encounter. Face-to-face communication, they think, is the intersubjective event *par excellence*.

We should not think, however, that our task has now been accomplished. For example, when Husserl speaks of the other subject as "not originally accessible" (CM, 114) we must keep in mind something that was established in Chapter 5. Husserl's phrase might seem to suggest that there is something meaningful and important that I cannot do here: some metaphysical wall that I cannot scale; some Cartesian realm to which I have no access. Of course, the uncertainties I may experience concerning another's thoughts, feelings, etc. are real enough. But ultimately, as I argued in Chapter 5, they are (or are based on) "constitutional" uncertainties. That is to say, they are *rules of the game* as such, and for that reason cannot meaningfully be construed as obstacles *within* the game. What we need, then, is an account of the perceptual presence of other subjects that avoids any suggestion that their mental lives are fundamentally "hidden" from me. At the same time, however, it must be an account that leaves a robust notion of the transcendence or "inaccessibility" of the other intact. I have not yet provided such an account.

The transcendence of the other 119

My discussion of the "transcendence" of the other, therefore, seems only to have made it more difficult to provide any solution to the problem of other minds. As long as we simply emphasize the essential intersubjective asymmetry, we have done nothing to solve or dissolve the problem of other minds. Quite the contrary, in fact, for, as Davidson has pointed out, to emphasize the asymmetry between self and other, including the way in which another's mental life somehow eludes me, only makes it harder to see how I could have access, in the case of another person, to the same phenomena – the mental states themselves – as I have access to in my own case (cf. Davidson 2001, 3–14, 16–17, 207). And this surely aggravates the problem of other minds rather than contributes anything to its (dis)solution. If Husserl and Levinas are right there must be a way of accounting for our perception of others that makes it intelligible that we perceive those other subjects *themselves*, rather than some external *Ersatz*, while still accommodating the fact that these other subjects somehow transcend our perception of them. But so far no such account has emerged. In fact, what I have said in this chapter might seem to cast doubt on the possibility of providing one. How can one combine the idea of the other subject's "transcendence" with the Wittgensteinian claim that "nothing is hidden?" Aren't these notions ultimately incompatible? To answer these questions, I will return to Wittgenstein.

7 The play of expression

> And if the play of *expression* develops, then indeed I can say that a soul, something *inner*, is developing.
>
> (LW I, § 947)

Introduction

One reason why it is hard to resolve all difficulties concerning other minds is that we seem to have two sets of conflicting yet equally fundamental intuitions about the accessibility of the mental lives of others. On the one hand we feel that Wittgenstein, behaviorists, and others are right when they observe that very often we do have reliable knowledge about the feelings and thoughts of other persons. Yet on the other hand there is also a sense in which skeptics and Cartesians are correct to say that the mental life of another is somehow inaccessible to us. We think that there are situations in which the fact that another is in pain is as plain as day, and yet we would also be inclined to agree that if another person does not tell us what she is thinking of and if she is not behaving in any particularly revealing way we are quite often in doubt as to what she is thinking. Most of us would thus be inclined to think there is something fundamentally wrong with Cartesian dualism and its apparent commitment to the view that the mental lives of others are essentially experientially inaccessible; but we do not want to fall into the opposite camp and claim, like the behaviorists, that everything lies completely open to view.

Probably philosophy can never again return to the blissful state of not knowing any problem of other minds, no matter how much effort we lavish on solving or dissolving the problem. But it also seems too facile just to ignore the difficulties that seventeenth-century philosophy has handed down to us – among them the problems of "mind and body" and "other minds." We have to reflect on these issues, even if complete solutions (or dissolutions) are unlikely to be found. Neither the quasi-Cartesian intuition nor the quasi-behaviorist one, however, seems to give way when reflection sets in. The idea that what we can observe in others at least sometimes leaves room for doubt regarding their thoughts, desires, and feelings, contrary to the claims of certain crude forms of behaviorism, still seems simply correct. On the other hand, there is something right about the notion that the thoughts, feelings, etc. of my friends and family are not entirely hidden and inaccessible to me. Both of these intuitions have something to do with the kinds of things we say about others and their mental states ("Look how angry she is"; "I can't figure out how she really feels about me"). But they also seem to be confirmed by experience. Part of our dissatisfaction with Cartesianism and behaviorism thus seems to turn on the fact that each position emphasizes only one set of intuitions and downplays, ignores, or even contests the other set, thereby contradicting some quite ordinary experiences and well-established ways of speaking. But if this is so, then it seems clear what our task is: we have to find a way of combining the intuitions apparently supporting and motivating each of these two extremes.

This is precisely what I aim to do in the present chapter. I will try to sketch an alternative to the Cartesian dualistic account of our knowledge of others, but one that does justice to the point developed in Chapter 6, that is, the point that there is a sense in which the mental lives of others transcend us. I will mainly rely on two philosophers to help me in this venture. First, I will present an alternative to Cartesianism that I think resembles what we find in the later Wittgenstein. Central in this regard is the idea that we *express* our mental lives in our bodily behavior. But then, in order to accommodate the quasi-Cartesian intuition, I turn to Emmanuel Levinas' account of expression. On the face of it, Levinas contradicts Wittgenstein. Whereas the latter claims that the expression of the other is what gives me direct access to her mental life, the former seems to claim that the other's expression is precisely what denies me full cognitive access to her. But Levinas' position is in crucial respects different from Cartesian dualism, and I shall try to show that Levinas' perspective can in fact be combined with Wittgenstein's view so as to provide a more adequate account of our experience of other human beings.

A point that I wish to call attention to here is the fact that I will be generalizing quite freely, and thereby it will sometimes appear as if I simply lump together emotion, thinking, sensation, etc. It is not, however, my intention to claim that all phenomena that philosophers have called "mental" are alike in all important respects. In fact, I think they are not, and Wittgenstein takes some important steps towards a clarification of the differences between them. But that is not my business here. Rather, just as elsewhere in this book, my point is more general: I want to provide some clues to a *model* of the appearance of other persons. If oversimplification is sometimes the price to pay for a clear presentation of the outline of such a model, then so be it.

The final thing to be noted here at the outset (even if it anticipates points to be established later) is the following. It is often argued – and quite rightly so – that Cartesians (and skeptics) are wrong in claiming that there is *always* room for uncertainty regarding the feelings etc. of others. *Sometimes*, so it is argued, we *can* know (or perceive, intuit, be certain, etc.) what others are feeling and sometimes we can't. This, I think, is true. But there is, nevertheless, a core of truth in the Cartesian claim, which is often overlooked by philosophers who reject the Cartesian generalization of doubt. There is an important *general* peculiarity that characterizes knowledge (or perception) of the feelings of others, in contrast to knowledge (or perception) of facts about physical objects. Even when we do *know* what another is feeling, her feeling is presented to us *as hers*, not ours; that is, she *feels* sad (or whatever it is that she feels), while we do not, or not necessarily. This seems to make room for the idea that our cognitive grasp of her feeling, if one may put it in this way, is less strong than the grasp we have of other types of fact, say facts concerning the colors of material objects clearly visible to us in broad daylight. Thus, even in the most favorable cases of "direct experience" of another's feelings we do experience what, following Husserl and Levinas, I have termed the "transcendence of the other." In such cases, too, we experience the other person eluding us in a particular way. This transcendence is at the basis of the various kinds of doubt and uncertainty that we may have concerning the mental lives of others. Therefore the most "favorable case" must already lay bare the foundations for both of the intuitions mentioned regarding other minds.

Against beetles in boxes: Wittgenstein on pain

In Chapter 1 I provided a first sketch of the Cartesian framework and gave some indications of what I think is wrong with it. Now I need to apply some of these points to the present discussion, which specifically concerns the perceptual appearance of other subjects. To this end, I will briefly return to Wittgenstein's story about the beetle in the box. The passage directly concerns sensations, but I think we can use it more generally to get a firmer grip on the kind of conception of the mind which we must avoid if we are to make sense of other minds. This is how the passage goes:

> Suppose everyone had a box with something in it: we call it a "beetle." No one can look into anyone else's box, and everyone says he knows what a beetle is only by looking at *his* beetle. – Here it would be quite possible for everyone to have something different in his box. One might even imagine such a thing constantly changing. – But suppose the word "beetle" had a use in these people's language? – If so it would not be used as the name of a thing. The thing in the box has no place in the language-game at all; not even as a *something*: for the box might even be empty. – No, one can 'divide through' by the thing in the box; it cancels out, whatever it is.

That is to say: if we construe the grammar of the expression of sensation on the model of "object and designation" the object drops out of consideration as irrelevant.

(PI, § 293)

As I mentioned in Chapter 1, some have argued that the conclusion to the argument is the sentence that we can "divide through" by the beetle in the box. And the sentences preceding it have been perceived by such commentators as the premises leading to that conclusion. Wittgenstein, in effect, would be saying that when we attribute pains to people what matters is their behavior rather than whatever might go on in their minds. But if Wittgenstein were simply trying to prove that the pain "cancels out" as irrelevant why would he repeat this conclusion again in a conditional, saying that *if* we construe such and such in such and such a way, *then* the conclusion follows? The last portion strongly suggests that Wittgenstein's argument is really a *reductio ad absurdum*. As I emphasized in Chapter 1, he is trying to show that a particular assumption has absurd consequences, and the point is, on the basis of its absurd consequences, to reject the assumption in question. The conclusion, then, is not that pain sensations are irrelevant to our attributions of pain to each other. Rather, since Wittgenstein takes the latter to be an absurd consequence he can reject the assumption from which it follows. In other words, Wittgenstein is saying something like the following: If we construe sensation talk in a certain way, then the absurd consequence follows that the sensations themselves are completely irrelevant. Since they cannot be irrelevant – indeed what could be more relevant to our attributions of pain to each other than the actual pains of actual people? – we should avoid construing sensation talk in that particular way. This conclusion, to be sure, is not stated explicitly; but then Wittgenstein often leaves it to his reader to draw the conclusions.

In the present context there is no need to discuss whether the argument is "valid" or whether Wittgenstein's premises fail to necessitate his conclusion; nor need we ask whether it is "sound" or whether some of the assumptions involved are false. I shall sidestep these questions. More interesting is the question what kind of conception of sensations, and ultimately of subjectivity or the mind, the passage is trying to dislodge. Let me first take a look at what seems to be the argumentative core of the passage. What Wittgenstein seems to be saying is this: If we construe sensations as inner objects, as beetles in boxes, accessible only to the owner of the box, then these sensations will turn out to be strangely irrelevant to our talk about sensations. Does this mean that only phenomena that have some kind of full public appearance can be relevant to our public language? Many philosophers have interpreted Wittgenstein as saying precisely this, and some have devised imaginative thought experiments to show that such a position is simply false – that it is merely the result of an unfounded "public-domain positivism" (G. Strawson 1994, 308–24). But it is not clear that Wittgenstein is making quite so strong a claim. I think his main point is just that we should take care not to interpret pain and other psychological phenomena as *completely, in principle* separated from everything observable (which is not to say that *everything* about such phenomena is *always* publicly observable). In Wittgenstein's story, everyone has a *box* with something – a "beetle" – in it. This is an interesting image, for it invites us to conceive of the beetle as cut off from the rest of the world, by the sides of the box, as it were. It is something completely "inner" to the individual person, isolated from everything outer. This idea of "self-containedness" is a target of Wittgenstein's criticism. (Another target, as we have seen, is the idea that pain is a kind of "inner object.") Note that the self-containedness that Wittgenstein associates with beetles in boxes is completely independent of any commitment to Cartesian immaterialism. One can be a hardnosed materialist and still think that pain (being nothing but C-fiber stimulation, say) is something "inner" in the sense of being completely independent of any behavioral manifestation.[1]

Proponents of the Cartesian position would presumably object along the following lines Surely, "'pain' is simply a general term for a certain class of unpleasant physical sensations, considered just as such, i.e. considered just as sensations and hence considered entirely independently of their typical causes or typical behavioral effects or expressions" (G. Strawson 1994, 215). And there is something right about this. "Pain" is a term for unpleasant sensations, rather than, say, for movements of the arm. The step that Wittgenstein would argue is problematic, I think, is the conclusion that "pain" refers to these sensations considered "entirely independently" of all bodily expressions. Not that this is entirely wrong either. If a monoglot Englishman asks me what I mean when I say, "*Ludwig hat Kopfschmerzen*" – whether I mean that Ludwig's head hurts, or that he is in a bad mood, or that he is constantly rubbing his forehead – I will reply that the first option is the right one. I don't mean that he is rubbing his forehead; I mean that his head hurts. The crucial thing is Ludwig's feeling of pain, not his behavior (RPP I, § 146). This is correct, but the question is whether this headache, as such, is really considered entirely independently of everything behavioral. By "pain" I don't *mean* "forehead rubbing," but that does not entail that what I mean is something that can be divorced completely from such phenomena as "forehead rubbing," "paleness," and so forth – let alone that what I mean I mean *as* divorced from these phenomena. To put it differently, the problem with the beetle conception is its claim that because "pain" denotes a type of sensation rather than a type of bodily movement it denotes such a sensation *as considered completely independently* of all behavior and bodily expression (cf. Pears 1988, 350, 357). That simply doesn't follow.

According to Wittgenstein, pain is best described as a "pattern in the weave of our lives" (cf. LW II, 42; Z, § 533). A similar view is defended by J. L. Austin in his paper "Other Minds." Discussing anger, Austin remarks:

It seems fair to say that "being angry" is in many respects like "having mumps." It is a description of a whole pattern of events, including occasion, symptoms, feeling and manifestation, and possibly other factors besides. It is as silly to ask "What, really, *is* the anger *itself*?" as to attempt to fine down "the disease" to some one chosen item [...]. That the man himself feels something which we don't (in the sense that he feels angry and we don't) is [;...] evident enough, and incidentally nothing to complain about as a "predicament": but there is no call to say that "that" ("the feeling") *is* the *anger*.

(Austin 1979, 109)

So when I say, "Ludwig has a headache," what I mean is something very intimately connected with his rubbing his forehead, his paleness, etc. – although I mean none of these things considered in isolation. The beetle interpretation holds that because "pain" denotes a sensation, and not (for example) a movement in space, it denotes a sensation *as completely isolated* from anything observable, that is, precisely as a beetle hidden inside a box. Wittgenstein's and Austin's point, in contrast, is this: How can something isolated in this way within a person have anything to do with our phenomenon of *pain*? Pain is, for instance, a very concrete, real phenomenon in emergency rooms, playgrounds, sports arenas, and so forth (cf. Pears 1988, 400), and the way it manifests itself in such contexts seems incompatible with the beetle model. Often we are quite able to tell, without having to draw inferences of any kind, that others are in pain; and this is something that the beetle model seems to exclude as a matter of principle. On the beetle model the pain is something inner, inside the box, visible only to one person. I might be able to *infer* that another is in pain on the basis of her bodily behavior, but the pain itself is directly available only to her. According to Wittgenstein, this is misguided. Pain is a phenomenon that stretches its arms out in many directions. Pain, considered just as a type of unpleasant sensation, plays many roles in publicly observable reality and Wittgenstein thinks that if we cut off these "external arms" of the phenomenon what we will be left with (beetles in boxes) will be so detached from our lives that it becomes hard to see how *it* could be what we mean when we talk about pain. A side effect is that the arms that are cut off are conceived as "mere matter," "mere behavior," or the like – deprived of all mental traces.

So Wittgenstein thinks the beetle framework will get us entangled in all kinds of philosophical problems (among them the problem of other minds) that are bizarre, to say the least, from the viewpoint of everyday experience: "Wouldn't it be ridiculous if a lawyer in court were to say that a witness couldn't *know* that someone had been angry, because anger is something inner? – Then one also cannot know whether hanging is punishment" (LW II, 84–85).[2] To push it to extremes, it would, on the beetle model, be a sensible and interesting question whether flogging can really be used to punish people. People scream and pant and make terrible faces when they are flogged; but that is all merely external. Who knows what they feel "inside?" On the beetle model it would even be a potentially distressful question whether they feel anything at all "inside" or whether their boxes are simply empty. In Wittgenstein's view, there is good reason to find these notions bizarre or ridiculous; because the place they assign to pain (anger, etc.) is quite far from the places it occupies in our actual lives.[3]

Expression: closing the gap

If the ideas just outlined are convincing we should have a rough notion of the kind of account to avoid: We should avoid construing the mental lives of others as something completely "inner," cut off from the body and the surrounding world. So the question now is how we are to articulate a positive alternative. In other words, how does pain (and how do other mental phenomena) reach out into our social lives?

As I mentioned in Chapter 1, it is sometimes claimed that Wittgenstein offers a "criterial" or "criteriological" account of our access to the mental lives of others. The precise structure of Wittgenstein's account is disputed. But an influential view states that, according to Wittgenstein, a criterion for something being in a certain way is "a logically necessary as well as logically sufficient condition of its being so" (Albritton 1966, 235), so that "[t]he satisfaction of the criterion of *y* establishes the existence of *y* beyond question" (Malcolm 1966, 84). Some have argued for a somewhat weaker link between the criterion for a state of affairs and the state of affairs itself (cf. Chihara and Fodor 1966, 387, 390, 397), but presumably all commentators who claim to find a criterial solution to the other minds problem in Wittgenstein would at least agree that the term "criterion" is supposed to pick out some kind of "logical" or "conceptual" relation between behavior (or statements about behavior) and mental states (or statements about mental states). It is clear, however that, as it is stated here, the "criterial" approach preserves precisely the dualistic picture that Wittgenstein, as he has been presented in the present book, is trying to overcome. As Peter Hacker has put it:

> [Wittgenstein's] argument that there must be behavioral criteria for what we call "the inner" was not an attempt to *preserve* that venerable picture by devising a new logical relation between two distinct domains, the one merely bodily behavior and the other consisting of ethereal objects, events and processes in the mind. On the contrary, he aimed to extirpate that very conception.
>
> (Hacker 1996, 254)

In addition, the criterial account seems to presuppose that it is Wittgenstein's agenda to refute other minds skepticism – to *prove* that we *can* have knowledge of that which the skeptic says we can only speculate about ("criteria" being the magical notion that accomplishes this). I believe this is the wrong way of construing Wittgenstein's intentions. As I will show later in this chapter (see pp. 132–8), Wittgenstein tries to stay faithful to the intuitions underlying the views of both the skeptic and her opponent – the intuitions I outlined at the beginning of this chapter (see pp. 120–1). We need an account of how our supposedly "private" and "inner" lives reach out into the social world; but one that remains sensitive to the genuine insights that tempt us to speak of the mental as "inner" or "private." Such sensitivity is incompatible with the ambition of refuting the skeptic.[4]

So instead of concentrating on what Wittgenstein says about criteria, I suggest that a more promising approach is to conceive of the human body and human bodily behavior as *expressive* of mind. The notion of "expression" is both intended to convey something more than a merely contingent relation between mind and body and to reflect a certain nonaccessibility of the mental lives of others. (My task will be, among other things, to make it plausible that these two things are not contradictory.) Developing such an expressive account, to put it in very simple terms, means bringing mind and body much closer to each other than in the Cartesian scenario, or, better, undermining the Cartesian split between mind and body from the outset. And this involves that we rethink not only the notion of mind, but also that of body. If we are to make sense of the idea, *pace* the beetle model, that the mental stretches many arms out to our social lives, then we have to give up the idea of the body as some merely mechanical appendix to the mind. To put it differently, we have to stop viewing the corpse as the paradigm of the human body[5] and focus instead on the lived and living body: the body of our loved one and the body of the person we greet in the street.

It involves a fundamental misunderstanding of expression to view it as an effect brought about by the presence of some purely "inner" state or process (cf. LW I, § 947).[6] Nor, more generally, should we understand the expression of (e.g.) anger as something distinct from the anger itself, as Sartre does in the following passage: "These frowns, this redness, this stammering, this slight trembling of the hands, these downcast looks which seem at once timid and threatening – these do not *express* anger; they *are* the anger" (BN, 346). Rather, we should understand "expression" as a term for the *way in which* the anger is manifest in the redness, the frowns, etc. That is, we must approach expression in the light of the discussions of intentionality and embodiment that we offered in Chapters 2 and 3. In the former I argued that to be a subject of experience is not be in possession of a special realm of private items, but rather to be "involved with the world" in a characteristic way. In the latter I tried to show that embodiment, bodily presence in the world, is essential to this world-involvement. I mentioned at one point that Heidegger conceives of subjectivity as itself essentially visible in making visible the world, without, however, providing much of an account of how these things hang together. My claim, now, is that the phenomenon of expression provides a very natural way of understanding the point Heidegger wants to make. Expression is the concrete way in which our intentional world-involvement, our "making-the-world-visible," itself becomes "visible." What we express may be called an "inner life" as long as we understand this life as inherently involved with other people and the world. As Levinas writes somewhere, "[w]e are not the subject of the world and a part of the world from two different points of view; in expression we are subject and part at once. To perceive [for example] is both to receive and to express" (CPP, 82).

As we attempt to develop further the structure of expression, the later Wittgenstein can supply some good material for the discussion. Consider the following familiar passages:

> "We *see* emotion." – As opposed to what? – We do not see facial contortions and *make the inference* that he is feeling joy, grief, boredom. We describe a face immediately as sad, radiant, bored, even when we are unable to give any other description of the features. – Grief, one would like to say, is personified in the face.
> (RPP II, § 570; cf. Z, § 225)

> Consciousness in another's face. Look into someone else's face, and see the consciousness in it, and a particular *shade* of consciousness. You see on it, in it, joy, indifference, interest, excitement, torpor, and so on. The light in other people's faces. Do you look into *yourself* in order to recognize the fury in *his* face? It is there as clearly as in your own breast.
> (Z, § 220; RPP I, § 927; cf. LW I, § 769)

Of course, part of what Wittgenstein is doing here is to combat the Cartesian conception. This is clearly why he rejects the inferential model and the suggestion that one has to look "into" oneself and notice one's own feeling of anger in order to establish that another is angry. But something else is going on as well. Wittgenstein almost poetically refers to "the light in other people's faces" and suggests that grief is something that can be "personified in the face." Grief, joy, anger, agony, and so forth are just as obviously present in the face of another person as in one's own breast, he says. Clearly, this involves a picture of the body that is quite different from the way the proponents of the beetle model would construe the external appearance and behavior of a person. The face, in fact the whole body of a human being, is not some mere material thing, and its movements not mere material movements, according to Wittgenstein. Rather, the bodily behavior of the other subject is itself, as it were, soaked with the meaning of mind:

> But what if I said that by facial exp[ression] of shame I meant what you mean by 'the fac[ial] exp[ression] + the feeling', unless I explicitly

distinguish between genuine and simulated fac[ial] expressions? It is, I think, misleading to describe the genuine expression as a *sum* of the expression and something else, though it is just as misleading [...] if we say that the genuine expression is a particular behavior and nothing besides.

(PO, 263)

The genuine expression is not a sum of something inner ("a beetle") and something outer (certain facial contortions). Rather, the joy, shame, or agony is simply what is, under suitable circumstances, expressed in the face. This not only pulls the "body" closer to the "mind"; it also drags the "mind" or the "mental" out into the body. Thus Wittgenstein emphasizes that we *see* in and through the facial expressions of others their mental lives, or at least part of their mental lives.

Naturally, Wittgenstein would be the first to stress that some caution is called for here. Not everything that we would classify as having to do with subjectivity or the mind finds expression in the same way. In fact, one should not assume that everything mental has characteristic expressions at all. Pain does seem to have characteristic expressions (facial as well as more broadly behavioral); joy likewise (especially facial); but what about such things as nostalgia, thinking, and knowing? Nostalgia presumably cannot be distinguished from, say, sadness if one only looks at a momentary facial expression. But once a person's expressive behavior and utterances are observed over a longer stretch of time one might well be able to make such a distinction. Whether I am thinking about last year's summer vacation or this year's, on the other hand, is something that seems not to find expression at all; and no one observing me ever so closely during my summer holidays would know whether I think Borges is a greater writer than Gabriel García Márquez (cf. RPP I, § 568). Yet there can be a characteristic expression of "thinking of something pleasurable"; and there certainly are a number of characteristic patterns of "being lost in thought." Likewise, while there is no telling whether I know the name of the capital of Mongolia as long as I keep quiet about it, my "knowing" that another is lying might be characteristically expressed in my face. The list can be extended infinitely, and the lesson to learn from all this, according to Wittgenstein, is that we should not lump all "mental" phenomena together and think that they are alike in all important respects. Our mental concepts are "widely branched" and the phenomena are widely dispersed (Z, § 110).

One important difference, ignored in the examples I have just given, concerns the difference between occurrent mental phenomena, which have a beginning and an end (e.g. sensations, perceptions, and emotions), and phenomena that seem rather to be dispositional in nature (e.g. understanding, abilities, beliefs, and knowledge), that is, phenomena that are "not interrupted by a break in consciousness or a shift in attention" (RPP II, § 45). But important in this context is that these dispositions, too, can, under suitable circumstances, be expressed (linguistically and otherwise). Even more importantly, as the examples given above should make clear, it would be a mistake to assume that only feelings and sensations, and not "cognitive" mental phenomena, find expression in (nonlinguistic) behavior. To mention just one simple example that we have already discussed, we see the eye of another human being as something that *looks*.

So what should be gained from all this, according to Wittgenstein, is the insight that the mental life of another is something that we can have cognitive access to; something that, under suitable circumstances, in various different ways and with varying degrees of certainty, can be directly seen in the facial and behavioral expressions of other persons. To use a familiar remark from the *Philosophical Investigations*, our perceptions of the mental state of another – when things go well – "do not stop anywhere short of the fact" itself (cf. PI, § 95).

Some, however, have found that this is moving too far in the direction of behaviorism. It might be apt as "a warning" against Cartesianism to say that we "see" the joys and pains of others, but it is nevertheless misleading insofar as a person's pain is different from the behavior that expresses it. Whereas one can "observe *that A* has toothache," one can "not see or hear his toothache," Peter Hacker argues (Hacker 1997, 313).[7] As another commentator emphasizes, "what I see is always behavior, not pain" (Rudd 2003, 121), and thus "[t]here remains a gap" between what I can see and the mental life of another (ibid.). Of course the suggestion that a toothache, as opposed to the fact *that* someone has a toothache, is something one might "see," just as one sees a wound or a cavity, is a very strange one indeed. And if we are pressed on this point we will undoubtedly feel inclined to admit that we do not really "see" the pain *itself*. It would seem right, then, to try to articulate the way that the pains and other mental states of others reach out into our social lives in such a way as to avoid the strong claim that our perceptual experiences can reach these mental states themselves.

But let us look more carefully at what is going on here. There are two problematic aspects to Hacker and Rudd's objection. First, when Hacker and Rudd insist on the difference between my seeing *that* someone is in pain or is angry and my seeing the pain or anger *itself*, what contrast are they actually highlighting? Granted that *I* do not see the other's pain, does *she* then see her pain? Perhaps Cartesians would be inclined to answer affirmatively; but what if we reverse the case? Do I "see," in some special "inner" sense of the word, my own toothache when I am suffering from it, for instance? Most would agree that this would be a very strange claim, and it is clearly at odds with Wittgenstein's view. Remember his remarks about "knowing" one's own pain: "It can't be said of me at all (except perhaps as a joke) that I *know* I am in pain. What is it supposed to mean – except perhaps that I *am* in pain?" (PI, § 246; cf. BB, 55). Wittgenstein, as we know by now, is strongly opposed to the inner observation model of our (default) relation to our own lives.[8]

The contrast, then, between my being able only to see *that* another is angry and her ability to "see" (or intuit, introspect) the anger itself seems only to make sense on the basis of something like the beetle model. It is on this model that there remains a gap between the thing (pain, anger, joy) itself and that which I can see; it is on this model that I always see only behavior and not pain. Thus it seems as if at least Rudd is lapsing into conceiving of pains as "inner objects" that only one person can see.[9] The pain itself is the "unpleasant sensation considered just as such" (G. Strawson 1994, 215), and the expression is then merely a link between the inner (that I don't see but the other does see) and the outer (that can be described in purely physical terms). But that seems wrong,[10] and it is certainly not Wittgenstein's view:

> But that which is in him, how can I see it? Between his experience and me there is always the expression!
> Here is the picture: He sees it immediately, I only mediately. But that's not the way it is. He doesn't see something and describe it to us.
> (LW II, 92; cf. PO, 288; RPP II, § 177)

Second, one might find that Hacker and Rudd's objection constitutes a good example of philosophical hairsplitting. After all, the reason why we notice and care about the toothaches of other persons is that we care about *other persons* (cf. Cockburn 1990, 67–68). That is, we care about how they are doing, what they are feeling, and so forth. And it seems that not even the objectors want to deny that we have some kind of perceptual access to how others "are doing"; indeed, they happily grant that we can see *that* another is feeling this or that. So what is the importance of the distinction they are pushing for?

I think it is fairly clear what motivates even philosophers sympathetic towards Wittgenstein to make such a distinction. It seems that denying the existence of a "gap" between expression and mind means violating the Cartesian intuition that there is a sense in which the other's mental life escapes us. If I see, in and through the other person's facial (and other) expressions, her pain, shame, and anger *as such*, then it seems no room is left for her transcendence. Such an impression is enhanced when one looks at how Wittgenstein proposes to deal with the notions of "mind" and "body." Recognizing that it makes little sense to say that it is the body that feels pain, Wittgenstein is also reluctant to say that it is the soul or the mind (PI, §§ 286, 573). He seems critical of both these notions, instead emphasizing that it is a "living human being" that has sensations, sees things, and is conscious (PI, § 281). But a human being, surely, is something that is present "out there" in the world; something extended, tangible, vulnerable, and perceivable. Emphasizing this notion, it seems, is to privilege public accessibility over privacy, and embodiment over mindedness. This seems to be confirmed by the fact that Wittgenstein often emphasizes that we have no interest in what goes on "inside" other persons (RPP II, § 561; LW II, 33, 68). Wittgenstein seems, in other words, to be guilty of some sort of "hostility to the doctrine of privacy," as P. F. Strawson (1966, 62) once claimed.

There is every reason to share the worry that an unbridled anti-Cartesian account may vitiate an important intuition.[11] But the beetle model, with its inventory of "gaps," "inner realms," and "private, singly observable things" (cf. Wisdom 1968, 216), is not the thing to opt for in order to alleviate that worry. Rather, the question we must ask is whether there isn't a way of staying faithful to the intuition in question without lapsing into the Cartesian position we seem to have overcome. The answer, I think, is affirmative. What we should do is look, once again, at what expression is and what it does.

Expression: transcendence without gaps

Expression is essentially nonstatic. A completely static face would not be an expressive face.[12] It is not an objection to this that we see painted or photographed faces as expressive, for these have a derived expressiveness; and when we look at a good photograph of a face we often feel that it could start to speak or change expression at any moment. If someone moved around in the world with a completely fixed "expression" (*any* completely fixed expression) we would not perceive her as expressing anything (cf. Z, § 527).[13] Expression only exists "in the play of the features," as Wittgenstein says (RPP II, § 356). But it is not just the limitless variability that makes expression what it is. Rather, the play of expression is *qualitatively* different from the (endlessly variable) movements of objects in space, Wittgenstein suggests (PI, § 284).

But what is the special quality of expression? Wittgenstein again provides us with an important clue. Consider what he says in one of his sets of remarks on the "philosophy of psychology," repeating his contention that I see emotions in the face of the other person, and at the same time introducing a quite different point:

> In general I do not surmise fear in him – I *see* it. I do not feel that I am deducing the probable existence of something inside from something outside; rather it is as if the human face were in a way translucent and that I were seeing it not in reflected light but rather in its own.
>
> (RPP II, § 170)

This is not the only place where Wittgenstein speaks of the "light" in the human face (cf. Z, § 220, quoted on p. 128). But in the present passage he is more specific. What is special about the "light" of the human face is that it is not something coming from the outside, something that the face merely reflects. Rather, the face emits "its own light," he says. But what might that mean? I think we can get a clearer picture of what Wittgenstein is hinting at if we compare his remarks with some of Levinas' ideas.

The play of expression 133

As we know, a distinctive feature of the philosophy of Levinas is the concern with the preservation of and respect for the alterity and separateness of the other person. According to Levinas, the mainstream of Western philosophy has generally failed to appreciate the fact that there is, and must be, a dimension of the other person that essentially eludes my cognitive grasp.[14] Throughout the centuries, philosophers have overlooked, ignored, or actively attempted to do away with this dimension, Levinas thinks, and he sees it as part of his task to bring a strong notion of this separateness or "transcendence" back into Western philosophy (cf. TI, 42–48).

All of this is clearly in line with what I have identified as one of the intuitions that underlie Cartesian dualism. Now, interestingly, Levinas tries to articulate the other's "transcendence" by emphasizing the very same phenomenon that interests Wittgenstein, namely the expressiveness of the human face. In order to do this, however, one would think Levinas must offer an interpretation of expression that differs fundamentally from that of Wittgenstein. Certain passages of Levinas' book *Totality and Infinity* seem to confirm this assumption: "The presentation of the face, expression, does not disclose an inward world previously closed, adding thus a new region to comprehend," he writes (TI, 212). "Expression does not consist in *giving* us the Other's interiority" (ibid., 202). But on the other hand Levinas also emphasizes that the face must not be conceived of as something outer that "hides" an inner "thing itself" (CPP, 102). This would seem to indicate that his point cannot be reduced to the claim that there is still a gap between the other's facial expressions and her inner life. Strange as it may seem at first sight, the peculiar nonrevelation of facial expression precisely has to do with the way the face appears "in its own light," as Wittgenstein says. In Levinas' somewhat enigmatic words:

> The face of the Other at each moment destroys and overflows the plastic image it leaves me, the idea existing to my own measure and to the measure of its *ideatum* – the adequate idea. It does not manifest itself by these qualities, but *kath' auto*. It *expresses itself*.
>
> (TI, 51)

The contrast that Levinas and Wittgenstein have in mind here is the contrast between the human face and any kind of object. A face appears in its own light. In contrast, "[o]bjects have no light of their own; they receive a borrowed light" (TI, 74), as Levinas puts it. Here we can reconfirm our claim that the Cartesian and the behaviorist actually share an important assumption – one that Levinas and Wittgenstein are both bent on overcoming. Cartesians and behaviorists, as we have already seen in Chapter 1, conceive of the mind – whether one's own or the mind of another – as object-like in an important sense. They conceive of the mental as something that simply occurs or "just stands there." Levinas and Wittgenstein disagree completely with this. *Pace* the behaviorist, another's mental life does not *lie* open to view. Objects "lie" open to view or "stand there," passively, awaiting inspection. But another's mental life does not present itself in such a way. On the contrary, it expresses itself, that is, it unfolds in a peculiarly personal dynamic that does not have me at its source. And *pace* the Cartesian, nothing is hidden either. The idea of something hidden from view is, once again, the idea of a realm of objects on display, just not on display for everyone; and this retains the problematic idea.

Thus, expression, on Wittgenstein and Levinas' view, is not some third term bridging the gap between inner state and external behavior, but rather the direct presentation of the mental life of another. Yet it is crucial to realize that the mental life of another is not some sphere of "inner" objects somehow displayed to my view – just as it cannot be reduced to external objects lying open to view. It is not something "lying" or "standing" there at all; it is nothing "present-at-hand." On the contrary, the other's mental life is something that, unlike any object, presents *itself*, expresses *itself*, that is, it appears as an independent and inalienable source of meaning (cf. TI, 51). On such an "expressive" model, in contrast to a beetle model, the inaccessibility or "transcendence" of the other person is not due to the fact that she has introspective access to private entities that I cannot perceive. Rather, her inaccessibility has to do with the circumstance that *she* is the one expressing herself, being expressed, or (perhaps better) *living expressively*, in her face; because she thereby always retains the potential to overturn – whether deliberately or inadvertently – every conviction I form of her.

Cartesians, however, will be inclined to make some objections at this point. Let me consider two such objections. First, some might argue that the uncertainty and doubt that I have been discussing precisely reflect the deeper fact that the other's mental life belongs to some private region that is not directly experientially accessible to me. John Wisdom writes:

> The peculiarity of the soul is not that it is visible to none but that it is visible only to one. Unless we understand this we cannot understand why people have so persistently clung to the model for the logic of the soul which gives rise to skepticism not only about the mental acts of others but also about their aches and pains, feelings of quickened heart beats, sensations as of voices, daggers, snakes.
>
> (Wisdom 1968, 237)

Our doubts about the true thoughts, feelings, or desires of the other surely concern something going on "inside" her, rather than her overt behavior (the latter, the objectors might also suspect, is what I have simply glossed by speaking of expression instead). My discussion of the beetle in the box should make it clear that I think some of this is all right as far as it goes (cf. LW II, 70). But we must be careful about how we, as Wittgenstein would say, "apply the picture" of "something going on inside a person."

According to Wittgenstein and Levinas, my doubts concerning her mental life have nothing to do with certain entities that I will never be able to see.[15] Thoughts, feelings, and desires are things that the other expresses and that play a number of important roles in our public lives; roles that could not be filled by beetles in boxes. So what Wisdom's objection should draw our attention to is, rather, the fact that there is a fundamental difference between first-person and third/second-person types of access to a person's mental life. As we have seen, Wittgenstein does not make the behaviorist mistake of arguing that "[t]he sorts of things that I can find out about myself are the same as the sorts of things that I can find out about other people, and the methods of finding them out are much the same" (Ryle 2000, 149).[16] Rather, he is concerned to emphasize the asymmetry between first-person and third-person types of access to the mind, though to be sure not as one of direct versus indirect types of access, nor indeed as a difference between firsthand knowledge and mere guesswork. What we have here, according to Wittgenstein, are simply two kinds of access that are essentially different; but one need not be epistemically superior to the other. Wittgenstein is clear about this:

> The characteristic sign of the mental seems to be that one has to guess at it in someone else using external clues and is only *acquainted* with it from one's own case.
> But when closer reflection causes this view to go up in smoke, then what turns out is not that the inner is something outer, but that "outer" and "inner" now no longer count as properties of evidence.
> (LW II, 61–62)

An alternative version of the last portion reads: "but for us direct inner and indirect outer evidence no longer exist" (ibid., 62). The point, then, is not to embrace behaviorism in exchange for Cartesianism, but to prevent the Cartesian move from different kinds of access to different types of evidence (with fundamentally different epistemic status). According to Wittgenstein, "[m]y thoughts are not hidden from [the other], but are just open to him in a different *way* than they are to me" (LW II, 34–35). It is not as if I had some infallible perceptual access to my own mind; that is not the reason why others ask *me* where it hurts when I'm in pain. Rather, they ask me because I am the one *who is in pain* (cf. PI, § 246). Putting the point in this way preserves an essential difference between being oneself in pain and observing the suffering of another; but at the same time it does not tempt us to cash out this difference in terms of some unique transparency of the mind to itself. This disarms the fundamental Cartesian idea that the intersubjective asymmetry reflects the essential isolation of the individual, inner "mind." For, according to Wittgenstein and Levinas, this is simply putting the cart before the horse. As Wittgenstein puts it, the relation between "inner" and "outer" is just a "picture-like representation" of the intersubjective asymmetry, and precisely not some metaphysical fact that *explains* the asymmetry (LW II, 68).

In fact, we can say more about the difference between these two "types of access," and this will reveal that what the Cartesian demands of us verges on a type of incoherence that we have already encountered. When another expresses sadness or joy she is herself the source of the expressed meaning; it is *her* feeling that is being expressed rather than mine. Presumably no one would disagree that there is a fundamental difference between *feeling* sad and observing the sadness of others (although such observations often call up emotional responses in oneself). And the observation of the sadness of others does leave room for doubts and uncertainties that do not arise concerning one's own feelings when one has them. But, as we saw in Chapter 5, it is crucial to realize that this does not, *pace* the Cartesian, indicate an imperfection or a defect in our access to the mental lives of others. For anything that would remedy such a supposed defect would *eo ipso* remove the alterity or transcendence of the other and thus make sociality a mere illusion. To evade the latter predicament obviously involves a commitment to the existence of an essential inaccessibility with regard to other minds. There are dimensions of the other's mental life that, because they are tied to her first-person perspective, are given to me in a way so different from the way they are given to her that they give the impression of being completely beyond my reach. I cannot know precisely *what it is like* for her to smell freshly brewed coffee or watch a funny movie.[17] I can often not know *what* she is thinking, for instance, although I can tell that she is caught up in thoughts, concentrating "on something," etc. But, as Wittgenstein says, these kinds of uncertainties are *constitutional* uncertainties (RPP II, § 657); they belong to the rules of the game, so to speak – the game of experiencing others *as others*.

Yet Cartesians will probably not be convinced by this. One thing they are likely to insist on is that we should not forget the twin possibilities of expressing things one does not feel (think, desire, etc.) and not expressing the thoughts, desires, pains, etc. that one does experience. Surely it is not just that the other – in and through her expressive manifestations – retains the ability to shock me; in addition, she has the ability to hide, in one way or the other, her mental life from me. One might feel that these possibilities have not received due attention in my account. And one might suspect that the reason why is that they do not sit well with the "expressive model" that I have outlined. What I have said about expression seems well suited to emphasize the unpredictability of the other person. Clearly, however, there is much more to the transcendence of the other than that. Prediction, for one thing, refers to the future. And the uncertainties I might experience concerning another's mental states do not only, or primarily, concern her future expressions and actions, but rather her thoughts, intentions, feelings, etc. *here and now*. Besides, I might develop the ability to predict a person's actions and responses with great accuracy and still feel that I do not really understand the person – that I still have no idea what she is feeling, why she says what she says, and so on (cf. LW I, § 192).

There is certainly something right in this objection. Again, however, we must be wary of the kind of pictures that we are working with and how we apply them:

> But it is *not* true that uncertainty in recognizing his irritation (for instance) is simply uncertainty about his future behavior. [...] So sometimes he is transparent, as it were, and sometimes he isn't. And it is misleading to think of the real irritation as a facial expression of an *inner* face, so to speak, such that this facial expression is defined completely clearly, and that it is only the outer face that makes it uncertain whether the soul really has this expression.
>
> (LW II, 70)

I think this passage contains more than one important point. First, it documents that Wittgenstein realizes that our uncertainty regarding the feelings (etc.) of others does not merely concern their future behavior. Second, the passage pinpoints the way in which we are tempted to make sense of what is going on in such a situation of uncertainty: namely as a question of the relation between an "outer expression" and an "inner" one. But is that the way it is? I think Wittgenstein is right to question this picture. The expression of irritation (angry glances, impatient movements and remarks, etc.) is the very *picture* of irritation; that is, when we feel inclined to make deception intelligible by driving a wedge between the (outer) expression and something inner, the natural way to do so is by imagining something like "inner glances," "inner impatient movements," and so forth. This indicates the central position that expression has in our lives. Third, however, it is also misleading, since we cannot separate feeling and expression in this way. To think that we can is to imagine that the "inner feeling" is completely clearly defined in isolation from any outward expression (to subscribe to the beetle model, in other words). Yet, paradoxically, the very way we try to conceive of and imagine this isolated "inner feeling" contains an essential reference to that (viz. expression) which we wanted to dispense with.

Thus, Wittgenstein and Levinas would ultimately argue that the possibilities of deception presuppose that mental life is originally something that is expressed:

> I can perhaps even imagine (though it is not easy) that each of the people whom I see in the street is in frightful pain, but is artfully concealing it. And it is important that I have to imagine an artful concealment here. That I do not simply say to myself: "Well, his soul is in pain: but what has that to do with his body?" or "After all it need not shew in his body!"
>
> (PI, § 391)

The hunger of the dog is visible in its behavior in a way that simply does not allow for the possibility of deception; the happy smile of the baby is there, as the very picture of joy, before honesty and deception have any foothold.[18] Deception, as Wittgenstein argues, can find a place only in a fairly complicated life-form (LW I, §§ 859–69). It is something we learn, and might be more or less good at, whereas some primitive expressions are there from very early on (pain, joy, hunger, anger; a little later, perhaps, confusion, amusement, etc.).

Moreover, the uncertainties that deception makes room for presuppose both that others are minded human beings *and* that their inner lives can, in suitable circumstances, be evident to me. As Wittgenstein says, "[t]hat an actor can represent grief shows the uncertainty of evidence, but that he can represent *grief* also shows the reality of evidence" (LW II, 67). That is, the existence of these uncertainties presupposes that feelings are something that we *express* and thereby make visible to others. Unless grief had characteristic expressions, one could hardly feign *it*.[19] In Levinas' words, "deceit and veracity already presuppose the absolute authenticity of the face [...] whose epiphany itself is somehow a word of honor" (TI, 202). It is only because human behavior in general, and facial expression in particular, presents "authentically" the mental life of human beings that deception becomes possible. If there were just a contingent relation between expression and feeling, why would anyone ever be fooled (cf. LW II, 35–36)?

Conclusion

Now we should be able to see how the "expressive model" can help us overcome the Cartesian position without jeopardizing the fundamental "Cartesian" intuition. The Cartesian ignores a crucial distinction between *degree* of access, certainty, evidence, etc. and *kind* of access. The Cartesian thinks the counterpart to my possible uncertainty regarding the mental states of another is her certainty, but precisely this is wrong. For I might be as certain about her mental states as is humanly possible, and still there would be a fundamental difference between us (LW I, § 963). It is quite possible to achieve as high a degree of certainty concerning another's mental states as about anything else in life, but clearly the kind of access remains different. I could not possibly occupy the other's perspective on the world, for then it would be my perspective. What I *can* (often) do, however, is to see, in and through her expressions, that she is feeling good, planning mischief, or whatever. But these expressions have her at their source, and they are therefore at the same time a vivid testimony to the fragility of my hold on her. Levinas tries to capture this point by emphasizing how the appearance of another person is a *personal* appearance in quite a different sense than the appearance of rocks, trees, and chairs:

In contradistinction to plastic manifestation or disclosure, which manifests something *as* something, and in which the disclosed renounces its originality, its hitherto unpublished existence, in expression the manifestation and the manifested coincide; the manifested attends its own manifestation and hence remains exterior to every image one would retain of it, presents itself in the sense that we say of someone that he presents himself by stating his name, which permits evoking him, even though he remains always the source of his own presence.

(TI, 296)

This passage is crucial to the argument I have tried to make in this chapter. One of the things it contains is the suggestion that expressing oneself is in a sense being extremely present. When the other person expresses herself she attends her own manifestation. An object does nothing of the kind. There is no one there to attend its manifestation; it lies passively open to view. The basic idea resonates, I think, with a point Stanley Cavell makes in the monumental final chapter of *The Claim of Reason*. Discussing the separateness of human beings (what I have spoken of under the rubrics of inaccessibility and transcendence), Cavell remarks that there is a sense in which the soul or mind of another *is* veiled or hidden. As he explains,

the soul may be hidden not because the body essentially conceals it but because it essentially reveals it. The soul may be invisible to us the way something absolutely present may be invisible to us. [...] So we might say: What hides the mind is not the body but the mind itself.

(Cavell 1979, 369)

What may be lacking or underexposed in Cavell's account, however, is the specifically *personal* nature of this "absolute presence" of the mind (cf. CPP, 20). Precisely because the other person, through expressing herself, is *personally present* at her own manifestation, as the dynamic source of that manifestation, all the indicators of an essential inaccessibility are there. Such personal presence, then, is the key to understanding how both of the intuitions mentioned in the introduction to this chapter can be accommodated (see pp. 120–1). It can account for both the other's accessibility and her strange inaccessibility. It is not that her mental life is hidden from me, but precisely that she *expresses* it that reveals both her inner life and the fact that it nevertheless eludes my grasp in an important sense. For, as expressed to me, it is precisely presented as her life, and not mine.[20]

Before concluding, let me emphasize that none of what I have said should be taken to imply that the other, being at "the source" of her expressions, being "personally present," and so forth, is completely transparent to herself and in complete control of her expressions. Neither is true. If my mental life is essentially something expressed, it can never be completely disclosed to me, and others may be in a better position than I am to tell what, for

140 *The play of expression*

example, my feelings and motives are on certain occasions. And controlling our expressions (to pick a somewhat unlucky phrase),[21] as most of us experience from time to time, can be rather difficult; yet our "personal presence" at least accounts for the possibility of controlling them. These consequences follow immediately from my account of expression. However, there is a further complication that must be noted. Expression is, of course, less purely personal than it would seem from the account presented here. Our expressions of feelings and emotions are culturally transmitted to us, and some may vary quite extensively from culture to culture. We do not create our own expressive patterns; we learn them as we are initiated into what Wittgenstein calls a life-form.[22] And those patterns of expression that appear to be innate rather than culturally transmitted (the smile of joy, the cry of pain, etc.) are, of course, not our personal creation either. And in any case, as Wittgenstein has pointed out, they are later supplemented and to some extent replaced by linguistic expressions ("It hurts!"). So there is a clear sense in which the other person is *not* the "source" of her own expressions. But all this notwithstanding, every expression in the face of another, being the expression of *another's mental life*, is also a creative event that reveals an alien source of meaning; a source that is extremely present, yet because of the nature of its personal presence remains beyond my grasp.[23]

So in this way our everyday experience of others reaches the other subjectivities themselves, without divesting them of their alterity. We can have all the knowledge of other minds that philosophers have ever wanted. But, being founded on expression, this knowledge nevertheless remains of such a character as to preserve "the otherness of others." Expression accomplishes both things at once. Expression, as Levinas memorably puts it, is what "at once gives and conceals the Other" (Levinas 1987, 78–79).

8 Responding to faces

> Look at your patients more closely as human beings in trouble [...]. I think in some sense you don't look at people's faces closely enough.
> (Wittgenstein, quoted in Drury 1984, 96)

Introduction

I want to begin this chapter by briefly returning to a remark of Wittgenstein's that, because of its behaviorist ring, has invited dissent from some readers. In the *Philosophical Investigations*, Wittgenstein rejects the idea that I "am certain" that others are minded, and he claims that my relation to another person is based on an "attitude towards a soul" rather than an opinion to the effect that the other has a soul (PI, 178). Referring to this passage, Kripke remarks that it "sounds much too behavioristic for me. I personally would like to think that anyone who does not think of me as conscious is wrong about the facts, not simply 'unfortunate', or 'evil', or even 'monstrous' or 'inhuman', in his 'attitude'" (Kripke 1982, 48–49). Surely, that others are minded is a *fact* that we ought to know about (and be *certain* about) rather than a mere projection of our feelings or attitudes. Shouldn't we, then, like Kripke, react with suspicion to any philosopher who calls such important truths into question?

I think there is an important insight behind Wittgenstein's provocative remarks, however. To see what I mean, recall Wittgenstein's contention that philosophical work is "work on oneself," on "how one sees things" (CV, 24). If we take this contention seriously, the purpose of the remark we began with cannot be to contest any obvious facts, but must rather be to get us to see certain things differently. What, then, is it about our approach to other minds that Wittgenstein is trying to get us to pay attention to? It must be something about how we, *as philosophers*, view things; something about how Kripke, for example, views things. Detectable in Kripke's response to Wittgenstein's remark, I want to suggest, is a tendency to think that "knowledge of facts" is somehow superior to, or more important than, "attitudes." But from one very natural point of view, it is more important, indeed *far* more important, whether a person is "evil," "monstrous," or "inhuman" in her "attitude" towards others than whether she is right or wrong about certain facts about others. (A kind and generous professed "solipsist" would in obvious ways be preferable to a sadist with perfect knowledge of the mental lives of others.) Could Kripke's insistence on the superiority of "knowledge of facts" be the symptom of a philosophical prejudice in favor of a purely theoretical viewpoint on questions concerning intersubjectivity?

If so, then it is a prejudice so deeply ingrained in our philosophical attitude to the theme of intersubjectivity as to be almost invisible to us. It seems natural to view the question of intersubjectivity or other minds as a fundamentally theoretical question: one that concerns our possible "knowledge" of certain "inner" (or possibly "outer") "facts." We think that before emotional responses and moral attitudes to others can make any sense we must have recognized these others as other minds. First we must establish that here is another person and that this person is in pain, say, and only then can we pity her and feel obligated to relieve her of her pain. This way of thinking inspires the way we rank the philosophical issues. That is, we are inclined to consider social emotions and moral attitudes secondary philosophical topics that presuppose a satisfactory resolution of primary questions of a more theoretical nature. First we have to provide an account of how one can have any knowledge of the existence of others, and of their mental states, and only then can questions arise as to how such others are to be treated.

I think Wittgenstein disagrees with these notions, evident as they may appear to be, and that he is trying to get us to recognize a prejudice at work in them. It is not right to say that sympathy and pity, for example, are emotional responses based on the prior observation or conviction that others are suffering. Rather, "[p]ity, one may say, is [itself] a form of conviction that someone else is in pain" (PI, § 287). More generally, the life of another human being is something "I (have to) *respond* to [...], or refuse to respond [to]. It calls upon me; it calls me out. I have to acknowledge it" (Cavell 1979, 84). It is fundamentally misguided, according to Wittgenstein, to view this call or demand for acknowledgment as something secondary, something founded on an original act of pure, neutral cognition. And it is equally misguided to think that as philosophers we can isolate a neutral epistemological question concerning such cognition from supposedly secondary questions concerning moral attitudes and responses.

If these ideas are on the right track, then an account of our relations to other minds cannot afford to ignore the ways in which these relations are intertwined with moral attitudes and responses.[1] Consequently, our account of Wittgenstein's thoughts on intersubjectivity cannot be concluded before we have said something about these issues. This is the task of the present chapter.

Moral phenomenology

It is not easy to provide a well-founded characterization of the ethical views of someone who writes so little on moral issues as does the later Wittgenstein. The sporadic remarks of an ethical nature that we encounter in manuscripts (most of them posthumously collected in *Culture and Value*) and in conversations recorded by students and friends do not seem to add up to a coherent full-blown moral philosophy. Presumably, this is because Wittgenstein never intended them to add up to anything of that sort. In fact, he impatiently dismissed the standard questions of ethics (and metaethics): "I think it is definitely important to put an end to all the claptrap about ethics – whether intuitive knowledge exists, whether values exist, whether the good is definable" (Wittgenstein 1979a, 68–69). Nevertheless, from the beginning of his philosophical itinerary until the end of his life Wittgenstein retained a keen interest in moral issues.[2] For him, being a good person (a "human being," as he would say) was a matter of the greatest importance – and the greatest difficulty. Toward the end of his life he would write despairingly of human beings as "poison" for one another, as "*all* wicked" (CV, 98). And he did not exclude himself from this characterization. Little more than a month before his death, he wrote: "God may say to me: 'I am judging you out of your own mouth. You have shuddered with disgust at your own actions when you have seen them in other people'" (CV, 99).

The absence of traditional moral philosophy in Wittgenstein's thought is thus not an absence of ethical concerns and considerations. Yet if we consult Wittgenstein for an answer to the question of *how* we are supposed to act, *how* we are supposed to live, we find little more than this: "Let us be human" (CV, 36). This, one is inclined to respond, may be where ethics begins; but it is surely not where it ends. It is not implausible to say that morality, in some sense, can be viewed as an appeal to be "human" (we speak, for example, about "humane" or "humanitarian" deeds, ideals, etc.). But the question is what principles and actions embody this ideal of the "human" – and here it seems Wittgenstein has little to tell us. This is presumably no accident on Wittgenstein's part, but rather has to do with his perspective on philosophical work. According to the *Philosophical Investigations*, our task as philosophers is to "do away with all *explanation*, and [let] description alone [...] take its place" (PI, § 109). So instead of offering theories about meaning, mind, moral action, and so forth, a philosopher working in the Wittgensteinian spirit should stick to describing the various patterns in the weave of human life that these concepts indicate. Applying this maxim to ethics, the philosophical job "does not involve presenting particular moral insights (or would-be insights), but rather consists in clarifying the area of ethics" (Johnston 1989, 24) by way of careful description.

One conception of "moral phenomenology," as the descriptive approach might be termed,[3] is the one we find in Levinas' philosophy. As a phenomenologist Levinas aims to offer descriptions from a first-person point of view. It is arguably common to all the major phenomenologists that they aim to describe the (social, material, practical, etc.) world "from the inside," *as it is experienced* by an agent, perceiver, and so on. That is, *pace* some rather widespread views, phenomenologists do not necessarily, and certainly not primarily, study their own experiences as such, introspectively. On the contrary, they are mainly interested in the world. The crucial point is just that their primary interest pertains not to the world as conceived by natural science, but rather to the world as it appears to us in everyday life. This is precisely the kind of interest underlying Levinas' perspective on morality or "ethics." In the interviews published as *Ethics and Infinity*, Levinas is asked to clarify the ethical "rules" that he is constructing. Levinas answers that he does not see it as his task to define or construct an ethics at all, although he considers it possible that one might use his works to do so. Rather, he sees his own task as that of uncovering the "meaning" of ethics (Levinas 1985, 90).[4] One way of explaining what this means is to say that Levinas is trying to describe ethical "space," just as Merleau-Ponty, say, is trying to describe perceived space. That is, Levinas is posing something like the following question: How does an ethical relation, just as such, without taking into account any sociological or other explanations about the social function of ethics, its historical development, and so forth; how does such a relation look from the "inside," as it were, from the point of view of a person standing in the relation? For Levinas, this kind of study of an ethical relation must be carried out in the first-person mode. An ethical relation, on Levinas' view, is a relation in which an ethical demand is addressed, and the addressee is in each case ultimately *me* – "me who am me and no one else" (OB, 14). Ethics in the Levinasian sense, then, is my personal business, and not something I can study from a safely detached distance. "Ethics is not a spectator sport," as Simon Critchley (2002, 22) has put it.

Levinas' agenda would have been congenial to Wittgenstein. The descriptive philosophical approach advocated by Wittgenstein is not a detached and insensitive observational approach. Rather, it often involves an attempt to understand something (a form of life, for example) from the perspective of a subject or several different subjects (e.g. from the perspective of someone living the kind of life in question). There is of course no reason why one cannot in this way approach phenomena in the life-form that is one's own, the form of life one is oneself involved in. In the words of one commentator, a Wittgensteinian approach to ethics "takes morality at face value and tries to understand it sympathetically, from the inside" (Gleeson 2002, 219). Note that this is different from simply giving expression to one's substantial ethical views. It might be the case that how I experience the moral significance of a particular situation contradicts the moral principles that I otherwise adhere to. I might *experience* a strong pull toward the view that the right thing to do in a particular situation is to tell a lie, although I have built my life around the moral ideal of honesty. To describe such experiences is the aim of Levinas' moral phenomenology; and

I think it is possible to detect a similar agenda in some of Wittgenstein's remarks.

Perhaps it would be better to speak of "proto-ethics" (cf. Llewelyn 1995, 4) instead of "ethics," since the approach we are considering is bound to disappoint those who expect from ethics a complete guide to moral action. Some might indeed question the ethical importance of a Levinasian or Wittgensteinian project. Shouldn't moral philosophy concentrate on providing us with some concrete answers to the real, ethical problems of our day?[5] What use do we have for an "ethics" that does not help us figure out the rights and wrongs concerning euthanasia and human cloning, or at the very least give us some general outline of how to behave? Further, one might perhaps even question the intelligibility and coherence of Levinas' project: Can one really detach the ethical relation from the wider social and historical contexts?[6] Such questions are legitimate and important, of course. But they are questions of an external nature, criticizing the Levinasian or Wittgensteinian perspective from the outside. One may also, out of curiosity if nothing else, try to adopt the perspective in question and see what mutation of "ethics" it leads to.

The latter is what I will attempt to do in the following. Several of the points I aim to establish here follow readily from what we have said in previous chapters. In fact, one may perceive much of what I am going to say as a translation of points previously made into an ethical vocabulary. In making a case for a Wittgensteinian ethical outlook I will rely more heavily on memoirs and personal remarks than has been the case previously in this book. Some philosophers might want to ignore such material on the ground that whatever can be classified as "personal" should be held apart from Wittgenstein's philosophical oeuvre. In the case at hand I must disagree. The reason is simple. Most Wittgensteinian remarks of any ethical interest are found in *Culture and Value*, memoirs, and notes from conversations.[7] To ignore these texts is thus to ignore the richest material we have available to us.

Looking at faces

The idea I wish to pursue in this section, and in the chapter as a whole, is that of a connection between ethics (or "proto-ethics") and what we said in Chapter 7 about mental life as something that is *expressed*. More precisely, I want to argue that the expressive face is – certainly for Levinas, but arguably also for Wittgenstein – an ethical category in that it embodies something like an ethical demand.

To get a first idea of how these things may be connected in a Wittgensteinian context, it is useful to consider the following remarks:

> Look at a stone and imagine it having sensations. – One says to oneself: How could one so much as get the idea of ascribing a *sensation* to a

> *thing*? One might as well ascribe it to a number! – And now look at a wriggling fly and at once these difficulties vanish and pain seems able to get a foothold here, where before everything was, so to speak, too smooth for it.
>
> (PI, § 284)

And read them in conjunction with these remarks:

> It is a help here to remember that it is a primitive reaction to tend, to treat, the part that hurts when someone else is in pain [...].
> But what is the word "primitive" meant to say here? Presumably that this sort of behavior is *pre-linguistic*: that a language-game is based *on it*, that it is the prototype of a way of thinking and not the result of thought.
>
> (Z, §§ 540–41)

> The game doesn't begin with doubting whether someone has a toothache [...]. In its most primitive form it is a reaction to someone's cries and gestures, a reaction of sympathy or something of the sort. We comfort him, try to help him.
>
> (PO, 381)

We see other humans (and animals) as expressive of mental lives. And our perception of such subjective lives is intimately connected with what Wittgenstein calls "primitive reactions" or "prototypes of ways of thinking." We might also speak of our primitive, natural "attitudes" to the expressive manifestation of others, as Wittgenstein himself does when he emphasizes that "[o]ur attitude to what is alive and to what is dead is not the same. All our reactions are different" (PI, § 284). I have stressed repeatedly in this book that to see that another is in pain is not, first and foremost, to record some special ghostly or behavioral fact. My further claim at this point is that seeing that another suffers is more like recognizing that (*ceteris paribus*) *something ought to be done*. That is, unlike the stone that cannot express suffering, joy, or anything else, possibly already the wriggling fly, by allowing pain (though not much else) "to get a foothold," embodies something like an *ethical demand*. This demand becomes infinitely more extensive as well as qualitatively different in the case of human beings, whose expressive lives are infinitely more complex and multifaceted. You cannot hurt a fly's feelings, or show it disrespect, as you can with humans. Nevertheless, some minimal ethical normativity is possibly already in place in the case of the wriggling fly.[8]

To put it differently, the kind of "seeing" that Wittgenstein speaks of in connection with the pain and grief of others is already intimately connected with our attitudes and reactions to others – and with something like moral concerns. However, it is important to view this connection in the right light.

It is not Wittgenstein's view that, for example, we recognize someone as a human being, with the ability to talk, think, feel pain, and so on, and *on the basis of this* respond with concern, pity, etc. That would make our reactions "the result of thought" rather than "a prototype of a way of thinking," and this amounts to putting the cart before the horse, according to Wittgenstein (cf. Z, §§ 541–42). The view I am attributing to Wittgenstein is much more radical. It involves the claim that to respond in a particular way, or to recognize that particular things are demanded of one, is part of what it *means* to recognize someone else as a human being. Such "moral" considerations constitute an essential part of our fundamental "attitude toward a human" (LW II, 38). Cora Diamond expresses this Wittgensteinian point aptly when she writes that having duties to other human beings "is not a consequence of what human beings are, it is not justified by what human beings are: it is itself one of the things which go to build our notion of human beings" (Diamond 1991, 324). As an extension of this point, we can say that it is part of our notion of the suffering of other human beings that it places an ethical demand on us; or, better, that "it is part of the 'grammar' of others' suffering that one is thereby placed under an obligation" (Plant 2005, 89).[9] One may of course refuse to accept this duty or obligation, but not to even notice that one is faced with a demand is "to not recognize suffering *qua* suffering" (ibid.).

The point here is not that there are "ethical properties" just as there are physical properties such as weight, size, and shape. Rather, to perceive an "ethical demand" in a situation is more like a particular way of being "*impressed* by an occurrence" (CV, 51).[10] I think it is natural for us human beings to be impressed in such a way by occurrences involving, for example, the suffering of innocent people. For us, it is close to impossible not to see such situations as presenting us with ethical demands or appeals, in the same way as "I might say 'It is impossible to see the face of this dog & not see that he is alert & full of attention to what his master is doing[']" (CV, 51–52). Not that there is anything necessary about this, of course; obviously, there could be people who are simply not impressed by an occurrence in this way. I think we would view them as "blind" to certain "aspects," as "blind to something important, indeed to what is most important of all" (cf. CV, 31).[11] That is, there would be some to us obvious, immediately given, meaningful features of a situation that they would not recognize in the same immediate way. To pursue the parallel with the dog's facial expression, some autistic persons seem to suffer from a kind of blindness to at least certain "aspects" of this kind (e.g. facial expressions and tones of voice of a certain complexity). They are therefore left with the extremely difficult task of trying to build a meaningful whole out of the objective, intrinsically meaningless data they perceive (a mouth curved in this particular way etc.).[12] Similarly for the "ethically aspect-blind": If they were willing to take part in our moral practices (and there is no special reason to think they would not be), then they would need some elaborate procedure of figuring out what the ethically repugnant or attractive features were in many situations in which most of us would "perceive" those features immediately.

To "normal" subjects, then, perceiving "faces" is not merely a question of gaining cognitive access to the mental lives of others (although it is also that). It is also a question of recognizing the ethical demand that faces express. Something along these lines seems to be the point of a letter Wittgenstein once wrote to his friend Maurice Drury. Drury was at the time a resident doctor in a hospital, but had expressed to Wittgenstein that he was dissatisfied with his own abilities and performance to the point of considering changing occupation. In response to Drury's worries, Wittgenstein writes: "I mainly think this: Don't think about yourself, but think about others, e.g. your patients" (Drury 1984, 95). He goes on to specify this suggestion in the following remarkable way:

> Look at your patients more closely as human beings in trouble and enjoy the opportunity you have to say "good night" to so many people. This alone is a gift from heaven which many people would envy you. And this sort of thing ought to heal your frayed soul, I believe. It won't rest it; but when you are healthily tired you can just take a rest. I think in some sense you don't look at people's faces closely enough.
> (Drury 1984, 96)

Obviously, when Wittgenstein speaks of "looking at people's faces" he does not mean noticing their physical features or anything of that sort. Rather, Wittgenstein links the notion of face with an ethical concern for others as "human beings in trouble."[13] The very last sentence is particularly revealing. Here Wittgenstein seems to indicate that if Drury would look more closely at people's faces he would get his priorities straight and realize the insignificance of his preoccupation with himself and his own abilities. The point, as I read it, is *not* that Drury's own troubles will be *outweighed* by those of others, as if it were a question of comparing needs and predicaments and realizing the insignificance of one's own problems compared with those of most hospitalized people. I think Wittgenstein would be opposed to the view that any such comparison of human agony is morally acceptable. As he says at one point in *Culture and Value*, "*no* distress can be greater than what a single person can suffer," and thus a "cry of distress cannot be greater than that of *one* human being" (CV, 52). If the distress of *one* individual cannot be superseded, then presumably it cannot be outweighed by anything either.[14] Wittgenstein's point in the letter is rather that by looking more "closely" at the faces of others I may realize that in some sense it is required of me that I think about the others and take care of them rather than myself. Not because they are in *greater* trouble than I am, but simply because they are *other human beings* in trouble.

All of this is clearly in line with much of what Levinas says about the face. As I mentioned in Chapter 6, Levinas' notion of the face (*visage*) is intimately connected with the idea of an ethical appeal or demand. Indeed, as I also indicated in that chapter, some commentators have gone as far as denying that what Levinas terms the face is something that can be seen at all. While I have argued that the latter claim is misguided, it is nevertheless true that more or less all that Levinas says about the face indicates that he has chosen to make this a key notion because of the ethical points that can be made intelligible with the help of it. A couple of these points can add valuable substance to the idea of an "ethics of expression" that I am trying to formulate here.

The first thing to note is that in some contexts the concept of "face" seems to be connected with the idea of people as *particular persons*. What I mean is not so much that we often recognize people by their faces. I am more interested in the kind of notion of face that we are working with when we speak, for example, of "putting faces" on the victims of a disaster. One might hear and read so much about third world tragedies that the victims tend to become mere numbers in the statistics. To put "faces" on the victims is to remind oneself that the lives of particular people – of real human beings of flesh and blood – are at stake. This is one important connotation that Levinas wants to evoke with the concept of face: relating to people as a gray ("faceless") mass is not relating ethically to them. To relate to people as mere specimens of *homo sapiens*, anonymous and replaceable, is not to relate to people *as people* (cf. TI, 22). To relate to people as *faces*, by contrast, is to relate to them as particular and in a certain sense irreplaceable human beings. Something akin to this respect for the particular person is, I think, echoed in Wittgenstein's statement that a "cry of distress cannot be greater than that of *one* human being" (CV, 52).

In Chapter 7 I quoted Wittgenstein's remark that the human face appears "not in reflected light but rather in its own" (RPP II, § 170) and connected this with the Levinasian point that an expressive face is something that shakes off or disturbs the characterizations we impose on it, in a way objects do not. Now, this thought, too, can be given an ethical interpretation. The expressive face in a sense suppresses a person's perceivable qualities, as well as the various social categories in the context of which she appears. As Levinas puts it,

> the Other, in the rectitude of his face, is not a character within a context. Ordinarily one is a "character": a professor at the Sorbonne, a Supreme Court justice, son of so-and-so, everything that is in one's passport, the manner of dressing, of presenting oneself. [...] Here, to the contrary, the face is meaning all by itself. You are you.
> (Levinas 1985, 86)

Not that any of these contexts ever really disappears, of course; we never relate to a person as completely devoid of skin color, nationality, sex, and the rest. The point is, rather, an ethical one. The other person has a right to be responded to *as a person*, that is, as someone who cannot be reduced to an exponent of a particular race, sex, nationality, social position, religious, political, or sexual orientation, and so on. Levinas expresses the point by saying that the best way to relate to the other is by not even noticing the color of her eyes (Levinas 1985, 85). This may seem to contradict the claim that a "face" is someone in particular, a concrete other human being; for concrete, particular human beings have a particular skin color, for example. But in fact there is no contradiction, since the concreteness Levinas associates with the face indicates the uniqueness and irreplaceability of each human being just as such – and not (which *would* generate a contradiction) that every aspect (height, hair color, temperament, etc.) about her concrete appearance and personality would influence the extent to which her life would be ethically important.

Hopefully, we can now glimpse the contours of an ethical perspective centered on the notion of expression. In the following sections I will try to fill in some more details. The question we should try to answer may be formulated in this way: If we suppose that to encounter human beings involves recognizing something like an ethical demand, then what – precisely – is demanded of us?

Stepping forth as an individual

Sometimes commentators on Wittgenstein – especially of the sort who endorse the "community interpretation" of the rule-following considerations – give the impression that the greatest achievement of the later Wittgenstein is to show us how vanishingly small is the active part the individual mind or subjectivity (grotesquely inflated in almost all post-Cartesian philosophy) plays in human life. The general validity of this anti-individualist portrait of Wittgenstein can be disputed, and has been throughout this book. But even its fiercest opponents must grant that it is not *completely* without textual support. Yet precisely when ethics is concerned the portrait is very far from the mark. Wittgenstein consistently held on to the view that ethics is a *personal* affair. In ethical matters it is, in a sense, only the individual subject that has any active part to play. This clearly comes out in the following remarks, recorded by Waismann: "At the end of my lecture on ethics I spoke in the first person: I think that this is something very essential. Here there is nothing to be stated any more; all I can do is to step forth as an individual and speak in the first person" (Wittgenstein 1979a, 117).

One might think that the right way to read this passage – an interpretation that would be in line with the early Wittgenstein's association of ethics and esthetics – is to interpret it as stating that ethics is personal in the same way as preferences are. Some people like Brussels sprouts and Truffaut movies; others don't. In the latter case we can, of course, state various things, give a number of reasons why Truffaut's films have the value we claim they have, etc. But in both cases we will, in the presence of articulate opponents, eventually have to admit that there is an element of personal taste in our judgments.

Clearly, however, ethics, for the later Wittgenstein, is not personal in *this* sense. It might be that the wrongness of murder is not something all people would recognize; but it is perverse to claim that it is merely a question of personal taste or preference. Wittgenstein is trying to express a completely different point – one that concerns a much more radical notion of "stepping forth as an individual" than whatever might be involved in expressing one's opinions on French cinema. For ethics is personal in the sense that the demands it involves place a responsibility on the individual's shoulders that the individual cannot transfer to anybody or anything else. For example, while it would make good sense to rely on an expert's opinion when I try to make up my mind about whether to go and see a particular French movie (although it is no guarantee that I would like the movie) and justify my going to the movie theater to see it with reference to that expert advice, there is no similar justification in the case of ethical decisions. As Lars Hertzberg, influenced by Wittgenstein, expresses the crucial point,

> moral seriousness, at least in one sense of the word, is precisely characterized by the recognition that there are some issues with respect to which I cannot hand over ultimate responsibility to anyone else. This gets expressed in our talking about such issues as matters of conscience. However, we are often tempted to flee responsibility, preferring to let the issues be resolved by an appeal to public opinion or to some sort of moral consensus or moral expertise. One might call this temptation moral escapism.
>
> (Hertzberg 2002, 253)

In moral matters, the ultimate responsibility for my actions stays with me. To affirm this personal indeclinable responsibility is precisely to "step forth as an individual and speak in the first person" in the sense Wittgenstein intends. A consequence of this is that there cannot be any ultimate set of moral rules, laws, or standards. Ethics is not something that can be studied and taught, according to Wittgenstein (Wittgenstein 1979a, 117); hence, not only can there be no moral experts, but there can be no ethical manuals and codes either. To think that there can be an ultimate code of conduct is to give in to the moral escapism of which Hertzberg speaks. For in that case I could always justify or excuse my actions by reference to my having followed the rules laid out in the code; and this would be no less a case of fleeing responsibility than would the reliance on "moral experts" (cf. Gleeson 2002, 220).

There is another way to reach the same conclusion. Remember what was said in the previous section about respect for the individual human being just as such (the "face"). Now, the idea of a moral code of conduct can be brought into conflict with this concern for the individual other. This is notoriously the case with the utilitarian principle of maximizing happiness or pleasure (which may prescribe the murder of innocent people), but we can pick just about any moral principle we like and generate a similar conflict. Refinements along the lines of "telling lies is wrong *unless* such and such" can take care of the most obvious disasters, but cannot remove the problem altogether. Rules and principles must have some degree of generality if they are to have any function (just as a map cannot be such as to capture all details of the area it maps, for then it would have to be a full-scale copy of it). And precisely this generality seems to be in tension with the notion that we have to answer to the individual person just as such. As Levinas puts it (rather bombastically), "how could universal [...] principles be opposed [...] to the face of the other, without recoiling before the cruelty of this impersonal justice!" (TI, 300). Rules and principles are inevitably faceless and impersonal, whereas the demands of ethics must be as particular and unique as the persons they concern (cf. Edwards 1982, 239).

The content of the "ethical demand" that the face expresses must, then, be such as to allocate full responsibility to the moral agent while (which is the reverse side of the same coin) giving her only a hint as to the direction she is to follow. I think the right notion of what ethics demands of us is summed up nicely in something Wittgenstein said in response to the political engagement of Fania Pascal (his teacher of Russian): "What you should do is to be kind to others. Nothing else. Just be kind to others" (Pascal 1984, 22).[15] From the perspective of normative ethics, to say this is to say next to nothing. But that there is this kind of emptiness or "silence" in the ethical demand is precisely an important ethical insight, and we should resist the temptation to fill it out with specific rules and principles. To succumb to the latter temptation is to misunderstand precisely the distinctive core of Wittgenstein's approach to ethics. The demand expressed by the face, to quote another moral phenomenologist, "does not bypass a person's own insight, experience, judgment, and imagination. It only indicates whom he or she is to serve through these abilities, namely, the other person rather than him or herself" (Løgstrup 1997, 105–6).

The ethical demand I am sketching here has a distinctly asymmetrical structure. In accordance with my repeated claim that there is an essential "intersubjective asymmetry" that philosophers must recognize if they want to come to grips with the problem of other minds, we might perhaps say that there is a corresponding "ethical asymmetry" that we, as moral phenomenologists, have to recognize if we want our descriptions to fit the way morality looks from the inside (cf. TI, 216).[16] It is generally recognized that there is a distinct first-person/third-person asymmetry in the moral significance of such things as "respecting a person's wishes," "pitying a person," or "being grateful to a person." "Self-pity," for example, has a completely different moral status than "pity directed at the person who is oneself" (cf. R. Moran 2001, xxxii). The view I am outlining here takes points such as these to their natural conclusion. Part of the idea is that to recognize the other person as another human being who has a claim on me strips me of my distinctions and "reduces" me to an ethical subject, that is, to someone who has to serve the other. Wittgenstein seems to be driving at this point in a passage in *Culture and Value*:

> Someone who [...] opens his heart to God in remorseful confession opens it for others too. He thereby loses his dignity as someone special & so becomes like a child. That means without office, dignity & aloofness from others. You can open yourself to others only out of a particular kind of love. Which acknowledges as it were that we are all wicked children.
>
> (CV, 52)

In losing one's dignity and aloofness and becoming like a child one does not (as it were) sink to the level of others (as if one were originally above them somehow), but in a sense to a *lower* level. Levinas makes this clear. He often quotes a passage from Dostoevsky's *The Brothers Karamazov* stating that "[w]e are all responsible for everyone else – but I am more responsible than all the others."[17] What Levinas wants to say with this reference is that the other might be responsible for me but this is ultimately her business and not mine (Levinas 1985, 98). Seen from *my* perspective (and this is ultimately the only perspective I can honestly adopt), I am in a sense more responsible than any other.[18] This does not rule out that others are responsible for me; but it does rule out that their responsibility for me can be something that figures explicitly in my ethical relation towards them. Ethics is not a matter of give and take. There must be some difference between the prudence of a businesswoman who knows that a good way of getting what one wants is to be generous to others and the kind of considerations guiding a person who is acting *ethically*. Not that the businesswoman necessarily deserves moral reproach; the point is, rather, that the "space" in which she operates, so to speak, is not a specifically ethical space. Levinas does seem to give expression to an important intuition when he emphasizes that ethics is not a matter of "calculations of deficits and compensations" (CPP, 92). Ethics is not bookkeeping; it is, rather, a matter of expending without worrying about the returns, as in Wittgenstein's advice to Drury: "Don't think about yourself, but think about others, e.g. your patients" (Drury 1984, 95).

This point too can be deepened with the help of the notion of the "face." If I expect the other to serve me in return, and if this is part of the reason why I treat her well, then the other no longer figures as a unique individual and nothing besides, but more as someone who can supply what I want. It is an insignificant step from here to a situation in which one treats others differently according not only to their willingness to return the favors but also to their power and ability to do so. If ethics is simply a matter of *quid pro quo*, then why should I be equally polite towards the Cambridge professor and the supermarket checkout assistant? Yet someone who is entertaining ideas like these is situated outside of "ethical space" as we have sketched it with the help of the notion of "face." That is, he or she is proposing to judge the others according to categories and contexts, instead of relating to them just qua other persons. No one is unique or irreplaceable in this scenario. Anyone who can supply what the agent wants will do; and there is little reason to care about those who either cannot or will not supply what the agent wants.[19]

The last thing I want to call attention to in this context is a point that, although it seems excessively radical, is actually implied by what I have already said. If what I have called the "ethical demand" cannot be translated into a set of standards or rules, but is rather simply the (unspecific) demand that I "be kind to others," then how can I know when I have done "enough," executed my duty? Levinas has an unambiguous – and, in the eyes of some, wildly problematic – answer to this: I can *never* say that I have done enough. As he formulates the claim (characteristically exaggerating):

> The self is a *sub-jectum*; it is under the weight of the universe, responsible for everything. The unity of the universe is not what my gaze embraces in its unity of apperception, but what is incumbent on me from all sides, regards me in the two senses of the term, accuses me, is my affair.
>
> (OB, 116)

As some commentators have noticed, this looks a lot like an ethical reinterpretation (or distortion) of the kind of claims transcendental philosophy makes about subjectivity.[20] While Husserlian transcendental philosophy conceives of subjectivity as the place where "all existing things" are constituted, Levinas conceives of subjectivity as the point subjected to infinite responsibility – indeed to *all* responsibilities in the world. Whatever plausibility the traditional transcendental claim has, the corresponding ethical claim seems deeply problematic. How can anyone manage such "infinite responsibility?" Would we not collapse under its weight? If we dig below the extreme rhetoric, however, Levinas is making the following simple point: there can be no fixed limit to what my ethical responsibility involves. Levinas himself emphasizes that "[t]*he infinity of responsibility does not denote its actual immensity*" (TI, 244). His point is thus not that there is, somewhere in a Platonic world of ideas, as it were, an infinitely long list of responsibilities that I have to administer and under the immense weight of which I have to suffer. Rather, as we have already seen, he is claiming that there can never be *any* list of duties or responsibilities that stipulates my obligations towards others, not even an infinite one.[21] My responsibility, in other words, is "infinite" in the sense that there can never be set any limit to what it involves (cf. OB, 47). Something similar seems to be expressed by Wittgenstein when, in a passage we have already encountered, he remarks that "*no distress can be greater than what a single person can suffer. Hence one human being can be in infinite distress & so need infinite help" (CV, 52). That Wittgenstein is speaking in general terms about the human condition, rather than about special situations that a person might find herself in, is suggested by other remarks of his. For example, he ends a letter to Norman Malcolm by expressing his wish that Malcolm be "in a position to be kind & *understanding* to all sorts of human beings who *need* it! Because we all need this sort of thing very badly" (Malcolm 1958, 37).

The last quotation from Wittgenstein is important in another way as well, for it illustrates a clarification that we ought to make here. When Levinas and Wittgenstein speak of "infinite responsibility" and "infinite help" one might get the impression that only truly great deeds can match these ethical demands. Yet in the quotation I have just given Wittgenstein speaks of "understanding" and "kindness." Similarly, in the letter to Drury already mentioned (see p. 148), in which Wittgenstein advises his friend to think about others, he especially emphasizes the opportunity "to say 'good night' to so many people" (Drury 1984, 96). Wittgenstein thus seems consistently to draw attention to very simple and ordinary moral phenomena that are a far cry from the heroic altruism that seems to interest Levinas. But the appearance of contrast here stems from a misunderstanding of Levinas. Despite the apparent excessiveness of much of what he says, Levinas ultimately claims that the asymmetrical structure he describes is simply what makes intelligible "the little humanity that adorns the world," "the little cruelty our hands repudiate" (OB, 185). In other words, like Wittgenstein, Levinas is trying to describe the meaning or structure of ethics as we experience it from within. He is attempting to describe what it means to respond ethically to another person, even in the most insignificant everyday ways, bordering on mere politeness and good manners (cf. Levinas and Kearney 1986, 32). Simple human kindness of the everyday sort that fascinated Wittgenstein is thus also a paradigm of what Levinas understands by an ethical response to another person (cf. OB, 141).

But are these claims about limitless responsibility reasonable claims, then? At least they arguably become more reasonable than they might look at first sight if we recall what was said earlier about the "face." To relate ethically to another is to relate to her just qua other person, but not abstractly, as if she were simply a replaceable specimen of a particular species. Rather, it is to relate to her as a unique individual person, and to respond to the appeal she embodies or expresses. To reject or ignore this appeal is to place oneself at the wrong end of "ethical space." That is, to respond to the other's face by saying, "This is no business of mine" is still *within* ethical space, since it is a response controlled by the original appeal; but at the same time it is obviously a refusal to uphold the ethical relation with her. But what is implied by the notion that my responsibility has determinate, fixed limits, if not precisely that there is a point beyond which it is ethically justifiable to say that her misery is not my business, that it no longer concerns me? To be sure, there are situations in which we say such things; where we feel "we have done what we could," and where no one would reproach us for shutting our door. But can we say that such actions are completely justified, as seen from within the ethical order? Don't I always wrong somebody when I shut my door to her? To put it slightly differently, if my responsibility is for the other just qua other, then it cannot have any fixed limits, like a list of duties that I can discharge so as to get the case off my desk; for to get the other's case off my desk is simply to close my eyes to her face, to respond to her appeal by refusing it. And while this might sometimes be the best thing to do, all things considered, it can never be *ethically* all right. Ethically, we are never through with the other person, because to be through with the other person is to no longer recognize and respond to her as a person. Therefore, the ethical demand has to be "impossibly demanding" (Critchley 2002, 28). It must be such that, as Wittgenstein says in a *Nachlass* remark, we simultaneously recognize this demand and realize that we do not (and I would add *cannot*) meet it.[22]

If we interpret Levinas' claim as I have suggested we should, then we have an easy reply to a type of criticism that has sometimes been leveled at him. As Putnam formulates this criticism, one should not carry ethical asymmetry as far as Levinas does, to the point where responsibility becomes limitless. For then ethics tends to monopolize one's life, to become "the *whole* of 'the true life'" (Putnam 2002, 56). And, as Putnam observes, "to be *only* ethical, even if one be ethical to the point of martyrdom, is to live a one-sided life" (ibid.).[23] However, Levinas is *not* claiming that ethics constitutes (or should constitute) all of "the true life"; and it is wrong to interpret his claim that responsibility is infinite as implying such a complete ethical domination of human existence. *Within* the ethical order, or from an exclusively ethical viewpoint, I am infinitely responsible. However, human life makes many other claims on me – "In the concrete, many other considerations intervene," as Levinas says (Levinas 1985, 99) – so that ethics becomes one voice among many. Levinas' point is that the ethical voice is univocal: it demands infinite responsibility. He is not claiming that one may lead a full human life by heeding to this voice alone.

Conclusion

In his memoirs, Norman Malcolm writes:

> Human kindness, human concern, was for [Wittgenstein] a far more important attribute in a person than intellectual power or cultivated taste. He related with pleasure an incident that happened to him in Wales. He had taken lodgings in the home of a preacher. The first time that Wittgenstein presented himself at this house the lady of the house had inquired of Wittgenstein whether he would like some tea, and whether he would also like this and that other thing. Her husband called to her from another room: "Do not ask; *give!*" Wittgenstein was

most favorably impressed by this exclamation. A characteristic remark that Wittgenstein would make when referring to someone who was notably generous or kind or honest was "He is a *human being*!"
(Malcolm 1958, 61)

I have argued in this chapter that one can make a link between the human concern suggested in Malcolm's story and the many things the later Wittgenstein says about the expressive face. It makes good sense to see the human face as the source of something like an ethical demand that – silent or empty as it is – simply summons us to face up to our personal, indeclinable, unlimited duty to be generous and kind towards other people.

To be a "human being" in this specifically moral sense is no easy task. In fact, I have argued that it is nothing that one can *be*, but something one can only strive to be. In reality, we are *"all* wicked" (CV, 98), at least part of the time and towards some people. And even when we are not exactly wicked we cannot honestly say that we are dutiful or good. Not only because, as Wittgenstein cautions, "something that you *might* be doing out of generosity & goodness is the same as you may be doing out of cowardice and indifference" (CV, 54); but also because morality is *insatiable*. Recall what Wittgenstein said to Drury about thinking about others rather than oneself: this might "heal" one's soul, but it will not "rest it" (Drury 1984, 96). Levinas also speaks of the ethical in terms of a "restlessness" that is "better than rest" (OB, 54). The life of a "human being" is a life in unrest, because living with others means being constantly presented with new demands. In a sense these demands reflect the endlessly new expressive manifestations we encounter when we encounter others. Yet, ethically speaking, the demands are all variations of the same, endlessly repeated appeal: "Let us be human" (CV, 36).

9 Concluding remarks

> Work on philosophy [...] is really more work on oneself. On one's own conception. On how one sees things.
>
> (CV, 24)

> If one doesn't want to SOLVE philosophical problems – why doesn't one give up dealing with them. For solving them means changing one's point of view, the old way of thinking.
>
> (LW II, 84)

I want to end this book by offering a brief summary of how I have attempted to "work on" our way of looking at or thinking about the problem of other minds.

In general terms, I have presented the Wittgensteinian contribution to a philosophical elucidation of intersubjectivity as consisting of a number of radical alternatives to the usual philosophical takes on a series of connected questions. The first step was to isolate a problematic assumption underlying much philosophizing about the mind – an assumption that in particular informs Cartesianism and behaviorism. Common to these positions, I argued, is the assumption that the mind is to be conceived of in terms of "things," "states of affairs," and "processes." In this way the dispute centers on the question whether the mental constitutes its own realm of peculiar "inner" things and processes or whether it is part of the physical world. To put it differently, both Cartesian dualists and behaviorists (and arguably many physicalists as well) conceive of mental life as consisting of items that "just stand there" inert and isolated from the rest of the world, like pearls on a string. Wittgenstein identifies this idea as the decisive movement in a "conjuring trick" that commits us to choose between a number of competing but ultimately equally misguided philosophical takes on mental life.

A further step was to challenge a corollary of the idea of subjectivity as a realm of things and processes, namely the notion that mental life can be adequately described in abstraction from the rest of the world. If it could be so described, then intentionality – our ability to perceive, think about, and intend things and states of affairs in the world – would be a total mystery.

We would be unable to reconstruct the normativity of intentional phenomena from the self-contained, isolated entities and processes we would be left with. But since we have already exposed the conjuring trick in play here we can view mental life as inherently open to the world, as world-involving.

The next move was to argue that only an embodied subjectivity could be world-involving in the required sense. This, however, should be understood in the right way. The point is not that a mind needs to be connected with a body in order to establish intentional contact with a world. Rather, the point is that we need to understand subjectivity itself as *bodily* – as a "living human being" or Dasein. To put it differently, to be involved *with* the world (intentionally) is only possible for a subject that is involved *in* the world, is placed in it, encompassed by it and exposed to it. In this is implied another kind of openness on the part of subjectivity: it can only have the world in view, so to speak, by itself being visibly present within the world. (This insight is obviously crucial to the later stages of the argument.)

Understanding subjectivity as world-involving and as embodied, however, still leaves intact one crucial element of Cartesianism, viz. the emphasis on individual subjectivity. Some philosophers have thought that in the context of the problem of other minds it is the very idea of an individual subject with a first-person perspective that causes the fundamental trouble, and not so much the notion of minds as distinct from the bodies they "inhabit." If we take our point of departure in our own first-person perspective, so these philosophers argue, solipsism is the inevitable result. This claim, interestingly enough, is one that is shared by commentators who think the later Wittgenstein remained sympathetic to solipsism and commentators who think he rejected solipsism altogether. Each party has a share in the truth. For the later Wittgenstein rejects solipsism while supporting the idea that each of us accesses the world through his or her individual, first-person perspective. What we must abandon, then, is the idea, common to the solipsists and their professed opponents, that the notion of a basic asymmetry between my first-person perspective on my own mental life and the third-person perspective I have on the mental lives of others involves some metaphysical point about the objective structure of the world. This self–other asymmetry is not an indication that only I really perceive the world, for example; rather, it merely indicates that we are separate finite individuals. And, far from entailing a commitment to solipsism, this insight, so I have argued, is essential to any viable (nonsolipsistic) account of social life.

The fact, then, that the kind of access I have to the mind of another person is different from the kind of access I have to my own mental life is not something that isolates me or elevates me as somehow "the unique" subject. On the contrary, it is precisely something that preserves the uniqueness of other subjects. For if I could occupy *their* first-person perspectives the way I occupy my own these would not be the first-person perspectives of *others*. In fact, the "others" would not be there at all: they would be absorbed by my subjectivity. So an important aspect of the aforementioned self–other asymmetry is the fact that other subjects *transcend* me. They (their first-person perspectives) necessarily elude me in a certain sense.

However, we should not jump to any Cartesian conclusions here. Specifically, we should hold on to the insight that subjectivity, in and through making the world manifest, is itself manifest. So the crucial (if seemingly impossible) task is to find room for both the point that, qua embodied, subjectivity has a public appearance in the world and the idea that it nevertheless (without being "hidden") eludes or transcends any third-person grasp of it. The Levinasian (and, arguably, Wittgensteinian) way to unite these two seemingly contradictory ideas revolves around the notion of mental life as *expressed* in bodily behavior. "Expression" is supposed to pick out the peculiar, personal, and dynamic way in which subjectivity becomes manifest, in such a way as to also make intelligible the fragility of any spectator's hold on it. To express oneself, or to be expressed, is to break into the world of visible objects as an independent and unique source of meaning. The expressive face of another intimates its own meaning to me; it appears "in its own light," to recall Wittgenstein's phrase. In so doing, it continuously challenges or disrupts the meaning that I discern in it. Even when it confirms, at least for the time being, the meaning I find in it ("she really is sad"), it does so by an act of grace, as it were. At any moment the other's expression might reveal to me that her sadness is approaching despair, or that she is really feeling nostalgic rather than sad, or perhaps that she was pretending all along.

The final (and ultimate) Wittgensteinian radicalization involved a challenge to the narrow conception of the nature of the problem of "other minds" characteristic of most philosophical approaches to intersubjectivity (including most of the discussions in this book). We tend to view the problem as either straightforwardly epistemological or else as conceptual/ontological. We think, in other words, that the primary question is theoretical and can be settled by a value-neutral account of what a mind is, in conjunction with a similarly neutral account of how we can know the contents of other minds. Whatever ethical or axiological questions there may be, they are secondary in relation to the ontological and/or epistemological issues. Levinas and Wittgenstein, however, urge us to view things in a different light. According to them, the question concerning our knowledge of the pain of another person is also a question about our recognition of an appeal or demand to alleviate the suffering. Similarly, the question of what the mind or subjectivity is is inseparable from a question concerning the kinds of reactions that are appropriate for this kind of entity. A "proto-ethical" demand, according to Wittgenstein and Levinas, is part of the expressive appearance of another mind; and hence there can be no complete description either of our knowledge of other minds or of the ontological structure of minds that is completely neutral and value free. To describe the expressive manifestation of others is already to enter the domain of ethics.

But it is not, of course, to provide anything like a complete guide to moral action. An "ethics of expression" of the kind I have claimed can be found in Levinas and Wittgenstein seems, in fact, to imply that any such guide is ethically problematic. The core of ethics, in the Wittgensteinian sense, is a demand that is part and parcel of the very appearance of another mind. But the demand in question is necessarily unspecific almost – but only *almost* – to the point of saying nothing at all.

Notes

Introduction

1 Another well-known problem in this vicinity is of course the mind–body problem. But in its most basic and general form the problem is that the dualistic picture threatens to isolate the mind from the rest of the world, thus making incomprehensible not merely how one mind can be given to another, or how a mind can be related to a body, but rather how mental life can be related to anything "external" at all.
2 In philosophical discussions, the term "zombies" does not refer to the familiar horror film personae of the "living dead," but rather to a type of creature that goes about acting just like ordinary people, but is really empty inside, has no mind, and (despite all appearances to the contrary) does not think, feel, or see anything (see Dennett 1991, 72–73).
3 I am thinking of someone like Oswald Hanfling, who formulates his dissent in the following way:

> It is sometimes thought that Wittgenstein's solution, or attempted solution, of the other minds problem, is one of his main contributions to philosophy. Yet it would be difficult to point even to a statement of the problem in his main work, let alone a "solution" of it by means of criteria.
> (Hanfling 2002, 48)

There are several things that we need to hold apart here: I submit that what Wittgenstein says about other minds *is* one of his main contributions to philosophy. But in saying this, I do not wish to imply that Wittgenstein thinks this is a single, easily formulated epistemological problem that has a straightforward solution (let alone one that relies mainly on some semi-technical concept of "criteria"). That is why Pears' casual reference to "the problem of other minds" is problematic.
4 I am alluding here to the famous remark that concludes *Wittgenstein's Lectures on the Foundations of Mathematics*: "The seed I'm most likely to sow is a certain jargon" (Wittgenstein 1989, 293). See also Wittgenstein's remarks on why he cannot "found a school" in CV (69–71).
5 For the idea of an opposition in such terms, see Burge (1979, 73).
6 Glendinning's book *On Being with Others* is one of very few books to stage a dialogue between Wittgenstein and key Continental thinkers on the problem of other minds. Glendinning's perspective, however, is fundamentally different from mine. Apart from the important fact that he, as I would put it, comes close to eliminating what has to be understood (the nature of the mind, or subjectivity) if we are to throw light on intersubjectivity, it should be mentioned that Glendinning

mainly draws on Continental thinkers such as Heidegger and Derrida, while I mainly exploit the thought of Husserl and Levinas.
7 In this regard my perspective differs fundamentally from another recent account of Wittgenstein's engagement with the problem of other minds. Mark Addis (1999) seems to think that Wittgenstein intends to provide a straightforward solution to the skeptical problem of other minds. I find it hard to believe that it was Wittgenstein's intention to do anything of that sort. I also think Addis' perspective may be partly responsible for preventing him from utilizing the rich resources that Wittgenstein's texts offer for rethinking other minds, leaving his account strangely fruitless. Most of Addis' book is dedicated to investigating whether a "criteriological solution" to the skeptical problem works, and whether such a solution can be attributed to Wittgenstein. Addis' answer to both questions eventually turns out to be negative (ibid., 139–45). But since he only manages to provide a very rough sketch of the alternative "non-criteriological" solution (scattered on pp. 127–56) one is left with the false impression that Wittgenstein has very little to offer on the question of other minds.
8 Richard Moran adopts a similar perspective in his recent book on self-knowledge. According to Moran, we have to acknowledge as fundamental the fact that there are a number of self–other asymmetries. While "a skeptical conclusion is often rendered as simply equivalent to a description of these features themselves" (R. Moran 2001, 156), to conceive of the asymmetries themselves as basic, in contrast, permits us to see that skepticism is merely "a particular *interpretation* of these differences (and the expression of a rather restricted interest in them)" (ibid.).

1 Exposing the conjuring trick

1 Hintikka and Hintikka (1986, 248) state that it is Wittgenstein's opinion that there is a beetle in every person's box!
2 One should hesitate to take this as McDowell's last word on the matter. In the revised and much expanded version of McDowell's 1989 text (published in McDowell 1998a, 297–321) the quoted formulation has been suppressed. In another, later text, McDowell unequivocally dismisses (and implies that Wittgenstein would too) the idea of "consciousness as a realm of states of affairs" (McDowell 2002, 288).
3 Ryle certainly rejects the view that "mental processes" are the same as "physical processes" (Ryle 2000, 23), and indeed deems what he calls "the Hobbes–Gassendi story about the mind" inferior to the Cartesian story (ibid., 310–11). But of course it is not entirely uncontroversial to claim that Ryle is a behaviorist.
4 "Cartesianism" is in fact a word that rarely appears in Wittgenstein's writings, if at all. Equally rare are references to Descartes – or to Locke, for that matter. Rather, Wittgenstein prefers to speak of the "picture" of "inner and outer," and as a philosophical advocate of such a picture he seems to have in mind someone like William James, rather than Descartes. Nevertheless, I shall use the convenient term Cartesianism throughout this book.
5 However, I am not persuaded that Wittgenstein would agree that a "basic, instinctive doubt" constitutes the "immediate expression of my natural attitude towards other people," as Joachim Schulte claims (Schulte 1993, 21). Just as immediate and natural, according to Wittgenstein, are trust and certainty (cf. Z, § 545).
6 Indeed, these possible uncertainties cannot coherently be viewed as defects that we ought to repair somehow. I explain why in Chapter 5.
7 Something like this interpretation is advanced in McDowell 1998b, 369–94. In the Wittgenstein literature, there has been some criticism of McDowell's position.

I take issue with this criticism in Chapter 7, where I also (briefly) offer some more reasons why we should not make too much of Wittgenstein's remark that an "inner process" needs outer criteria.

8 In a recent book, M. R. Bennett and P. M. S. Hacker argue that it does not make sense to say that one has *access* to a pain when one has a pain. They write:

> One has access to a library, for example, if one is permitted to use it; one has access to such-and-such a closed room or garden if one legitimately has a key to it; one has access to the president if one is permitted to see him on request; and one has access to information on the Web if one has a computer with appropriate facilities. But there is nothing comparable to these cases which can be characterized as "access" to one's pains.
> (Bennett and Hacker 2003, 92)

Bennett and Hacker may have a valid point here. I think, however, that we may without too much confusion retain the concept of "first-person access" if we understand it to refer simply to the first-person givenness of mental phenomena. We need to hold on to the important idea that neither my own pains nor the pains of others are beyond my cognitive reach; and "access" is a useful word to help convey this idea.

9 Perhaps one could also put this point in Sellarsian terms. Suppose it is correct that "in characterizing an episode or a state as that of *knowing*, we are not giving an empirical description of that episode or state; we are placing it in the logical space of reasons, of justifying and being able to justify what one says" (Sellars 1956, 298–99). If this is so, then it is awkward to claim that I *know* that I am in pain, for example. There really isn't much of interest that I can say in order to justify my statement that I am in pain, and hardly anyone would demand of me such a justification anyway.

10 As Michel ter Hark correctly notes, by rejecting this observational model Wittgenstein "brings out the diversity of 'feeling pain' and 'behaving in such-and-such a way' even more sharply than the [Cartesian] philosophy which sets itself against behaviorism" (Hark 1990, 102).

11 Interestingly, the detached attitude of constant self-monitoring or self-observation, rather than constituting the primary self-relation of the normal subject, seems to be an important element in the schizophrenic patient's illness. (See Sass 1994, especially 88–97, 116–30.)

12 This is opposed to claims recently made by David Bell. I agree with Bell that Wittgenstein does have a notion of "genuine subjectivity." I also agree that, on Wittgenstein's view, this genuine subjectivity "is that to which the entire conceptual machinery of objectivity is ultimately inapplicable" (Bell 1996, 157). But I disagree with Bell's way of characterizing Wittgenstein's idea of the asymmetry of first-person and third-person access. Bell speaks of "this vision of the asymmetry between the expressive, spontaneous aspects of genuine subjectivity, on the one hand, and the fully objective, assertoric, referential, criterial nature of our knowledge of the psychological states of others" (ibid., 170). Not only is this hard to square with certain central passages from Wittgenstein's opus. It also commits Wittgenstein – early *and late* – to solipsism, as Bell happily grants. I address the problem of solipsism in Chapter 5.

13 Marie McGinn, in a recent article, provides a good exposition of Wittgenstein's distinction between the fundamental attitude of being-with-others and the possibility of thematic knowledge of others (McGinn 1998). (I will later explore some ethical aspects of this fundamental nonintellectual "attitude" towards others.)

14 As already indicated, I think something like this interpretation is being advanced in Glendinning (1998), although he rejects the label of behaviorism.

15 However, it bears noting that at one point in his transition period Wittgenstein was very close to strong logical behaviorism. See his 1929–30 work *Philosophical Remarks* (PR, especially 94–95).
16 As this passage indicates, Wittgenstein might be sympathetic towards a form of "methodological behaviorism," i.e. roughly the view that psychologists should study the behavior of subjects rather than engage in introspective scrutinizing. But one should not lose sight of the fact that ultimately Wittgenstein is just as critical of the notion that human behavior can be identified with mere physical movements (or stimuli–response functions) as of the Cartesian conception of an introspectively given, private inner realm. Neither notion is, on Wittgenstein's view, adequate to the phenomenon of human, embodied subjectivity.
17 For the details of Wittgenstein's resistance towards materialism, see Johnston (1993, 211–23) and Rudd (1998).
18 Pitcher is not the only commentator to defend this interpretation. Consider, for example, the following statements:

> Wittgenstein has demonstrated that we do not know what "criteria" would be for "inner processes" [...]. Since it is impossible to stipulate criteria for "inner processes," it is impossible to establish their relevance to the grounds which warrant spectator sensation sentences. So even if there are "inner processes," they are irrelevant to the justification of such sentences.
> (Olscamp 1965, 246)

19 For Hull's view, see Cook (1969, 130–31). My short discussion of Chihara and Fodor is indebted to Cook's much more detailed discussion.
20 As will become clear towards the end of this chapter, there is one additional problem with Chihara and Fodor's claim: the very way they formulate Wittgenstein's position – without further ado speaking of the mental in such objective terms as "states" and "processes" – manifests their deep commitment to what Wittgenstein considers the error common to Cartesianism and behaviorism.
21 It scarcely needs to be emphasized that philosophical books and articles on the mind abound with such uncritical uses of "object-words" to characterize mental life. A convenient *Prügelknabe* here (and elsewhere in this book) is John Wisdom, who unconcernedly speaks of "objects in the mind," "mental things," and indeed "private, singly observable things" (Wisdom 1968, 210, 211, 216). (Note also Wisdom's claim that "[t]he soul is visible only to one" (ibid., 238).) The contrast with Wisdom is especially interesting in that on many specific points he is very close to the position defended in this book, while the essentials of his view are so different precisely because he overlooks the "decisive movement in the conjuring trick."

2 Catching reality in one's net

1 Some, however, have defended the view that also pains have their "intentional objects" (e.g. Tye 1997; Crane 2001, 78–83).
2 As Dennett puts it, "the standard means of individuation in folk psychology" is "individuat[ing] states (beliefs, states of consciousness, states of communicative intention, etc.) by their content" (Dennett 1991, 319).
3 "Quality" is the term originally suggested by Husserl in the *Logical Investigations* (Husserl 1970a, 586). "Mode" is the term adopted by Searle (1983, 6).
4 For a forceful statement of this point, see Putnam (1981, 2).
5 Discussing belief, Russell thus claims that "[t]he intrinsic nature of belief can be treated without reference to what makes it true or false," and he identifies belief (or believing) with "an actual experienced feeling" (Russell 1949, 232–33).

6 According to Michael Dummett, the problem of "objectless representations" was introduced to philosophy through Franz Brentano's theory of intentionality and constituted a major problem for subsequent thinkers such as Meinong, Husserl, and Russell (cf. Dummett 1996, 28–42). In fact, however, the problem is of ancient origin. According to M. F. Burnyeat, the problem that "typifies ancient philosophical enquiry" is precisely

> the problem of understanding how thought can be of nothing or what is not, how our minds can be exercised on falsehoods, fictions, and illusions. The characteristic worry, from Parmenides onwards, is not how the mind can be in touch with anything at all, but how it can fail to be.
> (Burnyeat 1982, 33)

7 Following Wittgenstein, I thus treat false thoughts as objectless thoughts. If my thought that King's College is on fire is false, then the state of affairs that is the intentional object of that thought ("King's College is on fire") does not obtain. In that sense the thought has no object.

8 The idea that there must be a loud report in one's expectation, even when this expectation is disappointed, thus implies that there is a sense in which one's expectations (and other intentional phenomena) never *really* misfire, a sense in which they are never *really* disappointed. After all, they successfully hit the "shadowy" targets, e.g. the report "in one's expectation."

9 Tim Thornton is thus right to point out that there is a problem in McDowell's interpretation of PI, § 95. McDowell interprets Wittgenstein as saying that, although "thought can be distanced from the world by being false, [...] there is no distance from the world implicit in the very idea of thought" (McDowell 1996, 27). This does not quite capture Wittgenstein's approach to false (and objectless) thoughts, according to which there is precisely "no difference in distance from the world of true and false thoughts. But if the thought that *such-and-such* is false then it is not the case that *such-and-such*" (Thornton 1998, 95).

10 I am alluding to the familiar claim of so-called "eliminative materialists." Paul Churchland, a leading advocate of this view, has argued that the idea that we have mental states that are "about" something is part of our quotidian "folk psychology" – a long-lived, but ultimately erroneous *theory* that is about to join phlogiston theory and alchemy in the repository of strange superstitious theories of the past. For an admirably clear statement of this view, see Churchland (1981). On different grounds, Hilary Putnam once argued that intentionality is a magical relation postulated by philosophers (he specifically mentions Brentano) in search of an easy solution to the problem of reference (Putnam 1981, 2, 17).

11 David W. Smith even finds Wittgenstein's "beetle in the box" an apt depiction of the way in which intentional content is "in the head" (Smith 2004, 287). Note that Smith's Fregean model conceives of content as the sense through which we intend objects in the world. That is, it does not construe the *objects* of intentional phenomena as shadowy entities inside our heads. Nevertheless, the model is not compatible with Wittgenstein's view, according to which intentional *content* does not stop anywhere short of matters of fact in the world.

12 Interestingly, Searle continues this sentence as follows: "because each of us is precisely a brain in a vat; the vat is a skull and the 'messages' coming in are coming in by way of impacts on the nervous system" (Searle 1983, 230). This suggests a robust Cartesian materialism, according to which the mind is simply identical with the brain and the rest of the body is considered a mere container for the brain. In the next chapter I will offer some reasons for thinking that this is not the right way to look at the mind (or the body).

Notes 167

13 It might seem that another way of reaching the same conclusion would be to point out that Husserl himself insisted on the fact that intentional experiences do not stop anywhere short of their objects in the real world (if any) while at the same time advocating a strong form of internalism. However, although it is fairly widely believed that Husserl's position is internalist if anything is (cf., e.g., Smith 1989, 144, 197–99; Keller 1999, 39–58, 111–31; Rowlands 2003, 56–75) there is reason to be suspicious of the claim (see Zahavi 2004).

14 Some commentators seem to view Wittgenstein's metaphilosophical outlook as deeply opposed to all forms of positive or substantive philosophy (see, e.g., Fogelin 1976, 127; M. McGinn 1997, 8, 28–31; McDowell 1996, 175–80). I cannot properly argue the point in this book, but I think this is a misunderstanding of Wittgenstein' metaphilosophical position, although, admittedly, Wittgenstein's irritation with much of what passes for academic philosophy sometimes got the better of him.

15 The same result seems to suggest itself if we ask how we should place Wittgenstein in relation to so-called "vehicle externalism" or "active externalism," as Clark and Chalmers (1998) call it. While clearly rejecting vehicle internalism, Wittgenstein does not seem to embrace the externalist position either: "'Where does thinking take place?' We can answer: on paper, in our head, in the mind. None of these statements of locality gives *the* locality of thinking" (BB, 16). This may not be satisfactory for those in search of "the most radical form of externalism on the block" (Rowlands 2003, 224); but Wittgenstein (rightly) suspects that if we view thinking as having a specific locality we conceive it as too object-like.

16 Some commentators have become mystified by Heidegger's concept of Dasein, concocting all kinds of strange theories about what it might designate. (For an argument that Dasein primarily designates institutions, with General Motors as an example, see Haugeland 1982). As I have argued elsewhere, however, Dasein is simply Heidegger's term for the individual human subject as thematized by phenomenology (Overgaard 2004, 87–90, 142–48). In fact, Heidegger himself says that Dasein is his *terminus technicus* for what is otherwise known as the "subject" or "subjectivity" (Heidegger 1996, 72, 115).

17 Yet this does not exhaust Heidegger's notion of being-in-the-world. (See Chapter 3.)

3 Being some body

1 It is ironic that philosophers who insist on a difference between the phenomenal what-it's-like-ness and brain processes sometimes defend themselves against the accusation (for that is what it almost always is nowadays) that they are Cartesians by emphasizing that they, in contrast to Descartes, would hold these things to be very intimately conjoined with each other. For no one is more emphatic on this point than Descartes himself.

2 For paradigmatic examples, see Lowe (2000, ch. 2, titled "Minds, Bodies, and People") and Crane (2001, ch. 2, titled "Body"). By the way, I do not intend this to be a criticism of these two excellent introductions to the philosophy of mind. It is precisely the point of an introduction to give some rough notion of the kinds of debates that have been and are going on within a specific field of research. My point is merely that much debate in the philosophy of mind has been shaped by this type of approach to the body.

3 Indeed, it has been suggested that Merleau-Ponty is the only philosopher who has "offered constructive alternatives to the concept of the body as an object" (Olafson 1995, 209). I do not wish to downplay Merleau-Ponty's achievement, but I do hope to show in the course of this chapter that this claim is exaggerated.

4 There is something profoundly right in Descartes' statement that "it is the ordinary course of life and conversation [...] that teaches us how to conceive the union of the soul and the body" (Descartes 1991, 227) – except of course for the circumstance that he is wrong to think that there are such two things in need of being united in the first place.
5 I will be oversimplifying slightly, concentrating on the case of visual perception. Most points, however, also hold, *mutatis mutandis*, for tactile perception. And if an Austinian should point out that my examples are always the familiar philosophical examples of "moderate-sized specimens of dry goods" (Austin 1962, 8), then I reply that most of what I say here also holds for "people, people's voices, rivers, mountains, flames, rainbows, shadows, pictures on the screen at the cinema, pictures in books or hung on walls, vapors, gases" (ibid.). For none of these things is perceived in splendid isolation from the rest of the world.
6 This intentional surplus, of course, could be considered a peculiar "grammatical" feature that cannot be analyzed and explained any further. As Wittgenstein says, explanations come to an end somewhere, and perhaps we have simply reached that point here. Husserl, however, would probably consider such postulates of inexplicable peculiarities a bad excuse for intellectual laziness.
7 I am unhappy both with the physiological notion of "muscular sensation" and with the concept of "visual space," which may give the impression that there is such a space, distinct from ordinary space. But one could interpret "space" here as merely indicating a horizon of visual possibilities – a visual *Spielraum*.
8 This is a situation that I may or may not have actualized voluntarily or intentionally. Of course, I can be kinesthetically aware of being moved without intentionally moving myself. If someone pushes me, for example, I am immediately aware of changing position, although I did not actively move. Husserl distinguishes three types of kinesthesia: compulsory or foreign, passive (but allowed), and active or free kinesthesia (cf. ZPI, 447).
9 For more on kinesthetic sensations and their function in Husserl's account of perception, see Drummond (1979–80) and Mulligan (1995). A good, concise introduction to the topic is found in Zahavi (2003, 98–109). Apparently independently of Husserl, analytical philosophers of perception have recently reached some of the same conclusions. For an excellent example, see the so-called "enactive approach" to perception advocated by Noë (2004).
10 In *Being and Nothingness*, Sartre criticizes Husserl's account, claiming that touching and being touched are "radically distinct, and [...] exist on two incommunicable levels" (BN, 304). Merleau-Ponty, in contrast, defends Husserl's perspective (Merleau-Ponty 1962, 93).
11 As Levinas provocatively writes, "Heidegger does not take the relation of enjoyment into consideration. [...] *Dasein* in Heidegger is never hungry" (TI, 134).
12 Among the first to be surprised by this fact was Heidegger's mentor Husserl (see Husserl 1997, 328). For a fierce, Husserl-inspired critique of Heidegger's refusal to discuss embodiment, see Alweiss (2003). Even commentators who are sympathetic towards Heidegger's philosophy as such have found reason to criticize his unwillingness to discuss the phenomenon of body. Hubert Dreyfus, for example, declares that on this point Heidegger's account is "unsatisfying" (Dreyfus 1991, 137).
13 According to Rorty, Heidegger's etymologies are "largely fake" (Rorty 1989, 131). It is not clear what evidence Rorty bases this claim on, and hence it is difficult to judge whether it is true or not. But in any case nothing turns on this question here.
14 Unless otherwise indicated, quotations from German titles are translated by me.
15 In everyday life, we also often speak of the body in contrast to something else. Sometimes that something else is a mind or a soul, but more often we intend

different contrasts, such as the contrast between the *body* of a person and that person's *face* (as in "she has a beautiful body"). See Cockburn (1985) for illuminating reflections on this.
16 Heidegger intends this as a general critique that applies to philosophers across the board. But arguably he targets one philosopher in particular, namely his one-time mentor Edmund Husserl (cf. Overgaard 2003b).
17 In the famous 1927 letter to Edmund Husserl, published in Husserl (1997, 136–39).
18 Furthermore, although Heidegger has important things to say about how (not) to use the concepts of body and embodiment, his extreme wariness in this area has a clear downside to it as well. As other commentators who are otherwise sympathetic to Heidegger's perspective have put it, "he does little to illuminate the way that the body is involved in a world being presented to a subject" (Gilbert and Lennon 2005, 106).
19 For, as Wittgenstein observes, unlike proper bodily sensations such as pains and itches, kinesthesia does not seem to have qualitative degrees ("scarcely perceptible – unendurable") (RPP II, § 63).
20 See Puhl (1999, especially 168–73). I am indebted to Puhl's account on this point.
21 In opposition to this, David Bell argues that if "genuine subjectivity" is something that cannot be captured with our standard repertoire of "object" concepts, then this must mean that "genuine subjectivity is not something that, as it were, *has* a place in nature" (Bell 1996, 156). Indeed, "[m]y subjectivity is clearly not, for me, something *in* the world" (Bell 1996, 168). Here I think Bell precisely misses the position the *later* Wittgenstein (like Heidegger) opts for: Genuine subjectivity *is* (of course) in the world; but it is not in the world *in the same way* as objects are. In the *Tractatus* and the *Notebooks*, however, Wittgenstein did appear to think along the lines suggested by Bell. (See Chapter 5.)
22 Nor, contra the views of some neuroscientists, is it "the brain" that thinks, perceives, and feels. To think that the brain (as opposed to the whole living human being) thinks is to commit what Bennett and Hacker call the "mereological fallacy" in neuroscience – i.e. to attribute to *parts* of a human being predicates that can only meaningfully be attributed to the *whole* human being (cf. Bennett and Hacker 2003, 73).

4 Externalism, realism, and Wittgenstein

1 I write "so-called" because of the familiar claim that Wittgenstein does not present any such *argument*. This claim is typically part of a more general claim concerning Wittgenstein's approach to philosophy, stressing the descriptive and (especially) "therapeutic" nature of Wittgenstein's philosophy and repudiating the idea that Wittgenstein aims to provide any "positive" philosophy at all. In the following discussion I shall omit the "so-called" for stylistic reasons. But my discussion should be read as noncommittal with regard to the questions of whether Wittgenstein's thoughts on private language constitute an "argument" (implies "theses"), whether Wittgenstein provides any "theory of (linguistic) meaning" (e.g. "meaning is use"), and so forth.
2 For some discussion of the potency of this argument, see Searle (1983, 202) and Putnam (1988, 29).
3 Actually, Putnam thinks this is impossible, since we have established scientifically that water *is* H_2O (cf. Putnam 1975, 233). But in any case we can just change the example. Putnam himself considers the possibility that the creatures we call "cats" might in fact turn out to be robots controlled from Mars. Here, so Putnam claims, we would *not* conclude that there are no cats, but that cats are really robots controlled from Mars (Putnam 1975, 243).

170   *Notes*

4 Burge (1979) argues that "incomplete understanding" is much more widespread than philosophers typically assume. In the same paper, Burge also offers an argument intended to show that social dependency holds also in cases where no vague or incomplete understanding is involved.
5 Putnam, remember, explicitly takes this step (cf. Putnam 1975, 238); and when McCulloch comments on this he expresses no reservations. In fact, he seems to think that the idealistic alternative is so unconvincing that it isn't even necessary to argue for Putnam's realistic position. He brushes the whole issue aside with the remark: "If you like, consider Putnam's argument to be qualified with an initial 'If realism is correct, then ... '" (McCulloch 1995, 174).
6 Some commentators have distinguished as many as five different private language arguments (Schroeder 2001); but to me it seems more obvious that there are some three distinguishable lines of argumentation to be found in Wittgenstein's text.
7 In his reply to the question Wittgenstein does not respond to the point about a single person, but only to the point about a single occasion. And in the *Remarks on the Foundations of Mathematics*, which contains similar remarks (Wittgenstein 1978, 322–23), Wittgenstein does not refer specifically to the idea of a single person following a rule. How this should be interpreted is itself disputed, of course. Maybe Wittgenstein thinks that it is too obvious even to deserve mention that an isolated individual cannot follow a rule. But then why does he think it worth posing the question in the *Investigations*? See also Wittgenstein (1978, 335): "In order to describe the phenomenon of language, one must describe a practice, not something that happens once, *no matter of what kind*."
8 But they are far from alone. See Kenny (1975, ch. 10), Budd (1989, chs. 2 and 3), and C. McGinn (1984, ch. 2) for examples of equally fierce opposition to the community interpretation.
9 I borrow this illuminating example from David Pears (1988, 333, 395). Wittgenstein's own example is that of someone who buys several copies of the same newspaper to assure himself of the truth of what it reports (PI, § 265).
10 Peter Hacker has also emphasized another point that is of importance to our discussion of Wittgensteinian externalism. In *Insight and Illusion* he argues against the "community interpretation" in the following way:

> Far from suggesting that a language of a socially isolated individual is inconceivable, because language is always a social activity involving rules that only a social institution can provide, Wittgenstein had no objection to following a rule privately (in solitude), but only to following a "private" rule, i.e. a rule which no one else *could in principle* understand or follow.
> (Hacker 1997, 252–53)

Undoubtedly it is correct that Wittgenstein had no objection to someone following a rule in solitude. But then it is not clear that any defender of the community view would claim this. Surely, what they would claim is that it makes sense for isolated individuals to follow rules only because of the stabilizing framework provided by their membership of (or onetime initiation into) a community. One might also feel that there is something strange about the positive side of Hacker's claim (though it seems corroborated in PI, § 256 and elsewhere). He writes: "What is ruled out in the private language argument is not the imaginary soliloquist (solitary or in groups) but one whose concepts, rules, and opinions are essentially unsharable rather than contingently unshared" (Hacker 1997, 253). And again: "What is essential is the *possibility* of another's mastering the 'language' that the solitary person 'speaks'" (Baker and Hacker 1985, 175). On this interpretation, what sort of view is Wittgenstein actually arguing against? To be more precise, what would it mean to conceive of a rule that only one person could *in principle* follow? Or of concepts (a "language") that only one speaker could *in principle* understand? If I were the most intelligent person alive, say, I might devise a code (or a rule) so complicated that no other existing person could possibly learn it. But still, it would not be impossible for others *per se* to understand my code (or rule); a *Wunderkind* could be born that would be able to figure it out. Note, however, which example Wittgenstein seems to be focused on throughout his discussion of private languages: he is focusing on a language for sensations or, rather, for sensations conceived of in a very special way. His reflections, in other words, concern rules and concepts that would be impossible for others to understand, *not* because they were too complicated (or whatever), because here it is hard to see what "in principle" might mean, but rather because the "objects" to which these rules and concepts would refer would essentially be accessible only to the private linguist and no one else (PI, § 243). Wittgenstein's idea of a "private language," then, is the idea of a language designed to refer to objects essentially inaccessible to a possible community. This is crucial to the "external" private language argument, which I will discuss shortly.

11 This Wittgensteinian "externalism," whatever its correct formulation, has obvious affinities with Kant's famous "refutation of idealism." Kant, too, was concerned to articulate (what we might call) a kind of externalism (cf. Rudd 2003, 49–53). In support of his statement that my consciousness of myself proves the existence of external spatial things, Kant argued:

> I am conscious of my own existence as determined in time. All determination of time presupposes something *permanent* in perception. This permanent cannot, however, be something in me, since it is only through this permanent that my existence in time can itself be determined. Thus perception of this permanent is possible only through a *thing* outside me and not through the mere *representation* of a thing outside me; and consequently the determination of my existence in time is possible only through the existence of actual things which I perceive outside me.
>
> (Kant 1929, B 275–76).

12 Indeed, McDowell claims that "the fundamental thrust of Wittgenstein's attack is not to eliminate the idea of a private language," but rather to establish "the general moral: a bare presence cannot be a ground for anything" (McDowell 1996, 19). As we will see shortly, the idea of grounding language on "a bare presence" is precisely what the stage-setting considerations push the would-be private linguist toward embracing.
13 This whole discussion bears striking resemblances to Hegel's discussion of "sense-certainty" in the *Phenomenology of Spirit* – a fact rarely noticed by commentators (but see Putnam 1981, 62). The purely "sensory" consciousness, in Hegel's scenario, "has" something, despite its complete lack of general concepts – but what? Well, *this*. But *everything* is a "this", so nothing in particular has been picked out (cf. Hegel 1977, 58–66).
14 See Stern (1995, 175–86) and M. McGinn (1997, 126–34) for good discussions of these issues.
15 I have corrected the translation here. Luckhardt and Aue write: "there is no grasping or understanding of an object, only the grasping of a technique." As if one cannot grasp the object – the colored patch – at all! Wittgenstein, however, writes: "Es gibt hier kein Erfassen, Auffassen des Gegenstandes, außer durch ein Erfassen einer Technik." That is, one can of course grasp the object, but *only through* grasping a technique.

16 This is not precisely Malcolm's way of putting it, but I think it preserves the structural distinction he makes. Note that Wittgenstein himself speaks of a "direct" and an "indirect" way of realizing the impossibility of a private ostensive definition (RPP I, § 397).
17 One philosopher who seems to draw this erroneous conclusion is Richard Rorty (1979, 111), but there are others as well, as was pointed out in Chapter 1.
18 But is this really convincing? Does it not just show that Wittgenstein's private language argument is "no more than a verificationist defense of logical behaviorism?" (cf. M. McGinn 1997, 130). McGinn does not endorse this interpretation, but she apparently thinks it is so close to home that it is better to look for an interpretation of Wittgenstein's argument that avoids mentioning "public criteria" for "inner processes" altogether. However, I don't think we need to be so uncomfortable with Wittgenstein's critique of the "inner." Chapters 1 and 7 will make clear why; but let me nevertheless emphasize one important point at this stage. In Wittgenstein's fable "pain" is conceived of as completely isolated from public life and the "external world." What Wittgenstein is sketching here, in other words, has a lot to do with what McCulloch describes as the idea that "the mind is self-contained" with respect to the social and material world (McCulloch 1995, 47; cf. 109). One should not assume that everyone who denies this self-containedness thesis is *eo ipso* a behaviorist. McCulloch has shown this very convincingly, emphasizing the crucial difference between behaviorism and *behavior-embracing mentalism* (McCulloch 2003, 12–13 and *passim*). Wittgenstein's beetle fable is designed to show the inadequacy of behavior-*rejecting* mentalism, to use this vocabulary – Wittgenstein in fact tries to show that such a position tends, strangely enough, to lead to a variant of behaviorism – and his agenda is to endorse something like behavior-embracing mentalism, not behaviorism. (I realize that "mentalism" may strike many as an extremely misleading term for Wittgenstein's position. But as McCulloch uses the term it just refers to the view that *there really are* pains, itches, thoughts, perception, and emotions.)
19 It should be clear, however, that he is *not* expounding a general theory of what meaning "is." Wittgenstein's choice of words is remarkable (see, e.g., PI, 220, § 421). He hardly ever says that meaning *is* or *consists* in use (or anything of the sort); rather, his remarks are of the type: "*one could explain* the meaning of the word 'meaning' by saying ... "; "*look upon* the use as ... "; "*let* the application teach you ... "; etc. His remarks are often more like stage directions in the text of a play than they are propositions expressing philosophical theses.
20 And in fact Rudd's brief but illuminating discussion of McCulloch's interpretation of Wittgenstein (Rudd 1997; 2003, 80–84) is an important source of inspiration for this discussion.
21 Incidentally, McCulloch's critical remarks on this aspect of Putnam's argument suggest that one should not assume out of hand that McCulloch's externalism is simply identical with "Putnamian externalism." Rudd, however, seems to me to do just that. That is probably also why he feels he can declare that Putnam has later "abandoned 'Putnamian externalism' altogether" (Rudd 1997, 502), when in fact Putnam reiterates the central points of his semantic externalism as late as 1999 (Putnam 1999, 119–20). What Putnam (of the 1999 vintage, and indeed already the 1981 vintage; cf. Putnam 1981, ch. 3) *has* abandoned is just the realism that McCulloch champions.
22 The two responses to Rudd that I have sketched here rest on misunderstandings of his argument, but misunderstandings that Rudd does not do enough to rule out.
23 Unsurprisingly, this is one of the passages Thomas Nagel cites in order to show that Wittgenstein is committed to idealism rather than realism (Nagel 1986, 107). The *locus classicus* of the idealistic interpretation of Wittgenstein is B. Williams

(1974). I will briefly address the question of idealism at the end of this chapter (see pp. 81–2).

24 McCulloch would respond fiercely to such a critique. As he writes,

> people who become irritated at such procedures [i.e. "imaginary counterexamples"] simply have no proper grasp of what enquiry is all about. Nor is this just a point about *philosophical* enquiry: thought-experiment is an integral part of scientific theorizing too. Only politicians and other simpletons who need the comfort of easy answers refuse to consider hypothetical questions.
> (McCulloch 1995, 174)

There are thought experiments and then there are thought experiments, however, and one might accept the procedure of imaginary counterexamples as indispensable to philosophy and yet remain skeptical about the value of the more exotic specimens of philosophical science fiction. Prominent contemporary philosophers have argued that there is reason to be unwilling to conclude *anything* from fictions as fantastic as that of Twin Earth (cf. Dennett 1982, 230; Davidson 2001, 199). And even if one does not share this skeptical attitude, one might argue that there are serious *limitations* on what thought experiments such as those of Putnam and Burge can establish. The scenarios, after all, have to be interpreted, and if there is anything the history of Twin Earth shows, then it is that it is rarely obvious what the correct interpretation of the relevant details of the scenario is.

25 Incidentally, so would phenomenologists such as Husserl, Heidegger, and Levinas.

26 See Putnam (1999, 54). It is interesting that Putnam himself, following the lead of Wittgenstein and Austin (among others), has recently adopted this view, abandoning metaphysical realism but (unlike in Putnam 1981) upholding what he calls "natural realism." See also the illuminating discussion in Hutto (2003, 174–90).

27 In his critique of metaphysical realism in *Reason, Truth and History*, Putnam emphasizes that realism presupposes what he calls "a God's Eye point of view" (Putnam 1981, 49–50). In this book it is the metaphysical realistic outlook that Putnam labels "externalism" (precisely because it holds that it is possible to achieve an external point of view on mind, language, and world), while his own perspective is labeled "internalism" (holding that no such external viewpoint is possible). On such a classificatory scheme, of course, the Wittgenstein I have presented does come out as an "internalist." A good discussion of these two very different internalism–externalism oppositions – together with the interesting suggestion that Searle's argument in favor of a full-blooded internalism trades on confusing the two oppositions – is found in McDowell (1998b, 270–74).

5 The opposite of solipsism

1 For a good example of this, see Cook (1972). Despite the title of the piece Cook hardly says two sentences about solipsism, and he completely ignores Wittgenstein's discussions of intersubjective asymmetry. His article is simply an elaboration of the private language argument.

2 Anita Avramides seems, at first glance, to insist merely that solipsism results if one takes "reflection on one's own mind as one's starting point in thinking about the mind more generally" (Avramides 2001, 3). In other words, the idea seems to be that it is not so much the emphasis on the first-person perspective as the idea of *beginning* one's philosophical account of the mind from this perspective that causes problems. Yet in her critical engagement with John Searle, Thomas Nagel, and Galen Strawson, Avramides also suggests that "[t]he first-person

174 Notes

element that Nagel, Searle, and Strawson are so keen to emphasize is precisely what makes it so hard to see just *how* we can have one unified general concept of mind" that applies to both self and other and thus avoids conceptual solipsism (ibid., 286). This is an expression of the stronger view that it is the very notion of emphasizing the first person that leads to solipsism. In a similar vein, Marie McGinn speaks of a "conception of being-in-the-world in which the idea of the first person no longer occupies its traditional (and problematic) position of privilege" and in which, consequently, "the idea of the presence of one consciousness to another no longer appears as a paradox" (M. McGinn 1998, 49–50). See also Pihlström (2004, 59–60, 80, 180, and *passim*). Pihlström argues at length, however, that it is not possible completely to get rid of the problem of solipsism.

3 All the authors I mention in note 2 think their worry is shared by Wittgenstein.
4 But, as we will see, this Husserlian perspective finds a surprising corroboration in Levinas' philosophy.
5 See PR (88, 286), where Wittgenstein emphasizes that a phenomenological description may only refer to "data," not to material objects. Bearing this in mind, one should not assume that Wittgenstein's own eventual abandonment of phenomenology necessarily holds consequences for phenomenology of the Continental variety.
6 Nor should we think that the world is the *active creation* of a transcendental ego. Husserl's talk of constitution is fundamentally distorted if it is interpreted as an "attempt to ground all forms of intentionality in the meaning-giving activity of a detached transcendental subject" (Dreyfus 1991, 141). As Robert Sokolowski points out in his classical study *The Formation of Husserl's Concept of Constitution*, Husserl's texts abound with uses of the verb "constitute" in the reflexive form. Mostly, Husserl does not write that subjectivity constitutes the world, but rather that the world and worldly objects *constitute themselves* (*sich konstituieren*) in or for me. This expression, as Sokolowski points out, "is not used for things which are totally caused by something else" (Sokolowski 1964, 216).
7 *Pace* Edith Wyschogrod (1974, 49), among others. I will develop this point more fully in Chapter 6.
8 Despite many differences, both terminological and substantial, Husserl's perspective is not totally alien to that of Donald Davidson (2001, 205–20). Davidson's insistence that only a creature that is part of a community can have knowledge of an objective world; his point that intersubjectivity, conversely, presupposes that a world is given; and his claim that all this essentially hangs together with a creature's immediate knowledge of itself; all of this would be congenial to Husserl. So would Davidson's insistence that none of this compromises "our personal, private outlook," since the community in question is not *im*personal, but *inter*personal, and thus precisely requires our personal, individual outlook (ibid., 219). For an account of how these "three varieties of knowledge" are connected in a Husserlian context, see Zahavi (1999).
9 In addition to Chapter 6, see the discussions of Levinas' critique of Husserl in Derrida (1978, 79–153), Cohen (1994, 274–86), Bernasconi (2000, 67–74), Drabinski (2001), Bernet (2002), and Overgaard (2003a).
10 Such criticism of Husserl is found, for example, in Waldenfels (1971, 12–51).
11 Hacker devotes a chapter to the issue in his *Insight and Illusion* (Hacker 1997, ch. 4). He openly admits that he finds Wittgenstein's solipsistic ruminations "enigmatic," "obscure," and "mysterious" (ibid., 89, 91, 95, 96). Elsewhere, Hacker even complains that "[i]t is doubtful whether one can make sense of [the early Wittgenstein's] dark sayings" (Hacker 1993, 230). For a contrasting, patient, and lucid account of the reasoning that led Wittgenstein to embrace solipsism, see Sluga (1996).

12 It might be that Wittgenstein only appears to embrace such views, without really holding them. After all, the solipsistic pronouncements of the *Tractatus* are part of the "ladder" that, according to the penultimate section of the book, eventually must be "thrown away" (T, § 6.54). And according to one recently very influential reading of the *Tractatus* Wittgenstein must be taken at his word when he declares that the "propositions" of the *Tractatus* are nonsensical (cf. Conant 1989; Diamond 1991, 179–204).
13 In *The Blue Book*, for example, Wittgenstein still says that there is "no objection to adopting a symbolism in which a certain person always [...] holds an exceptional place," as when I would say that "only I really see" (BB, 66). But he stresses that there can be no justification for such a choice.
14 My reading of Wittgenstein's response to solipsism converges to a considerable extent with that of William Child. I agree with Child that

> Wittgenstein's aim is not to deny the existence of the [first-person and third-person] asymmetries; it is to get us to understand them correctly. If we do so, he thinks, we will no longer be subject to the temptation to express the distinctive character of our own first person viewpoint by saying, for example, "only my pain is real pain."
>
> (Child 1996, 143)

However, I do not agree with Child that Wittgenstein tries to achieve this aim by "block[ing] the suggestion that there is something that would count as knowing another's experience directly" (ibid.). Child does not want to say that we *only* have *indirect* knowledge of the mental lives of others, for his suggestion is precisely that we should erase the word "only" here, the word that tempts us to imagine a more direct route to other minds. But still, it does not seem right (and it does not seem quite faithful to the spirit of Wittgenstein) to say that we know the experiences of another "indirectly." Perhaps the difference is merely terminological, but I think we should hold on to the idea that we can know another's experience "directly." What we should add, and what the talk of "indirect knowing" is awkwardly trying to get at, is that there is nothing that would count as knowing another's experiences *as she "knows" them*.
15 Some will object that in this example we feel the *same pain*, for when pains are qualitatively identical then it is a mistake to claim that they are still numerically different (cf. Hacker 1997, 239). The latter sort of claim (so it will be urged) gives the misleading impression that a pain is something like an object that I might own or have, as if having a pain is like having a red marble in one's pocket; here another might have a qualitatively identical marble in her pocket, but my marble would still be mine and hers would still be hers. For the sake of argument, I will accept this critical point (but see the sustained discussion in Cavell 2002, 238–66). However, notice that my example may be easily be described in such a way as to make our pains qualitatively different. Suppose my knee only hurts a little and that the other gives every sign of being in severe pain. Here I can surely imagine (strong) pain I do not feel straightforwardly on the model of (the weaker) pain that I do feel.
16 In fact, there are additional questions we would have to ask before we could tell for certain whether this scenario is actually meaningful. For example, I could hardly *experience* the pain as being in that other arm (as opposed to merely feeling pain in *my own* arm, when the other arm is stung by a bee) unless this arm was part of my "experienced, subjective body" – my "body image," in Merleau-Ponty's terminology (Merleau-Ponty 1962, 98) – in some sense and to some degree. But to what extent would it then be presented to me as the arm of *another*?

176 *Notes*

17 Cavell's statements that there is a "truth of skepticism" concerning other minds (Cavell 1979, 7) and that "I live my skepticism" (ibid., 437; cf. 447) are closer to the truth. I must make room for the mental lives of others as in some sense eluding or evading me, and this evasion must be an essential part (as opposed to a contingent fact) of my living-with-others.
18 The two correspond roughly to Malcolm's "internal" and "external" arguments against private language (see Malcolm 1966, 75, as well as Chapter 4).
19 A similar interpretation of the private language argument is offered in Rudd (1998, 456–57). In line with this interpretation, Rudd argues persuasively against the view – defended, e.g., in Hanfling (2002, 118–27) – that there is no place for "qualia" or "what-it-is-like-ness" in Wittgenstein's account. The question turns on whether or not we construe qualia as inner objects of some sort. I offer a few more remarks on this topic in Chapter 7.
20 For an interesting argument that Husserl's use in this connection of the word "only" (*einzig*) rather than "unique" (*einzigartig*) suggests that his account is incompatible with solipsism, see Held (1966, 161–63).
21 Pihlström speaks of an unavoidable "dialectics of non-solipsistic enlightenment" (Pihlström 2004, 118, 179), implying that a solipsistic or at least quasi-solipsistic "affirmation of the primacy of the individual ego" re-emerges here (ibid., 180). I think this is precisely the wrong conclusion to draw. Pace Pihlström, the intersubjective asymmetry we are sketching here is a necessary part of the very *opposite* of solipsism.
22 Something to this effect is what McDowell himself says in response to a criticism expressed by Robert Brandom (cf. McDowell 2002, 280–81).
23 Francis Jacques seems to move dangerously close to this type of solipsism. For example, he objects to the following (alleged) consequences of Husserl's position: "We each really exist in our own interiority, which is accessible only to the meditating ego. Any knowledge of others as they know themselves is closed off" (Jacques 1991, 134). The last sentence, suitably interpreted, is correct as a description of Husserl's position (and Levinas, too, would be sympathetic); but this is not something to be lamented, for it saves Husserl's position from being vulnerable to the kind of solipsism just introduced.

6 The transcendence of the other in Husserl, Sartre, and Levinas

1 A telling (if outrageous) example of this is Adorno's critique of Husserl's theory of "horizon intentionality" (see Chapter 3). Adorno writes:

> A Husserl inspired sociology has hastened to deduce from [the theory] the necessity of [social] classes. They are supposed to be the expression of psychological consolidations which correspond to the current events of consciousness. A classless society presupposes universal currency of the life of consciousness of all of its members and just that is excluded by Husserl's essential insight. Husserl's theory must bear the responsibility for philosophemes of this sort. However harmless and formal it may appear, it can never sustain the claim of an unvarying "structure of pure consciousness."
> (Adorno 1982, 220–21; translation modified)

2 And we will see in Chapter 7 that Wittgenstein was no stranger to these issues either.
3 An engaging account of how this basic separateness is a fundamental precondition for, rather than an obstacle to, human relations of friendship and love is found in Dilman (1987), especially in the chapter on Proust (ibid., 93–108).

4 Heidegger might be a case in point. And in Levinas' optic, so might Merleau-Ponty. In his paper "The Philosopher and His Shadow," Merleau-Ponty writes: "My two hands 'coexist' or are 'comprescent' because they are one single body's hands. The other person appears through an extension of that comprescence; he and I are like organs of one single intercorporeality" (Merleau-Ponty 1964b, 168). Levinas responds by raising the question whether "the ethical relation is not imposed across a *radical separation* between the two hands, which precisely do not belong to the same body, nor to a hypothetical or only metaphorical intercorporeality" (Levinas 1990, 59). I think one can appreciate Levinas' worry here, even if he neglects other passages in Merleau-Ponty's article that point in a different direction (e.g. Merleau-Ponty 1964b, 171: "The other person's life is not given to me with his behavior. In order to have access to it, I would have to be the other person himself").
5 I should add that the theory of *Fremderfahrung* is not Husserl's only contribution to a phenomenology of intersubjectivity. The perception of other subjects constitutes only one type of intersubjectivity, and in fact there is evidence that it might not even be the most fundamental form of intersubjectivity on Husserl's view (see Steinbock 1995; Zahavi 2001a). Nevertheless, I will concentrate here on Husserl's account of the perception of others, not only because it is this account that Levinas and Sartre criticize, but also because the point of this chapter is precisely to argue that it is essential not to sever all bonds between the transcendence of the other and some kind of perceptual manifestation.
6 The *locus classicus* of "reasoning by analogy" is Mill (1979, 204–06). A recent defense of this approach to the other minds problem is found in Hyslop (1995).
7 Whereas being-in-itself and being-for-itself are ontological categories, subject and object are relational or, perhaps, epistemological categories for Sartre. I therefore think Sartre is less ambiguous or inconsistent here than Alfred Schutz has argued (Schutz 1962, 199–200). Schutz argues that Sartre is inconsistent when he claims that being-for-itself, in its being-for-others, is in some sense a being-in-itself, insofar as it is an object. Admittedly, part of the confusion is due to the fact that Sartre sometimes says things that seem to imply that being-for-others is a sort of being-in-itself. What Sartre mostly says, however, is that being-for-others means being an *object*. It makes good sense to claim that in shame I discover my being-looked-at, my being-objectified. But it would be absurd to say that I discover my being-in-itself. This is obviously ruled out by the very facts that *I discover* my being-objectified and that *I feel* shame. But in being-objectified I also discover a new mode of existence, viz. my being-for-others.
8 Heidegger's idea may be illustrated by such expressions as "One [German: *man*] does not sit like that at the table!" No one in particular is referred to in such a remark, but the point is supposed to apply to everyone: what *one* does (or does not), *you* are supposed to do (or not do) as well. Heidegger thinks much of human life is controlled by this monster of convention that he calls "the One" or "the They" (*das Man*) (cf. BT, 164).
9 It is worth emphasizing that it is not my claim here that Sartre's analysis of the look should be met with wholesale rejection. In fact, I am inclined to agree that there is much of value for a philosophical account of other minds to be found in what Sartre has to say about the look (as is persuasively argued, for example, in Sacks 2005). My target here is exclusively Sartre's strict dichotomy of the other as subject and the other as object, from which much of Sartre's analysis of the look could in principle be detached.
10 For a critique of Sartre's account of intersubjectivity based on recent empirical findings in child psychology, see Wider (1999).
11 That said, however, there is something special about the expressiveness of the face. The handshake that Levinas refers to, for example, derives much of its

expressive significance from the mutual look in the eyes that usually accompanies it. In addition to Chapter 7, see Cockburn (1985) for an elaboration of the special role of the face.
12 It has been argued that these different senses of nakedness are very hard to combine with each other (cf. Visker 1999, 136–38; 2003). But I think Levinas is on to something quite important here. The presence of another *is* such an ambiguous presence: at the same time "infinitely" transcendent and exposed and vulnerable.
13 It should be noted that my response cannot be merely in the form of "words." As Levinas emphasizes, "[n]o human or interhuman relationship can be enacted outside of economy; no face can be approached with empty hands and closed home" (TI, 172). Some ethical consequences of the present discussion are elaborated in Chapter 8.
14 Indeed, Visker thinks Levinas does not successfully free himself of Sartre's account of subjectivity at all (ibid., 134–43). I think there is reason to be skeptical of this latter claim.
15 This is emphasized, for example, in Ricœur (1992, 189) and Waldenfels (2002, 69).
16 Dermot Moran's reading, in his recent *Introduction to Phenomenology*, is very uncharitable towards Levinas on this point. Moran argues that Levinas' "entirely unsupported, not to say downright contradictory, claims about this so-called non-disclosive encounter with the face" will not "add up to a coherent picture." Furthermore, it is, according to Moran, entirely unclear how Levinas' thought can be said to be phenomenological at all (D. Moran 2000, 352). As I argue in this chapter, however, Levinas' descriptions of the face only express the phenomenological realization, also found in Husserl, that the appearance of the other has something paradoxical to it – that it is a "living contradiction."
17 In *Otherwise than Being* the emphasis is on the face being "too weak [to appear], non-phenomenon because less than a phenomenon" (OB, 88), rather than something that overwhelms or overflows appearance. This might seem to imply an effort on Levinas' part to move the "epiphany of the face" farther away from appearance and manifestation. But I doubt that he wants a total divorce (cf. OB, 90).

7 The play of expression

1 A good example of a materialist "beetle view" is the position defended by Putnam (1975, 325–41). A more recent prominent defender is Galen Strawson, who happily refers to his own position as "naturalized Cartesianism" (G. Strawson 1994, xi). Thus Wittgenstein is not just attacking straw men or flogging dead Cartesian horses. There are "beetle-like" elements in several currently fashionable positions in the philosophy of mind. Incidentally, the same goes for the views defended by many cognitive neuroscientists (see Bennett and Hacker 2003, ch. 3).
2 This quotation contradicts the interpretation of Michel ter Hark, according to which it is Wittgenstein's view that I cannot know about the mental states of others, but only about my attitudes and reactions to others (Hark 1990, 154).
3 Wittgenstein's reply to the well-known philosophical doubts concerning whether others are minded *at all* is similar. As he says:

> "I believe that he is suffering." – Do I also *believe* that he isn't an automaton? It would go against the grain to use the word in both connexions. (Or is it like this: I believe that he is suffering, but am certain that he is not an automaton? Nonsense!)
>
> (PI, 178; LW I, § 324).

It makes perfect sense for me, in certain situations, to doubt whether my wife is hiding some strong pain from me or whether she is in fact feeling all right. But it is hard to imagine the circumstances under which I might be able to seriously entertain the notion that she might not be a minded, sentient creature at all, but merely a robot or a zombie. This is simply not an option.

4 Hanfling suggests a further reason to be suspicious of the "criteriological" reading of Wittgenstein. In PI (§ 580), Wittgenstein writes: "An 'inner process' stands in need of outward criteria." As Hanfling remarks, "it should be noted that the expression 'inner process' is enclosed in scare quotes, indicating that there is something wrong with describing the feelings in question in that way" (Hanfling 2002, 16; cf. 45). The point, I take it, is that *if* we postulate peculiar inner items and processes, *then* we had better be able to provide outer criteria for them; but at the same time Wittgenstein is indicating that it is better not to conceive our mental lives this way in the first place. Needless to say, this interpretation ties in nicely with the account of Wittgenstein offered in the present book.

5 I borrow this way of expressing the point from Sartre (BN, 348).

6 This is, for example, the view of Franz Brentano. He writes: "In addition to the direct perception of our own mental phenomena, we have an *indirect knowledge of the mental phenomena of others*. The phenomena of inner life usually express themselves, so to speak, i.e. they cause externally perceivable changes" (Brentano 1973, 37).

7 Hacker is explicitly arguing against John McDowell here. McDowell has defended the view that our perceptual experiences can reach the mental states of others, claiming this to be a Wittgensteinian insight (cf. McDowell 1998b, 370–71). Others have derived a similar message from Wittgenstein's texts. As İlham Dilman summarizes his findings,

> anger or joy is not only what a person *feels* when he is angry or joyful and says so, but also what we *see* when he is angry or feels joy and does not hide it. What he feels and what we see are thus *one and the same thing*.
> (Dilman 1987, 33).

8 This is a point Crispin Wright has argued for in several papers (e.g. C. Wright 1989, 1998). The point remains valid even if McDowell is right that it is not Wittgenstein's only or main concern (cf. McDowell 1998c, 48–49).

9 In contrast to Rudd, Hacker insists that there is no gap (Hacker 1997, 314). Moreover, he appears to revise his position in a later text:

> One might object: to be sure, we can see *that* another person is in pain, but one cannot see his pain; surely that is inferred! The objection is incorrect. First, do we not say "I could see his agony" or "I was witness to his suffering"? Is it elliptical to say "I saw the pain in his face"? (Although, to be sure, the pain I see in his face may well be the pain of a broken leg.) Secondly, in so far as it is true that I cannot *see* or otherwise perceive his pain, neither can he. I see the manifestations of pain which he exhibits; but when he exhibits pain, it is *manifest*.

(Hacker 1993, 132; note that this was written several years after Hacker 1997)

10 How would one, for instance, make sense of the place confession occupies in our lives, on such a view? If it *were* simply a question of looking inside and honestly describing what one sees would we then not be distrustful of the confessions of people whom we know in general to be very poor observers? Yet we do accept the confessions of absentminded people and people who give poor descriptions (cf. RPP II, § 562). This shows something important about the nature of mental life.

180 *Notes*

11 David Cockburn's otherwise careful and illuminating account seems to violate the "Cartesian" intuition. Cockburn repeatedly (and correctly) emphasizes the importance of "the extended, tangible human being" (Cockburn 1990, 57, 62, 107, 117, 129), but when this is coupled with an attempt to downplay the importance of the fact that others have a point of view (ibid., 128) one almost gets the impression that there is nothing essential about other human beings that is not straightforwardly "extended and tangible."

12 In his recent book *About Face*, neurophysiologist Jonathan Cole describes a rare condition called Möbius syndrome, characteristic of which is the inability of those afflicted to move their facial muscles in any way. In other words, people with Möbius really do have completely static, fixed faces. Other people find the people with Möbius completely inscrutable; they cannot tell how a person with Möbius is feeling, whether she is lying, and so forth (cf. Cole 1998, 140). Interestingly, people with Möbius feel that their feelings, moods, and emotions themselves are weak or damped (ibid., 128, 136–40, 145). On the basis of interviews with Möbius patients, Cole therefore concludes that "losing facial animation mean[s] not only losing expression and communication with others but [leads] to a reduced intensity and delineation of feeling within oneself" (ibid., 150). (Fortunately, people with Möbius syndrome typically have other means of expression, such as body language and voice.)

13 But *how* would she move around, then, if all her expressions were completely fixed? There is a lot of expression in the way we walk, for example; so we have to imagine this person moving in some essentially nonhuman way (say, rolling on wheels, or gliding over the ground) in order for this thought experiment to be even coherent. Thanks to Lisa Käll for drawing this point to my attention.

14 Levinas thinks this type of approach to alterity constitutes the essence of "ontology." Western philosophy, he writes, "has most often been an ontology: a reduction of the other to the same by interposition of a middle and neutral term that ensures the comprehension of being" (TI, 43). And, in opposition to this philosophical mainstream, Levinas launches his own philosophy under the slogan "ethics as first philosophy" (cf. TI, 304; Levinas 1989). One must not misconstrue Levinas' agenda, however. For example, when Hilary Putnam claims in a recent book that "[the book's] title, 'Ethics without Ontology', could well have been the title of one of Levinas's works" (Putnam 2004, 23), I think he expresses a view that, though not uncommon, is fundamentally mistaken. Levinas does not want to banish ontology from philosophy; nor does he think his phenomenological ethics would even be possible without ontology. As Simon Critchley presents Levinas' view, "[o]ne can see nothing without [ontological] thematization, and all talk of an ethics without ontology is blind" (Critchley 1992, 169). What Levinas wants, then, is merely to question the legitimacy of our (often implicit and unacknowledged) philosophical priorities in favor of supposedly morally neutral "theoretical" issues. This agenda, as I hope to make clear in Chapter 8, is one he shares with Wittgenstein.

15 It seems to me worth considering what the nature of such an interest in essentially hidden entities would be. Would it not be a perversely theoretical interest, very far removed from our usual practical and emotional involvement with the lives of others?

16 He explicitly criticizes this view, in fact. One philosopher sympathetic to behaviorism whom Wittgenstein might have had in mind is Russell. In *The Analysis of Mind*, Russell endorses the behaviorist point of view (even if he thinks "the behaviorists somewhat overstate their case") in the following words:

> [The behaviorist] maintains that our knowledge of ourselves is no different in kind from our knowledge of other people. We may see *more*, because our

own body is easier to observe than that of other people; but we do not see anything radically unlike what we see of others.

(Russell 1949, 29)

The idea that our own body is easier to observe than that of others is so plainly false that it is incredible that anyone should ever have endorsed it. Clearly, facial expressions play a rather large part in the way we determine the mental states of others; and we are generally in a much worse position to observe our own face than the faces of others. And, as Wittgenstein shows in various places, it is absurd to claim that we constantly observe our own behavior (listen to the words that come out of our mouths, for instance; or watch our own eyes to determine what we are looking at!) in order to determine our own mental states (cf. PI, 192; LW II, 9–12). In *The Big Typescript*, indeed, Wittgenstein openly makes fun of the idea: "Behaviorism. 'It seems to me as if I'm sad, my head is drooping so'" (Wittgenstein 2000, 340; translation from Gier 1981, 135).

17 These are the famous (or infamous) "qualia" so much discussed in the philosophy of mind. Yet I think there are reasons why the term qualia is best avoided. Some seem to think that qualia are roughly equivalent to what Russell, Ayer, and a host of others used to call "sense-data" (the neutral stuff out of which both the mental and the physical were taken to be constructed). Some even think that the word "qualia" designates some mysterious inner objects, postulated by philosophers attempting to avoid complete naturalization of the mind (a good discussion of this is found in Rudd 1998). Along with the later Wittgenstein, I have of course no wish to populate the world with such beetles in boxes. But that does not mean that it is not *like something* to perceive goldfinches and do mental arithmetic; and this "what-it-is-like-ness," I think, is something essentially tied to the first-person point of view, and for that reason less accessible to others than my seeing goldfinches or my doing mental arithmetic. For the original formulation of the issue of "what-it-is-like," see Nagel (1979).

18 The smile of an infant is a very good example to show why it is a mistake to claim (as Stuart Hampshire [1976] seems to do) that expression can universally be understood as the "residue" that remains when actions aimed at bringing about changes in the world are inhibited for one reason or another. The smile of an infant is surely not such a residue. Rather, it is simply a primitive natural expression of joy.

19 Good actors, indeed, can be so convincing that it can be hard to believe that they are not feeling something like the emotions that they are displaying. And incidentally, many of the actors whom we admire on the screen today have been trained in so-called "method acting," in which a central idea is that the best way to portray feelings and emotions is precisely to call forth, in a controlled fashion, the appropriate feelings and emotions in oneself.

20 Jonathan Cole argues that the reason why people with autism or Asperger's syndrome hardly ever look at other people's faces is not, as some have thought, that they are not interested in faces. On the contrary, it has to do with the fact that watching other people's faces is a very disturbing experience for autistic subjects. According to Cole, this is precisely because of the way the face expresses. One pervasive problem thus seems to be that autistic subjects experience an overload of information when they look at the face of another person. As Cole says, summing up his findings,

[f]aces make many subtle movements simultaneously, too many for autistic persons to process. A single expression, like a simple musical theme, might be learned and understood by rote, but the complex, almost symphonic use of the face we all engage in was just too difficult.

(Cole 1998, 107)

But this is not all. One autistic person explains why she prefers a static face to a moving one in the following words: "The static one is socially easier to handle [...] because it won't blah at you or grab you and try to force eye contact. The static face of a picture is controllable and able to be abandoned without consequence" (ibid., 103). The same person also states: "I could tell mood from a foot better than from a face. Facial expression [...] was so overlaid with stored expression, full of so many attempts to cover up or sway impression that the foot was much truer" (ibid., 96). Indeed, while apparently maintaining that the faces of other people were a source of information overload, this autistic person also complains that the people whose faces she would watch "were somehow dangerous because their real self was not accessible" (ibid., 94). The problem here seems to concern not just the amount of information, then, but also the peculiar *nature* of the information. The face, to some of these subjects, is not simply an overwhelming flood of data to be processed, but rather "an overwhelming presence of another" (ibid., 91), precisely because, unlike static pictures and objects, it is something uncontrollable and difficult to abandon once it has gotten hold of you.

21 In fact we more often speak of controlling or repressing our *feelings* and *emotions* (or failing to do so). This seems significant, indicating precisely that by preventing our feelings from being expressed we are not merely repressing some external accompaniment of the feeling, but the *feeling itself* (cf. Austin 1979, 108).

22 And of course the language, gestures, and perhaps partly even facial expressions of people from other cultures can be so different that they are a completely mystery to us (cf. Z, § 219).

23 Thus I do not want to embrace the allegedly Davidsonian position that McDowell criticizes on the final pages of *Mind and World* (McDowell 1996, 184–87). That is, I do not claim that expression can be conceived of as something that takes place between "self-standing individuals" equipped *ab initio* with everything they need (and thus in no need of initiation into a tradition). On the other hand, however, I think we should hold on to the idea that there is a sense in which individual subjects *are* "self-standing." Even though we are perhaps heirs to the same tradition and culture, I am I and the other is the other. If one denies completely the independence and separateness of subjects there is ultimately no way of making *inter*subjectivity intelligible, and the result is some kind of higher-order solipsism. This, of course, is a recurring point in Levinas' writings, and in the argument of the present book. It is also a point that, if I am not mistaken, is neglected or at least underemphasized in most allegedly Wittgensteinian accounts of the role of bodily expression in a social context (such as, e.g., the otherwise fine account by Schatzki [1996, 41–53, 58–69]).

8 Responding to faces

1 Cockburn (1990) offers a similar interpretation of Wittgenstein, as well as a defense of the inseparability of questions in philosophy of mind from ethical questions.

2 Just how much importance the early Wittgenstein attached to ethical issues is clear from his statement that the point of the *Tractatus* as a whole "is an ethical one" (cf. G. H. von Wright 1971, 16). This is a fairly surprising statement given the brevity of the discussion of ethics in the early magnum opus (cf. T, §§ 6.4–6.5). The ethical views of the early Wittgenstein will not be discussed here; but for a brief overview of them, see Phillips (2001, 348–54).

3 "Moral phenomenology" often refers simply to the commonsense moral intuitions that most of us share, and which any moral philosophy must take into

account, even if they are not the final word (see, e.g., Nagel 1986, 179–80). As I am using the term, however, it refers to a particular philosophical approach to moral issues – a descriptive first-person approach. A similar notion of moral phenomenology is central to Anne-Marie Christensen's account of Wittgenstein's conception of ethics (Christensen 2005, 158–66).
4 Levinas apparently overhears or ignores the interviewer's suggestion that ethics consists of rules, and thus Levinas only responds to the point about "constructing an ethics." As we will see later (see pp. 150–2), it is a crucial point for Levinas (and I think for Wittgenstein too) that ethics does not consist of rules at all.
5 As Gleeson formulates this objection (which he does not endorse) in a Wittgensteinian context, it amounts to the claim that

> while Wittgenstein had a personal ethical sensibility that informed at least the early work, this was of a vague, unsystematic sort that has nothing to do with philosophical ethics, because philosophical ethics is about working out a comprehensive *theory* of morality that will tell us how to *behave*: and Wittgenstein's private, poetic musings do not help us do that.
> (Gleeson 2002, 217).

6 I am here treating Wittgenstein and Levinas as having much the same perspective. But one question that might reveal disagreement here is this: Is there any single way an ethical relation looks "from the inside?" Wittgenstein would presumably emphasize the *variety* of cases (cf. Rhees 1965, 25), whereas Levinas would insist on there being a basic structure that all cases have in common.
7 Duncan Richter says that Wittgenstein's more personal remarks are "seemingly crazy" (Richter 2002, 324–25). Although ultimately Richter generously concludes that Wittgenstein's ideas are "compatible with sanity" (ibid., 329), he still feels entitled to say that Wittgenstein's attitude was "more aesthetic than humanist" – indeed "almost inhuman" (ibid., 327). The examples of Wittgensteinian views that Richter gives are admittedly idiosyncratic and *seemingly* difficult to reconcile with a humanist outlook, but I have the feeling that many of them are taken out of context, and in any case there is an abundance of remarks in which Wittgenstein displays a distinctly humanist attitude – all of which Richter completely ignores.
8 I will, however, omit the question of the ethical status of animals from my discussion in this chapter. But the way I am introducing the expressive perspective should already have made it clear that it *is* ethically important how we treat animals. This, incidentally, makes it possible to reply to a criticism that has sometimes been leveled at Levinas, viz. that there is no place, or at best only a secondary place, for animals in his conception of ethics (cf., e.g., Plant 2005, 171–79). Nevertheless, the ethical approach I am sketching does restrict the domain of the ethical in certain ways. For example, if we adopt the view I am suggesting, we cannot say that plants (as such, isolated from the roles they play in the lives of humans and animals) literally make ethical demands on us. I don't think this constitutes a problem for the view I am presenting, however. What sense could we make of the suggestion that we should pity the grass for drying out in midsummer and consider it a human duty to alleviate this "suffering?" Not much, I think; and to the extent that we can make sense of it we do so by viewing the brownish color or hanging leaves of plants as somehow "expressive" of thirst. In contrast, many of us are immediately impressed in such a "moral" way by the predicaments of dogs, birds, and perhaps even beetles. Human corpses are a different sort of example. Corpses are not, I take it, expressive in the sense that interests me here (although one can say of a dead person that she has a calm expression on her face, for example). But I would think that the ethical

demands that corpses make on us have to do with the fact that corpses are not mere things to us, but dead *persons*. Persons qua persons make numerous ethical demands on us. The fact that other persons appear as persons to us and the fact that they make ethical demands on us are two sides of the same coin. I have suggested in this book that both of these facts should be made intelligible with the notion of expression. But that does not commit me to the (outrageous) view that once expression ceases (or becomes fixed), as happens when someone dies, we cease to perceive any connection to the person, and thus also cease to attribute any ethical significance to the corpse that remains. Corpses are not mere things; so of course we may not treat them as such. I am grateful to David Cockburn for drawing these issues to my attention.
9 Similar views are advocated in Cavell (1979, 81–82) and Cockburn (1990, 209–10).
10 I would prefer not to have to impose any specific metaethical labels on this view. Suffice it to say that I think it is just as opposed to the emotivist claim that when we say that the suffering of a person ought to be relieved we are merely expressing our feelings or attitudes as it is to the realist view that would posit the existence of ethical norms or values independent of human attitudes and reactions. *For someone who lives the kind of life we live* (though not necessarily for someone who inhabits a different life-world) the wrongness of harming innocent people can, however, be a cognizable "fact." (If we must have a label for this position, perhaps we may call it an "internal realism.")
11 I am not thinking of people who are sadistic or indifferent to the suffering of others. I think most people who profess that the suffering of others does not concern them (or that it brings them joy or pleasure) precisely are not blind to the fact that the situation demands something of them. They just think that they are entitled to let their egoistic interests overrule the interests of others. The "blind" person I am thinking of here would have a special "innocence" that egoists and sadists usually do not have. He or she might, for example, be willing to do what is morally right in most situations.
12 One autistic subject described by Cole (1998) explains her reluctance to look at faces by reference to "the meaningless[ness] of their component parts," and she complains that in general "everything comes in disconnected and in often meaningless bits and pieces" (ibid., 95, 100). The Wittgensteinian concept of aspect perception is usefully discussed by Mulhall (1990); Mulhall defends the plausible thesis that we continuously perceive aspects. This claim is criticized by Johnston (1993, 240–45). But Johnston's attempts to provide a *reductio* of Mulhall – e.g. questions of this type: If we bump into a table does that mean we are momentarily aspect-blind? (ibid., 245) – are too facile and unconvincing.
13 Apparently unaware of this passage (but in perfect accordance with it), B. R. Tilghman suggests that it is in line with Wittgenstein to "describe the human body and especially the human face as a moral space, that is as the locus of the possibility of all those expressions that are at the basis of moral life" (Tilghman 1991, 115).
14 Obviously, then, Wittgenstein would be opposed to the ethical outlook of utilitarianism. In particular, if *nothing* can outweigh an individual's cry of distress it cannot make sense to attempt to calculate the positive and negative consequences of one's actions the way (act) utilitarianism proposes to do.
15 This is opposed to Johnston, who claims that Wittgenstein would contend that, from an ethical point of view, "there is a set of uniquely correct standards according to which everyone should act" (Johnston 1989, 120).
16 And it would be just as erroneous to claim that the ethical claim entails a commitment to "ethical solipsism" (*contra* Pihlström 2004, 144–45, 148, 162–65) as it is to advance the corresponding claim regarding the intersubjective asymmetry generally.

17 Cf. Levinas (1985, 98, 101; OB, 146). It is not, as Levinas sometimes claims (cf. Levinas and Kearney 1986, 31), Alyosha Karamazov who says this. Rather, the statement is attributed to Father Zossima's late brother Markel (Dostoevsky 1952, 149–50). For a very illuminating study of the many points of convergences between the *Karamazov* novel and Levinas' ethics, see Toumayan (2004). (An interesting fact that Toumayan does not mention is that it seems Dostoevsky gradually worked his way toward the idea of "I more than the others." In the major novel preceding *The Brothers Karamazov*, the novel known as *Devils* or *The Possessed*, three different characters declare that all humans are guilty and that they themselves are as guilty as everyone else; but no character claims that he is *more* guilty or responsible than everyone else. Such a twist, it seems, is only added in *The Brothers Karamazov*.) Incidentally, Wittgenstein too is reported to have been fascinated by Dostoevsky's work and in particular by *Karamazov*. Ray Monk writes that Wittgenstein was especially taken with the character of Father Zossima, "who represented for him a powerful Christian ideal" (Monk 1990, 136).

18 Perhaps if one emphasizes more clearly that this is Levinas' point there is less reason for commentators to feel so uncomfortable about the asymmetry claim (cf. Peperzak 1997, 126, 226; Waldenfels 2002, 69). It all turns on Levinas' insistence that I cannot ultimately adopt a view from nowhere on ethics; I can only really see things from my own, personal perspective. And from that perspective, surely, I am more responsible than any other person. To add that of course the other is equally responsible for me is again to adopt the perspective of an outside spectator.

19 Indeed, Levinas seems to think that the peaceful *quid pro quo* of commerce, as long as it stands alone, is ultimately just a modification of the "struggle of each against all" (OB, 4). References to Hobbes are relatively rare and unspecific in Levinas (cf. CPP, 57, 94; Levinas 1998, 101), but often one gets the impression that Hobbes must lurk somewhere in the background. Of the condition of war of each against all that he thinks is "the state of nature," Hobbes writes:

> For he that should be modest, and tractable, and performe all he promises, in such time, and place, where no man els should do so, should make himself a prey to others, and procure his own certain ruine, contrary to the ground of all Lawes of Nature, which tend to Natures preservation.
> (Hobbes 1985, 215)

This passage resonates with a lot of things Levinas repeatedly says. Levinas agrees more with it than one might think: the law of being and nature is *conatus*; so "going to the other without concerning oneself with his movement toward me" is both dangerous, because one exposes oneself and becomes vulnerable, and positively against nature. But this is precisely what ethics consists in, according to Levinas. The Hobbesian solution of ensuring reciprocity is just a continuation of war with other means. The true transcendence of war lies in going against nature (cf. Levinas and Kearney 1986, 24–25). Incidentally, this constitutes a significant point of disagreement between Wittgenstein and Levinas, in that Wittgenstein considers the ethical response part of our repertoire of "natural reactions." See Plant (2005, 159–71) for a useful discussion of this difference.

20 The interpretation of Levinas' work as "an ethical transcendental philosophy" is forcefully presented in Theo de Boer's article of that very name (Boer 1986). In a later essay, de Boer seems to modify his claim, arguing that while Levinas' confrontation with Western philosophy "at first took the shape of an 'ethical transcendental philosophy'" Levinas gradually developed his own unique style of philosophizing (Boer 1997, 160).

21 In a similar vein, Cavell denies that the "acknowledgment" that he claims is crucial to the very encounter with another human being can be conceived in terms of duties we have "to others of a universal kind, duties [we have] to them apart from any particular station we occupy" (Cavell 1979, 435), on the following ground: "Duties are dischargeable. The surmise of which I speak is of an acknowledgment that is not dischargeable; it is something I will, or will not, see and live with" (ibid.).
22 The *Nachlass* passage I refer to is quoted by Christensen (2005, 178). Christensen argues persuasively that Wittgenstein is committed to this idea of the ethical demand as one that cannot be met.
23 The problem is also one Bernard Williams has called attention to in his writings (without mentioning Levinas, of course). In *Ethics and the Limits of Philosophy*, Williams discusses it in connection with the idea that "*only an obligation can beat an obligation.*" Once we start thinking about morality in this way, Williams argues, we "get into trouble – not just philosophical trouble, but conscience trouble – with finding room for morally indifferent actions." Surely, if anything, I am obligated to help people in need; but if that is so how can I then possibly justify going on holidays or dining out, given the way the world is? In this way, morality comes to "dominate life altogether," leaving no room for me to lead a human life of my own (cf. B. Williams 1985, 180–82).

Bibliography

Addis, M. (1999) *Wittgenstein: Making Sense of Other Minds*. Aldershot: Ashgate.
Adorno, T. W. (1982) *Against Epistemology: A Metacritique*. Trans. W. Domingo. Oxford: Blackwell.
Albritton, R. (1966) "On Wittgenstein's Use of the Term 'Criterion'." In: G. Pitcher (ed.), *Wittgenstein: The Philosophical Investigations*, 231–50. Garden City, NY: Anchor Books.
Alweiss, L. (2003) *The World Unclaimed: A Challenge to Heidegger's Critique of Husserl*. Athens, OH: Ohio University Press.
Ammereller, E. (2001) "Wittgenstein on Intentionality." In: H.-J. Glock (ed.), *Wittgenstein: A Critical Reader*, 59–93. Oxford: Blackwell.
Aristotle (1984) "On the Soul." Trans. J. A. Smith. In: J. Barnes (ed.), *The Complete Works of Aristotle*, vol. 1, 641–92. Princeton: Princeton University Press.
Austin, J. L. (1962) *Sense and Sensibilia*. Ed. G. J. Warnock. Oxford: Oxford University Press.
—— (1979) *Philosophical Papers*. Ed. J. O. Urmson and G. J. Warnock. Oxford: Oxford University Press.
Avramides, A. (2001) *Other Minds*. London: Routledge.
Baker, G. P. and P. M. S. Hacker (1984) *Skepticism, Rules and Language*. Oxford: Blackwell.
—— (1985) *Wittgenstein: Rules, Grammar, and Necessity*. Oxford: Blackwell.
Bell, D. (1996) "Solipsism and Subjectivity." *European Journal of Philosophy* 4: 155–74.
Bennett, M. R. and P. M. S. Hacker (2003) *Philosophical Foundations of Neuroscience*. Oxford: Blackwell.
Berkeley, G. (1988) *Principles of Human Knowledge. Three Dialogues between Hylas and Philonius*. Ed. R. Woolhouse. Harmondsworth: Penguin Books.
Bernasconi, R. (2000) "The Alterity of the Stranger and the Experience of the Alien." In: J. Bloechl (ed.), *The Face of the Other and the Trace of God*, 62–89. New York: Fordham University Press.
Bernet, R. (2002) "Levinas's Critique of Husserl." In: S. Critchley and R. Bernasconi (eds.), *The Cambridge Companion to Levinas*, 82–99. Cambridge: Cambridge University Press.
Boer, T. de (1986) "An Ethical Transcendental Philosophy." In: R. A. Cohen (ed.), *Face to Face with Levinas*, 83–115. Albany: SUNY Press.
—— (1997) *The Rationality of Transcendence: Studies in the Philosophy of Emmanuel Levinas*. Amsterdam: J. C. Gieben.

Bibliography

Brentano, F. (1973) *Psychology from an Empirical Standpoint*. Ed. O Kraus and L. L. McAlister, trans. A. C. Rancurello, D. B. Terrell, and L. L. McAlister. London: Routledge and Kegan Paul.

Budd, M. (1989) *Wittgenstein's Philosophy of Psychology*. London: Routledge.

Burge, T. (1979) "Individualism and the Mental." *Midwest Studies in Philosophy* 4: 73–121.

Burnyeat, M. F. (1982) "Idealism and Greek Philosophy: What Descartes Saw and Berkeley Missed." In: G. Vesey (ed.), *Idealism: Past and Present*, 19–50. Cambridge: Cambridge University Press.

Cavell, S. (1979) *The Claim of Reason: Wittgenstein, Skepticism, Morality, and Tragedy*. New York: Oxford University Press.

—— (2002) *Must We Mean What We Say? A Book of Essays*. Updated edition. Cambridge: Cambridge University Press.

Cerbone, D. R. (2000) "Heidegger and Dasein's Bodily Nature: What Is the Hidden Problematic?" *International Journal of Philosophical Studies* 8: 209–30.

Chihara, C. S. and J. A. Fodor (1966) "Operationalism and Ordinary Language: A Critique of Wittgenstein." In: G. Pitcher (ed.), *Wittgenstein: The Philosophical Investigations*, 384–419. Garden City, NY: Anchor Books.

Child, W. (1996) "Solipsism and First Person/Third Person Asymmetries." *European Journal of Philosophy* 4: 137–54.

Christensen, A.-M. (2005) *"Entschuldige nichts, verwische nichts, sieh und sag, wie es wirklich ist": Wittgenstein's Conception of Ethics*. Ph.D. dissertation, University of Aarhus, Denmark.

Churchland, P. (1981) "Eliminative Materialism and the Propositional Attitudes." *Journal of Philosophy* 78: 67–90.

Clark, A. and D. Chalmers (1998) "The Extended Mind." *Analysis* 58: 7–19.

Cockburn, D. (1985) "The Mind, the Brain, and the Face." *Philosophy* 60: 477–93.

—— (1990) *Other Human Beings*. Basingstoke: Macmillan.

Cohen, R. A. (1994) *Elevations: The Height of the Good in Rosenzweig and Levinas*. Chicago: The University of Chicago Press.

Cole, J. (1998) *About Face*. Cambridge, MA: The MIT Press.

Conant, J. (1989) "Must We Show What We Cannot Say?" In: R. Fleming and M. Payne (eds.), *The Senses of Stanley Cavell*, 242–83. Lewisburg: Bucknell University Press.

Cook, J. W. (1969) "Human Beings." In: P. Winch (ed.), *Studies in the Philosophy of Wittgenstein*, 117–51. London: Routledge and Kegal Paul.

—— (1972) "Solipsism and Language." In: A. Ambrose and M. Lazerowitz (eds.), *Ludwig Wittgenstein: Philosophy and Language*, 37–72. London: Allen and Unwin.

Crane, T. (2001) *Elements of Mind: An Introduction to the Philosophy of Mind*. Oxford: Oxford University Press.

Crary, A. (2000) "Introduction." In: A. Crary and R. Read (eds.), *The New Wittgenstein*, 1–18. London: Routledge.

Critchley, S. (1992) *The Ethics of Deconstruction: Derrida and Levinas*. Oxford: Blackwell.

—— (2002) "Introduction." In: S. Critchley and R. Bernasconi (eds.), *The Cambridge Companion to Levinas*, 1–32. Cambridge: Cambridge University Press.

Cunningham, S. (1976) *Language and the Phenomenological Reductions of Edmund Husserl*. The Hague: Martinus Nijhoff.

Davidson, D. (2001) *Subjective, Intersubjective, Objective*. Oxford: Clarendon Press.

Dennett, D. C. (1982) "Reflections." In: D. R. Hofstadter and D. C. Dennett (eds.), *The Mind's I: Fantasies and Reflections on Self and Soul*, 230–1. Toronto: Bantam Books.
—— (1991) *Consciousness Explained*. Harmondsworth: Penguin Books.
Derrida, J. (1978) *Writing and Difference*. Trans. A. Bass. London: Routledge.
Descartes, R. (1984) *The Philosophical Writings of Descartes*, vol. II. Trans. J. Cottingham, R. Stoothoff, and D. Murdoch. Cambridge: Cambridge University Press.
—— (1991) *The Philosophical Writings of Descartes*, vol. III. Trans. J. Cottingham, R. Stoothoff, D. Murdoch, and A. Kenny. Cambridge: Cambridge University Press.
Diamond, C. (1991) *The Realistic Spirit: Wittgenstein, Philosophy, and the Mind*. Cambridge, MA: The MIT Press.
Dilman, İ. (1987) *Love and Human Separateness*. Oxford: Blackwell.
Donagan, A. (1966) "Wittgenstein on Sensation." In: G. Pitcher (ed.), *Wittgenstein: The Philosophical Investigations*, 324–51. Garden City, NY: Anchor Books.
Dostoevsky, F. M. (1952) *The Brothers Karamazov*. Trans. C. Garnett. Chicago: Encyclopaedia Britannica, Inc.
Drabinski, J. E. (2001) *Sensibility and Singularity: The Problem of Phenomenology in Levinas*. Albany: SUNY Press.
Dreyfus, H. L. (1991) *Being-in-the-World: A Commentary on Heidegger's Being and Time*. Cambridge, MA: The MIT Press.
Drummond, J. J. (1979–80) "On Seeing *a* Material Thing *in* Space: The Role of Kinaesthesis in Visual Perception." *Philosophy and Phenomenological Research* 40: 19–32.
Drury, M. O'C. (1984) "Some Notes on Conversations with Wittgenstein." In: R. Rhees (ed.), *Recollections of Wittgenstein*, 76–96. Oxford: Oxford University Press.
Dummett, M. (1996) *Origins of Analytical Philosophy*. Cambridge, MA: Harvard University Press.
Edwards, J. C. (1982) *Ethics Without Philosophy: Wittgenstein and the Moral Life*. Tampa: University Presses of Florida.
Fogelin, R. J. (1976) *Wittgenstein*. London: Routledge.
Gier, N. F. (1981) *Wittgenstein and Phenomenology: A Comparative Study of the Later Wittgenstein, Husserl, Heidegger, and Merleau-Ponty*. Albany: SUNY Press.
Gilbert, P. and K. Lennon (2005) *The World, the Flesh, and the Subject: Continental Themes in the Philosophy of Mind and Body*. Edinburgh: Edinburgh University Press.
Gleeson, A. (2002) "Introduction." *Philosophical Papers* 31: 217–25.
Glendinning, S. (1998) *On Being with Others: Heidegger – Derrida – Wittgenstein*. London: Routledge.
Glock, H.-J. and J. M. Preston (1995) "Externalism and First-Person Authority." *Monist* 78: 515–33.
Hacker, P. M. S. (1993) *Wittgenstein: Meaning and Mind. Part I: Essays*. Oxford: Blackwell.
—— (1996) *Wittgenstein's Place in Twentieth-Century Analytic Philosophy*. Oxford: Blackwell.
—— (1997) *Insight and Illusion: Themes in the Philosophy of Wittgenstein*. Bristol: Thoemmes Press.
Hampshire, S. (1976) "Feeling and Expression." In: J. Glover (ed.), *The Philosophy of Mind*, 73–83. Oxford: Oxford University Press.
Hanfling, O. (2002) *Wittgenstein and the Human Form of Life*. London: Routledge.
Hark, M. ter (1990) *Beyond the Inner and Outer: Wittgenstein's Philosophy of Psychology*. Dordrecht: Kluwer.

Haugeland, J. (1982) "Heidegger on Being a Person." *Noûs* 16 (1): 15–26.
Hegel, G. W. F. (1977) *Phenomenology of Spirit*. Trans. A. V. Miller. Oxford: Oxford University Press.
Heidegger, M. (1976) *Logik: Die Frage nach der Wahrheit*. Ed. W. Biemel. Frankfurt a. M.: Vittorio Klostermann.
—— (1982) *The Basic Problems of Phenomenology*. Trans. A. Hofstadter. Bloomington: Indiana University Press.
—— (1984) *The Metaphysical Foundations of Logic*. Trans. M. Heim. Bloomington: Indiana University Press.
—— (1985) *History of the Concept of Time: Prolegomena*. Trans. T. Kisiel. Bloomington: Indiana University Press.
—— (1987) *Zur Bestimmung der Philosophie*. Ed. B. Heimbüchel. Frankfurt a. M.: Vittorio Klostermann.
—— (1990) *Kant and the Problem of Metaphysics*. Trans. R. Taft. Bloomington: Indiana University Press.
—— (1994) *Einführung in die phänomenologische Forschung*. Ed. F.-W. von Herrmann. Frankfurt a. M.: Vittorio Klostermann.
—— (1996) *Einleitung in die Philosophie*. Eds. O. Saame and I. Same-Speidel. Frankfurt a. M.: Vittorio Klostermann.
—— (2003) *Four Seminars*. Trans. A. Mitchell and F. Raffoul. Bloomington: Indiana University Press.
Held, K. (1966) *Lebendige Gegenwart: Die Frage nach der Seinsweise des transzendentalen Ich bei Edmund Husserl*. The Hague: Martinus Nijhoff.
—— (2003) "Husserl's Phenomenological Method." Trans. L. Rodemeyer. In: D. Welton (ed.), *The New Husserl: A Critical Reader*, 3–31. Bloomington: Indiana University Press
Hertzberg, L. (2002) "Moral Escapism and Applied Ethics." *Philosophical Papers* 31: 251–70.
Hintikka, J. and M. Hintikka (1986) *Investigating Wittgenstein*. Oxford: Blackwell.
Hobbes, T. (1985) *Leviathan*. Ed. C. B. Macpherson. Harmondsworth: Penguin Books.
Husserl, E. (1959) *Erste Philosophie (1923/24). Zweiter Teil*. Ed. R. Boehm. The Hague: Martinus Nijhoff.
—— (1969) *Formal and Transcendental Logic*. Trans. D. Cairns. The Hague: Martinus Nijhoff.
—— (1970a) *Logical Investigations*, vol. II. Trans. J.N. Findlay. London: Routledge and Kegan Paul.
—— (1970b) *The Crisis of European Sciences and Transcendental Phenomenology*. Trans. D. Carr. Evanston, IL: Northwestern University Press.
—— (1973) *Zur Phänomenologie der Intersubjektivität. Dritter Teil: 1929–1935*. Ed. I. Kern. The Hague: Martinus Nijhoff.
—— (1982) *Ideas Pertaining to a Pure Phenomenology and to a Phenomenological Philosophy. First Book: General Introduction to a Pure Phenomenology*. Trans. F. Kersten. Dordrecht: Kluwer Academic Publishers.
—— (1989) *Ideas Pertaining to a Pure Phenomenology and to a Phenomenological Philosophy. Second Book: Studies in the Phenomenology of Constitution*. Trans. R. Rojcewicz and A. Schuwer. Dordrecht: Kluwer Academic Publishers.
—— (1991) *Cartesianische Meditationen und Pariser Vorträge*. 2nd edition. Ed. S. Strasser. Dordrecht: Kluwer Academic Publishers.

—— (1997) *Psychological and Transcendental Phenomenology and the Confrontation with Heidegger (1927–1931)*. Ed. and trans. T. Sheehan and R. E. Palmer. Dordrecht: Kluwer Academic Publishers.
—— (2001) *Analyses Concerning Passive and Active Synthesis*. Trans. A. J. Steinbock. Dordrecht: Kluwer Academic Publishers.
Hutto, D. D. (2003) *Wittgenstein and the End of Philosophy: Neither Theory nor Therapy*. Basingstoke: Palgrave Macmillan.
Hyslop, A. (1995) *Other Minds*. Dordrecht: Kluwer Academic Publishers.
Jacobsen, R. (1996) "Wittgenstein on Self-knowledge and Self-expression." *Philosophical Quarterly* 46: 12–30.
Jacques, F. (1991) *Difference and Subjectivity: Dialogue and Personal Identity*. Trans. A. Rothwell. New Haven: Yale University Press.
Johnston, P. (1989) *Wittgenstein and Moral Philosophy*. London: Routledge.
—— (1993) *Wittgenstein: Rethinking the Inner*. London: Routledge.
Kant, I. (1929) *Critique of Pure Reason*. Trans. Norman Kemp Smith. London: Macmillan.
Keller, P. (1999) *Husserl and Heidegger on Human Experience*. Cambridge: Cambridge University Press.
Kenny, A. (1959) "Aquinas and Wittgenstein." *Downside Review* 77: 217–35.
—— (1975) *Wittgenstein*. Harmondsworth: Penguin.
—— (1991) "The Homunculus Fallacy." In: J. Hyman, *Investigating Psychology: Sciences of the Mind after Wittgenstein*, 155–65. London: Routledge, 1991.
Kripke, S. A. (1982) *Wittgenstein on Rules and Private Language*. Oxford: Blackwell.
Levin, D. M. (1999) "The Ontological Dimension of Embodiment: Heidegger's Thinking of Being." In: D. Welton (ed.), *The Body: Classic and Contemporary Readings*, 122–49. Oxford: Blackwell.
Levinas, E. (1985) *Ethics and Infinity*. Trans. R. A. Cohen. Pittsburgh: Duquesne University Press.
—— (1987) *Time and the Other*. Trans. R. A. Cohen. Pittsburgh: Duquesne University Press.
—— (1989) "Ethics as First Philosophy." Trans. S. Hand and M. Temple. In: S. Hand (ed.), *The Levinas Reader*, 75–87. Oxford: Blackwell.
—— (1990) "Intersubjectivity: Notes on Merleau-Ponty." Trans. M. B. Smith. In: G. A. Johnson and M. B. Smith (eds.), *Ontology and Alterity in Merleau-Ponty*, 55–60. Evanston, IL: Northwestern University Press.
—— (1998) *Entre Nous: On Thinking-of-the-Other*. Trans. M. B. Smith and B. Harshav. New York: Columbia University Press.
Levinas, E and R. Kearney (1986) "Dialogue with Emmanuel Levinas." Trans. R. Kearney. In: R. A. Cohen (ed.), *Face to Face with Levinas*, 13–33. Albany: SUNY Press.
Llewelyn, J. (1995) *Emmanuel Levinas: The Genealogy of Ethics*. London: Routledge.
Løgstrup, K. E. (1997) *The Ethical Demand*. Trans. T. I. Jensen, ed. A. MacIntyre and H. Fink. Notre Dame, IN: University of Notre Dame Press.
Lowe, E. J. (2000) *An Introduction to the Philosophy of Mind*. Cambridge: Cambridge University Press.
McCulloch, G. (1995) *The Mind and Its World*. London: Routledge.
—— (2002) "Phenomenological Externalism." In: N. H. Smith (ed.), *Reading McDowell: On Mind and World*, 123–39. London: Routledge.
—— (2003) *The Life of the Mind: An Essay on Phenomenological Externalism*. London: Routledge.

McDowell, J. (1989) "Wittgenstein and the Inner World." *Journal of Philosophy* 86: 643–4.
—— (1996) *Mind and World*. 2nd expanded edition. Cambridge, MA.: Harvard University Press.
—— (1998a) *Mind, Value, and Reality*. Cambridge, MA: Harvard University Press.
—— (1998b) *Meaning, Knowledge, and Reality*. Cambridge, MA: Harvard University Press.
—— (1998c) "Response to Crispin Wright." In: C. Wright, B. C. Smith, and C. MacDonald (eds.), *Knowing Our Own Minds*, 47–62. Oxford: Clarendon Press.
—— (2002) "Responses." In: N. H. Smith (ed.), *Reading McDowell: On Mind and World*, 269–305. London: Routledge.
McGinn, C. (1984) *Wittgenstein on Meaning: An Interpretation and Evaluation*. Oxford: Basil Blackwell.
McGinn, M. (1997) *Wittgenstein and the Philosophical Investigations*. London: Routledge.
—— (1998) "The Real Problem of Others: Cavell, Merleau-Ponty and Wittgenstein on Skepticism about Other Minds." *European Journal of Philosophy* 6: 45–58.
Malcolm, N. (1958) *Ludwig Wittgenstein: A Memoir*. Oxford: Oxford University Press.
—— (1966) "Wittgenstein's *Philosophical Investigations*." In: Pitcher (ed.), *Wittgenstein: The Philosophical Investigations*, 65–103. Garden City, NY: Anchor Books.
Merleau-Ponty, M. (1962) *Phenomenology of Perception*. Trans. C. Smith. London: Routledge.
—— (1964a) *The Primacy of Perception and Other Essays on Phenomenological Psychology, the Philosophy of Art, History and Politics*. Ed. J. M. Edie. Trans. A. B. Dallery, J. M. Edie, J. Wild, *et al.* Evanston, IL: Northwestern University Press.
—— (1964b) *Signs*. Trans. R. C. McCleary. Evanston, IL: Northwestern University Press.
Mill, J. S. (1979) *An Examination of Sir William Hamilton's Philosophy. Collected Works*, vol. IX. Ed. J. M. Robson. Toronto: University of Toronto Press.
Monk, R. (1990) *Ludwig Wittgenstein: The Duty of Genius*. New York: The Free Press.
Moran, D. (2000) *Introduction to Phenomenology*. London: Routledge.
Moran, R. (2001) *Authority and Estrangement: An Essay on Self-Knowledge*. Princeton: Princeton University Press.
Mulhall, S. (1990) *On Being in the World: Wittgenstein and Heidegger on Seeing Aspects*. London: Routledge.
Mulligan, K. (1995) "Perception." In: B. Smith and D. W. Smith (eds.), *The Cambridge Companion to Husserl*, 168–238. Cambridge: Cambridge University Press.
Mundle, C. W. K. (1966) "'Private Language' and Wittgenstein's Kind of Behaviourism." *Philosophical Quarterly* 16: 35–46.
Nagel, T. (1979) "What Is It Like to Be a Bat?" In: *Mortal Questions*, 165–80. Cambridge: Cambridge University Press.
—— (1986) *The View from Nowhere*. New York: Oxford University Press.
Noë, A. (2004) *Action in Perception*. Cambridge, MA: The MIT Press.
Olafson, F. A. (1995) *What Is a Human Being? A Heideggerian View*. Cambridge: Cambridge University Press.
Olscamp, P. J. (1965) "Wittgenstein's Refutation of Skepticism." *Philosophy and Phenomenological Research* 26: 239–47.

Overgaard, S. (2003a) "On Levinas' Critique of Husserl." In: D. Zahavi, S. Heinämaa, and H. Ruin (eds.), *Metaphysics, Facticity, Interpretation*, 115–38. Dordrecht: Kluwer Academic Publishers.
—— (2003b) "Heidegger's Early Critique of Husserl." *International Journal of Philosophical Studies* 11: 157–75.
—— (2004) *Husserl and Heidegger on Being in the World*. Dordrecht: Kluwer Academic Publishers.
Pascal, F. (1984) "Wittgenstein: A Personal Memoir." In: R. Rhees (ed.), *Recollections of Wittgenstein*, 12–49. Oxford: Oxford University Press.
Pears, D. (1988) *The False Prison: A Study of the Development of Wittgenstein's Philosophy. Volume II*. Oxford: Clarendon Press.
Peperzak, A. T. (1997) *Beyond: The Philosophy of Emmanuel Levinas*. Evanston, IL: Northwestern University Press.
Phillips, D. Z. (2001) "Ethics, Faith, and 'What Can Be Said.'" In: H.-J. Glock (ed.), *Wittgenstein: A Critical Reader*, 348–66. Oxford: Blackwell.
Pihlström, S. (2004) *Solipsism: History, Critique, and Relevance*. Tampere, Finland: Tampere University Press.
Pitcher, G. (1964) *The Philosophy of Wittgenstein*. Englewood Cliffs, NJ: Prentice-Hall.
Plant, B. (2005) *Wittgenstein and Levinas: Ethical and Religious Thought*. London: Routledge.
Puhl, K. (1999) *Subjekt und Körper: Untersuchungen zur Subjektkritik bei Wittgenstein und zur Theorie der Subjektivität*. Paderborn: Mentis.
Putnam, H. (1975) *Mind, Language, and Reality: Philosophical Papers*, vol. 2. Cambridge: Cambridge University Press.
—— (1981) *Reason, Truth and History*. Cambridge: Cambridge University Press.
—— (1988) *Representation and Reality*. Cambridge, MA: The MIT Press.
—— (1999) *The Threefold Cord: Mind, Body, and World*. New York: Columbia University Press.
—— (2002) "Levinas and Judaism." In: S. Critchley and R. Bernasconi (eds.), *The Cambridge Companion to Levinas*, 33–62. Cambridge: Cambridge University Press.
—— (2004) *Ethics without Ontology*. Cambridge, MA: Harvard University Press.
Rhees, R. (1965) "Some Developments in Wittgenstein's View of Ethics." *Philosophical Review* 74: 17–26.
Richter, D. (2002) "Whose Ethics? Which Wittgenstein?" *Philosophical Papers* 31: 323–42.
Ricœur, P. (1967) *Edmund Husserl: An Analysis of His Phenomenology*. Trans. E. G. Ballard and L. E. Embree. Evanston, IL: Northwestern University Press.
—— (1992) *Oneself as Another*. Trans. K. Blamey. Chicago: Chicago University Press.
Rorty, R. (1979) *Philosophy and the Mirror of Nature*. Princeton: Princeton University Press.
—— (1989) *Contingency, Irony, and Solidarity*. Cambridge: Cambridge University Press.
Rowlands, M. (2003) *Externalism: Putting Mind and World Back Together Again*. Chesham: Acumen.
Rudd, A. J. (1997) "Two Types of Externalism." *Philosophical Quarterly* 47: 501–7.
—— (1998) "What It's Like and What's Really Wrong with Physicalism: A Wittgensteinian Perspective." *Journal of Consciousness Studies* 5: 454–63.

—— (2003) *Expressing the World: Skepticism, Wittgenstein, and Heidegger*. Chicago: Open Court.
Russell, B. (1949) *The Analysis of Mind*. London: Allen & Unwin.
Ryle, G. (2000) *The Concept of Mind*. Harmondsworth: Penguin Books.
Sacks, M. (2005) "Sartre, Strawson, and Others." *Inquiry* 48: 275–99.
Sass, L. A. (1994) *The Paradoxes of Delusion: Wittgenstein, Schreber, and the Schizophrenic Mind*. Ithaca, NY: Cornell University Press.
Savigny, E. von (1996) *Der Mensch als Mitmensch: Wittgensteins "Philosophische Untersuchungen."* Munich: Deutscher Taschenbuch Verlag.
Schatzki, T. R. (1996) *Social Practices: A Wittgensteinian Approach to Human Activity and the Social*. Cambridge: Cambridge University Press.
Schroeder, S. (2001) "Private Language and Private Experience." In: H.-J. Glock (ed.), *Wittgenstein: A Critical Reader*, 174–98. Oxford: Blackwell.
Schulte, J. (1993) *Experience and Expression: Wittgenstein's Philosophy of Psychology*. Oxford: Oxford University Press.
Schutz, A. (1962) "Sartre's Theory of the Alter Ego." In: *Collected Philosophical Papers*, vol. I, 180–203. Ed. M. Natanson. The Hague: Martinus Nijhoff.
Searle, J. (1983) *Intentionality: An Essay in the Philosophy of Mind*. Cambridge: Cambridge University Press.
Sellars, W. (1956) "Empiricism and the Philosophy of Mind." In: H. Feigl and M. Scriven (eds.), *Minnesota Studies in the Philosophy of Science, Volume 1: The Foundations of Science and the Concepts of Psychology and Psychoanalysis*, 253–329. Minneapolis: University of Minnesota Press.
Shoemaker, S. (1968) "Self-Reference and Self-Awareness." *Journal of Philosophy* 65: 555–67.
Sluga, H. (1996) "'Whose House Is That?' Wittgenstein on the Self." In: H. Sluga and D. G. Stern (eds.), *The Cambridge Companion to Wittgenstein*, 320–53. Cambridge: Cambridge University Press.
Smith, D. W. (1989) *The Circle of Acquaintance: Perception, Consciousness, and Empathy*. Dordrecht: Kluwer Academic Publishers.
—— (2004) *Mind World: Essays in Phenomenology and Ontology*. Cambridge: Cambridge University Press.
Sokolowski, R. (1964) *The Formation of Husserl's Concept of Constitution*. The Hague: Martinus Nijhoff.
Steinbock, A. J. (1995) *Home and Beyond: Generative Phenomenology after Husserl*. Evanston, IL: Northwestern University Press.
Stern, D. G. (1995) *Wittgenstein on Mind and Language*. New York: Oxford University Press.
Strawson, P. F. (1966) "Review of Wittgenstein's *Philosophical Investigations*." In: G. Pitcher (ed.), *Wittgenstein: The Philosophical Investigations*, 22–64. Garden City, NY: Anchor Books.
Strawson, G. (1994) *Mental Reality*. Cambridge, MA: The MIT Press.
Theunissen, M. (1984) *The Other: Studies in the Social Ontology of Husserl, Heidegger, Sartre, and Buber*. Trans. C. Macann. Cambridge MA: The MIT Press.
Thornton, T. (1998) *Wittgenstein on Language and Thought: The Philosophy of Content*. Edinburgh: Edinburgh University Press.
Tilghman, B. R. (1991) *Wittgenstein, Ethics, and Aesthetics: The View from Eternity*. Basingstoke: Macmillan.

Toumayan, A. (2004) "'I More than the Others': Dostoevsky and Levinas." *Yale French Studies* 104: 55–66.

Tye, M. (1997) "A Representational Theory of Pains and Their Phenomenal Character." In: N. Block, O. Flanagan, and G. Güzeldere (eds.), *The Nature of Consciousness: Philosophical Debates*, 329–40. Cambridge, MA: The MIT Press.

Vinci, T. (1995) "Solipsism." In: R. Audi (ed.), *The Cambridge Dictionary of Philosophy*, 751. Cambridge: Cambridge University Press.

Visker, R. (1999) *Truth and Singularity: Taking Foucault into Phenomenology*. Dordrecht: Kluwer Academic Publishers.

—— (2003) "Is Ethics Fundamental? Questioning Levinas on Irresponsibility." *Continental Philosophy Review* 36: 263–302.

Waldenfels, B. (1971) *Das Zwischenreich des Dialogs: Sozialphilosophische Untersuchungen in Anschluss an Edmund Husserl*. The Hague: Martinus Nijhoff.

—— (2002) "Levinas and the Face of the Other." In: S. Critchley and R. Bernasconi (eds.), *The Cambridge Companion to Levinas*, 63–81. Cambridge: Cambridge University Press.

Wider, K. (1999) "The Self and Others: Imitation in Infants and Sartre's Analysis of the Look." *Continental Philosophy Review* 32: 195–210.

Williams, B. (1974) "Wittgenstein and Idealism." In: G. Vesey (ed.), *Understanding Wittgenstein*, 76–95. London: Macmillan.

—— (1985) *Ethics and the Limits of Philosophy*. London: Fontana Press.

Williams, M. (1999) *Wittgenstein, Mind, and Meaning: Towards a Social Conception of Mind*. London: Routledge.

Wisdom, J. (1968) *Other Minds*. Berkeley: University of California Press.

Wittgenstein, L. (1961) *Notebooks 1914–1916*. Ed. G. H. von Wright and G. E. M. Anscombe, trans. G. E. M. Anscombe. Oxford: Basil Blackwell.

—— (1969) *On Certainty*. Ed. G. E. M. Anscombe and G. H. von Wright, trans. D. Paul and G. E. M. Anscombe. Oxford: Basil Blackwell.

—— (1978) *Remarks on the Foundations of Mathematics*. Ed. G. H. von Wright, R. Rhees, and G. E. M. Anscombe, trans. G. E. M. Anscombe. Oxford: Blackwell.

—— (1979a) *Ludwig Wittgenstein and the Vienna Circle: Conversations Recorded by Friedrich Waismann*. Ed. B. McGuinness, trans J. Schulte and B. McGuinness. Oxford: Basil Blackwell.

—— (1979b) *Wittgenstein's Lectures: Cambridge, 1932–1935*. Ed. A. Ambrose. Oxford: Blackwell.

—— (1989) *Wittgenstein's Lectures on the Foundations of Mathematics: Cambridge, 1939*. Ed. C. Diamond. Chicago: The University of Chicago Press.

—— (2000) *The Big Typescript*. Ed. M. Nedo. Vienna: Springer.

Wright, C. (1989) "Wittgenstein's Later Philosophy of Mind: Sensation, Privacy, and Intention." *Journal of Philosophy* 86: 622–34.

—— (1998) "Self-Knowledge: The Wittgensteinian Legacy." In: C. Wright, B. C. Smith, and C. MacDonald (eds.), *Knowing Our Own Minds*, 13–45. Oxford: Clarendon Press.

Wright, G. H. von (1971) "Historical introduction." In: L. Wittgenstein, *Prototractatus: An Early Version of Tractatus Logico-Philosophicus*, 1–34. Ed. B. F. McGuinness, T. Nyberg, and G. H. von Wright, trans. D. F. Pears and B. F. McGuinness. London: Routledge.

Wyschogrod, E. (1974) *Emmanuel Levinas: The Problem of Ethical Metaphysics*. The Hague: Martinus Nijhoff.

Zahavi, D. (1999) *Self-Awareness and Alterity.* Evanston, IL: Northwestern University Press.
—— (2001a) *Husserl and Transcendental Intersubjectivity.* Trans. E. Behnke. Athens, OH: Ohio University Press.
—— (2001b) "Beyond Empathy: Phenomenological Approaches to Intersubjectivity." *Journal of Consciousness Studies* 8: 151–67.
—— (2002) "Intersubjectivity in Sartre's *Being and Nothingness.*" *Alter* 10: 265–81.
—— (2003) *Husserl's Phenomenology.* Stanford: Stanford University Press.
—— (2004) "Husserl's Noema and the Internalism-Externalism Debate." *Inquiry* 47: 42–66.

Index

aboutness *see* intentionality
Addis, M. 163
Adorno, T. W. 176
Albritton, R. 126
Alweiss, L. 168
Ammereller, E. 28, 37
analogy: argument from 105, 177
analytical conception of the human being 57–59
animals 56, 146, 183
appeal 9, 115–16, 118, 143, 147, 149, 155–57, 160; *see also* ethical demand
Aristotle 56, 58, 86
asymmetry: first-person and third-person 4, 7–8, 15, 27, 83, 85, 89–93, 96–102, 119, 135–36, 152, 159–60, 164, 173, 176 ethical 152, 156, 184–85
attitude: to a human 9, 17–18, 147 to others 2, 18, 141–42, 146–47, 163, 165, 179, 184 to a soul 17, 141–42, to what is alive 146
Austin, J. L. 68, 79–80, 124–25, 168, 173, 182
autism 147, 181–82, 184
automata 1–2, 178; *see also* zombies
Avramides, A. 1–2, 84–85, 173

Baker, G. P. 70, 170
beetle in a box 22, 24, 74, 78, 122–29, 131–32, 134–35, 137, 163, 166, 172, 178, 181
behaviorism 5–6, 9, 10–11, 14, 25–26, 33–34, 41, 46, 61, 76–77, 120–21, 130, 133, 135, 141, 158, 163–65, 172, 180–81, eliminative 18–19 logical 18–24, 165,172, methodological 18, 165, ontological 18 reductive 18, 20
being: question of 58; mode of 43, 56–59, 62

being-for-itself 108, 110, 177
being-for-others 109, 177
being-in-the-world 41, 43, 53–57, 59–60, 62, 167, 174
being-in-itself 108, 177
being-with-others 17–18, 164, 176
Bell, D. 85, 164, 169.
Bennett, M. R. 164, 169, 178
Berkeley, G. 48–49, 87
Bernasconi, R. 174
Bernet, R. 174
body 94–95, 111, 126, 131, 137, 139, 159, 162, 167–69, 177, 181; affective 51–53; behaviorist conception of 20, 24; Cartesian conception of 2, 12, 45, 62, 127, 166, 168; ego inhabiting a 6, 45–46, 57–60, 62–63; expressive 14, 24, 114, 127–29, 184; image 175; lived 7, 55, 105, 127; physical (*Körper*) 55, 105; as picture of the soul 26; moving (*see* kinesthesia); as point of view 47, 56; as thing 55, 57, 167; *see also* embodiment
Boer, T. de 185
Brandom, R. 176
Brentano, F. 29–30, 33, 86, 166, 179
Budd, M. 170
Burge, T. 162, 170, 173
Burnyeat, M. F. 166

Cartesianism; 5, 10–12, 14, 17–18, 20, 24–25, 46, 58–59, 61, 99–100, 121, 130, 135, 158–59, 163, 165 (*see also* dualism); naturalized 178
Cavell, S. 2–3, 139, 142, 175–76, 184, 186
certainty 12–13, 15, 100, 130, 138, 163
Chalmers, D. 167
Chihara, C. S. 23–24, 126, 165

Child, W. 175,
Christensen, A.-M. x, 183, 186
Churchland, P. 166
Clark, A. 167
Cockburn, D. x, 99, 131, 169, 178, 180, 182, 184
Cohen, R. A.
Cole, J. 180–81, 184
common sense 81, 91
community: account of the mental 4–5; account of rule-following 68–71, 74, 76, 150, 170–71 (*see also* rule-following); communicative 107; linguistic 64–71; transcendental 87
Conant, J. 175
conceptual problem of other minds 2, 160
Continental philosophy 4, 27, 162–63, 174
Cook, J. W. 165, 173
content *see* intentionality
Crane, T. 39, 44, 165, 167
Crary, A. 81
Critchley, S. 144, 156, 180
criteria 2, 14, 22–24, 61, 126–27, 162, 164–65, 172, 179
criteriological solution 126–27, 162–63, 179
Cunningham, S. 86

Dasein 42–44, 53–57, 59–61, 159, 167–68
Davidson, D. 119, 173–74, 182
deception 136–38
Dennett, D. C. 162, 165, 173
Derrida, J. 163, 174
Descartes, R. 1–2, 12, 45, 163, 167–68
Diamond, C. 147, 175
Dilman, İ. 176, 179
disclosedness 43, 60; *see also* openness
Donagan, A. 25
Dostoevsky, F. M. 153, 185
Drabinski, J. E. 174
Dreyfus, H. L. 60, 168, 174
Drummond, J. J. 168
Drury, M. O'C. 141, 148, 153, 155, 157
dualism 2, 5–6, 10–11, 24–25, 41, 45, 57–59, 62, 113, 120–21, 126, 133, 158, 162
Dummett, M. 166

Edwards, J. C. 152
embodiment 6–7, 45, 62, 98, 127; in Heidegger 53–60, 168–69; in Husserl 46–53; in Levinas 52–53; in Merleau-Ponty 46–47; in Sartre 46–47; in Wittgenstein 60–62
epistemological problem of other minds 2–3, 142, 160, 162
ethical: demand 9, 144–57, 160, 183–84, 186; relation 144–45, 153, 155, 177, 183
expression: of emotions 80, 129–30, 137–38, 140, 180–81; ethics of 149–50, 161, 184; in Levinas 8–9, 121, 133–34, 139–40; of mental life 85, 120, 126–30, 132, 136–37, 138–40, 148, 160, 180–82, 184; of sensations 13, 22, 80, 123–24, 129–31, 138, 140; of thoughts 129–30, 135–36; in Wittgenstein 8, 13, 19, 22, 80, 120–21, 123, 128–32, 137; *see also* face
externalism 7, 38–41, 63, 65, 67–68, 71, 73–81, 170–73; active 167; minimalist 40; vehicle 167

face 8, 134, 140, 145–57, 160, 169, 177–84; in Levinas 113–18, 133, 138, 145, 148–50, 152, 178; in Wittgenstein 13–14, 128–29, 132–33, 137, 141, 145, 147–48, 157
Fichte, J. G. 106
first-person perspective 4–5, 7, 15–17, 24, 27, 77, 84–85, 89–95, 97–100, 102, 106, 135–36, 143–44, 152, 159–60, 164, 173–75, 181, 183; *see also* asymmetry
Fodor, J. A. 23–24, 126, 165
Fogelin, R. J. 72, 167

Gier, N. F. 181
Gilbert, P. 169
Gleeson, A. 144, 151, 183
Glendinning, S. 5, 11, 99, 162, 164
Glock, H.-J. 40
grammar 7, 16, 19, 22, 72, 91, 93–94, 96, 99, 101–2, 123, 147, 168

Hacker, P. M. S. 70, 83, 89, 92, 126, 130–31, 164, 169–70, 174–75, 178–79
Hampshire, S. 181
Hanfling, O. 162, 176, 179
Hark, M. ter 164, 178
Haugeland, J. 167
Hegel, G. W. F. 108, 110, 171
Heidegger, M. 4, 17, 41–44, 46, 53–62, 109–11, 127–28, 163, 167–69, 173, 177
Held, K. 86, 176
Hertzberg, L. 151

Index 199

Hintikka, J. 10, 163
Hintikka, M. 10, 163
Hobbes, T. 11, 163, 185
homunculus fallacy 21
Hull, C. F. 24, 165
human being: living 6, 26–27, 46, 62, 99, 131, 159, 169; moral category of 143, 157
Husserl, E. 4–5, 8, 29–30, 46–53, 60, 85–92, 98, 100–101, 103–9, 112–13, 116–19, 122, 154, 163, 165–69, 173–74, 176–78
Hutto, D. D. 173
Hyslop, A. 2, 177

idealism 81–82, 86–87, 91, 170–73
immunity from error 15
intentionality 6, 21, 28, 46, 127–28, 158–59, 165; in Brentano 29–30, 33; intentional content 30–31, 34, 39–40, 80, 166; in Heidegger 41–44, 55; horizon 46–51, 87, 168, 176; in Husserl 29–30, 86–88, 91, 107, 113, 116–17, 167, 174; as internal relation 34–35; as magic 6, 28, 32–33, 38, 166; normativity of 6, 33–34, 36, 38, 159; objectless 35–38, 166; and propositional attitudes 30; intentional quality 30–31, 39, 165; in Russell 33–34; in Wittgenstein 31–41, 44
internalism 7, 38–41, 80, 167, 173
internal relation *see* intentionality
intersubjectivity 3–5, 7, 89–90, 97–105, 108–11, 113, 142, 158, 160, 162, 174, 177, 182; intersubjective asymmetry (*see* asymmetry); transcendental 87–88
introspection 24, 131, 134, 144, 165
intuitions about other minds: 5, 120–22, 127, 131–33, 138–39, 180

Jacobsen, R. 16
Jacques, F. 89, 176
James, W. 163
Johnston, P. 143, 165, 184

Käll, L. x, 180
Kant, I. 59–60, 171
Kearney, R. 155, 185
Keller, P. 167
Kenny, A. 3, 21, 170
kinesthesia 46–47, 49–50, 52, 60–61, 105, 168–69

knowledge: of one's own mind 15–17, 23–24, 61, 74, 84, 92, 95–96, 122, 130, 135, 163–64, 174, 180–81; of other minds 2, 15–18, 23–24, 31, 44, 92, 95–96, 104–6, 109, 111, 113, 120–22, 125–27, 129, 135–36, 140–42, 160, 164, 174–76, 178–81; of the world 41–44, 174
Kripke, S. A. 69, 84–85, 141–42

language game 16, 22–23, 66, 80, 97, 122, 146
Lennon, K. 169
Levin, D. M. 60,
Levinas, E. 4–5, 8–9, 52–53, 88–89, 91, 102–4, 111, 113–19, 121–22, 128, 132–35, 137–38, 140, 143–45, 148–50, 152–57, 160–61, 163, 168, 173–74, 176–78, 180, 182–83, 185–86
Llewelyn, J. 145
Locke, J. 163
Løgstrup, K. E. 152
look: in Sartre 108–16, 177
love 29–30, 107, 109, 153, 176,
Lowe, E. J. 167

McCulloch, G. 7, 30, 39, 63, 65–68, 71, 75–81, 97, 170, 172–73
McDowell, J. 10, 25, 33, 41, 43–44, 81, 86, 99, 163, 166–67, 171, 173, 176, 179, 182
McGinn, C. 170
McGinn, M. 62, 74, 77, 95, 164, 167, 171–72, 174
Malcolm, N. 74, 126, 155–57, 172, 176
materialism 6, 11, 41, 124, 165; Cartesian 166, 178; eliminative 18, 20, 166; reductive 18, 20–21, 25–26
Meinong, A. 166
memory 20–21, 26, 35, 70
Merleau-Ponty, M. 46–47, 51, 96, 112, 144, 167–68, 175, 177
metaethics 143, 184
metaphysics 1, 7, 10, 32, 105, 136; metaphysical realism (*see* realism); metaphysical self 90; metaphysical solipsism (*see* solipsism)
Mill, J. S. 177
mind-body problem 45–46, 120, 163
Möbius syndrome 180
Monk, R. 185
Moran, D. 178
Moran, R. 152, 163
Mulhall, S. 184

Mulligan, K. 168
Mundle, C. W. K. 19

Nagel, T. 172–74, 181, 183
need 51–53
neuroscience 169, 178
Noë, A. 168

objectivistic conception of subjectivity 25–26, 41; *see also* presence-at-hand
Olafson, F. A. 167
Olscamp, P. J. 165
openness 41, 43, 86–87, 159
ostensive definition 72–74, 172
Overgaard, S. 90, 167, 169, 174

pain 2–3, 13–17, 19, 22–26, 29–30, 61–62, 72, 80, 93–96, 100–101, 120, 129–31, 134–38, 140, 142, 146–47, 160, 164–65, 169, 175, 179; beetle model of 74, 122–26, 131, 172 (*see also* beetle in a box)
Parmenides 166
Pascal, F. 152
Pears, D. 3, 16, 70–71, 124–25, 162, 170
Peperzak, A. T. 185
perception: aspect 184; of other minds 8–9, 12–14, 17–18, 87, 104–10, 113–14, 116–19, 122, 130–32, 134, 146–48, 177, 179; of our own minds 17, 24, 135, 179 (*see also* introspection); of physical objects 28–31, 34–35, 38, 41, 43, 46–52, 55, 58, 87, 128, 168, 171
phenomenalism 108
phenomenology 13, 15, 17, 43, 52–53, 58–59, 88, 167, 177–78, 180; moral 143–44, 152, 182–83; phenomenological tradition 4–5, 29, 46, 52–53, 86–87, 103–4, 144, 173, 174; in Wittgenstein 86, 174
picture: of embodiment 60, 62; of inner and outer 12–13, 17, 24, 126, 135, 137, 163; of the mental 31, 35, 131, 134; of the soul *see* body
Phillips, D. Z. 182
Pihlström, S. x, 174, 176, 184
Pitcher, G. 22, 165
Plant, B. x, 147, 183, 185
Plato 154
presence-at-hand 41–43, 55, 57–61, 134
Preston, J. M. 40
private language argument 7, 63, 68–78, 83–85, 96–97, 169–73, 176

process: chemical 32; inner 10–11, 14, 22, 41–42, 127, 158, 164–65, 172, 179; mental 6, 23, 25, 29, 30–33, 126, 163; physiological 20–21, 167; supernatural 32–33, 41–42
propositional attitude *see* intentionality
proto-ethics 3, 9, 145
Puhl, K. 169
Putnam, H. 63–67, 71, 75–76, 79, 156, 165–66, 169–73, 178, 180

qualia *see* what-it-is-like
quietism 38, 40, 43–44

realism 7, 63, 66–68, 75, 81, 83, 96,170, 172–73, 184
responsibility 9, 115, 151–56, 185
Rhees, R. 183
Richter, D. 183
Ricœur, P. 106, 178
Rorty, R. 168, 172
Rowlands, M. 167,
Rudd, A. J. 75–77, 130–31, 165, 171–72, 176, 179, 181
rule-following 68–71, 150, 170–71
Russell, B. 4, 33–34, 49–50, 165–66, 180–81
Ryle, G. 23, 135, 163

Sacks, M. 177
Sass, L. A. 164
Savigny, E. von 11, 16, 69
Schatzki, T. R. 182,
schizophrenia 164
Scholasticism 29
Schroeder, S. 170
Schulte, J. 23, 25, 163
Schutz, A. 177
science 18, 77, 144, 169, 173
Searle, J. 39–40, 165–66, 169, 173–74
Sellars, W. 164
Shoemaker, S. 15
skepticism 2, 95, 120, 122, 126–27, 134, 163, 176
Sluga, H. 174
Smith, D. W. 39, 166–67
Sokolowski, R. 174
solipsism 97–101, 103, 106, 142, 159, 173–74, 176, 182; conceptual 93; epistemological 84, 92; ethical 184; in Heidegger 109; in Husserl 85, 88–89, 91, 108, 112, 116, 176; in Levinas 89, 116; in Merleau-Ponty 96; metaphysical 84, 91–92;

psychological 85; transcendental 89; in Wittgenstein 7, 70, 81, 83–86, 89–96, 101–2, 159, 164, 173–75
Steinbock, A. J. 177
Stern, D. G. 171
Strawson, G. 123–24, 131, 173–74, 178
Strawson, P. F. 132

Theunissen, M. 107, 111
third-person perspective 4, 7, 15, 17, 24, 27, 76–77, 85, 93, 135, 152, 159–60, 164; *see also* asymmetry
Thornton, T. 28, 40, 166
thought 13–15, 17, 20, 28, 31–32, 35–41, 47, 58, 61, 72, 92, 95–96, 100–102, 118, 120–21, 134–35, 146–47, 166, 172; *see also* expression; intentionality
thought experiment 48, 79, 123, 173, 180
Tilghman, B. R. 184
Toumayan, A. 185
transcendence: of objects 46–47, 49–50, 87, 105–6; of others 8, 87, 103–4, 106–7, 109–10, 113, 115–16, 118–19, 122, 131–34, 136, 139, 177–78 (*see also* asymmetry)
transcendental: intersubjectivity (*see* intersubjectivity); philosophy 154, 185; solipsism (*see* solipsism); subjectivity 60, 87–89, 174
Twin Earth 63–65, 67, 75, 80, 173
Tye, M. 165

uncertainty 12–13, 122, 134, 136–38, 163; constitutional 100–102, 118, 136; *see also* asymmetry; transcendence of others
understanding 7, 65–68, 73, 75–81, 129, 170–71
Ur-Ich 87–89, 92, 98, 100, 102

veil of ideas 36
verificationism 172
Vinci, T. 84–85, 102
Visker, R. 116, 178

Waldenfels, B. 174, 178, 185
what-it-is-like 136, 176, 181
Wider, K. 177
Williams, B. 172, 186
Williams, M. 4, 69
Wisdom, J. 132, 134–35, 165
wishes 28–29, 31–32, 34–38, 41, 43; *see also* intentionality
world-involvement 5–6, 28, 35, 38–41, 43–44, 46, 62, 127–28, 159; *see also* being-in-the-world; disclosedness; intentionality
Wright, C. 179
Wright, G. H. von 182
Wyschogrod, E. 174

Zahavi, D. x, 106, 111, 167–68, 174, 177
zombies 2, 99, 162, 179

CPSIA information can be obtained
at www.ICGtesting.com
Printed in the USA
BVHW04s0049241018
531043BV00002B/54/P